When I Was Young

Raymond Massey

When I Was Young

LITTLE, BROWN AND COMPANY · BOSTON · TORONTO

FIRST AMERICAN EDITION
T 09/76

ISBN 0-316-54977-0

LIBRARY OF CONGRESS CATALOG CARD NUMBER 76-21929

PRINTED IN THE UNITED STATES OF AMERICA

To Dorothy

1

"And each half-lives a hundred different lives."

Matthew Arnold did not have actors especially in mind when he wrote that line from *The Scholar Gypsy*. Still, it does express the disjointed course of an acting career. So I lift the poet's words from context and let them stand alone as a comment on my profession. Again, Arnold's thought suggests the disunity most of us find in the time of our growing up, a disunity that troubled the first quarter century of my own life before I became an actor.

Not that I was conscious of any confusion or frustration. I was a child of privilege; my family were well-to-do and well known in Toronto where I was born in 1896 and grew up. I thought my early years were as happy as could be. It was only later on that I became aware of the knocks I had received and the mistakes I had made.

Like most actors I have a photographic memory. Recall has always been visual to me. My recollections are a sequence of flashbacks.

These memories of mine begin in 1899. I had apparently abandoned my go-cart and was able to make my daily inspections of Jarvis Street on fairly steady feet when accompanied by my mother. Jarvis Street was a broad, tree-lined avenue running north and south from King Street to Bloor Street in Toronto.

The way I first remember our street is that it had a rough,

macadam surface with shallow ditches and gravel pathways on each side. There were houses, big and medium sized, all along Jarvis Street from Queen to Bloor. There were three churches and two schools north of Gerrard Street. It was a fine street, all right: the houses all had wide lawns and some had flower beds. The lines of great elm trees on both sides of the street gave good shade in summer and when the bare branches were covered with snow the street was really beautiful. It was beautiful all year round.

Our house was on Jarvis Street, number 519, the second north of Wellesley Street on the east side. It was a nice big house with the stables at the back. Grandma Massey's house was next door, number 515, on the corner, a big house with a greenhouse and a conservatory. There were stables, too, with living quarters for her coachman and gardener. Grandma's house had a lot of venturesome things in it.

I had discovered Toronto in 1899. I was not yet four and my discovery was not in any sense an operation in depth. My world consisted of those two properties on Jarvis Street; a proprietary interest in Jarvis Street from Carlton Street north to Isabella Street; and certain other outposts or spheres of influence: a house at the northwest corner of Jarvis and Isabella Streets belonging to my Uncle Walter and my Aunt Susie, where four cousins lived; T. A. Crow's livery stable and smithy on Isabella Street; Mr. W. H. Lee's drugstore at Church and Wellesley; the Church Street Station of the Toronto Fire Department, where two big fire engine horses accepted periodic gifts of sugar; the Riverdale Zoo, where father's polar bear resided; the Metropolitan Methodist Church, where my restlessness and incontinence were tested weekly during interminable prayers and sermons.

There were also the several shops to which I often accompanied mother who, although possessed of one of Mr. Bell's recently invented instruments listed as North 2, preferred to do her shopping in person. I knew Stitt's, the dressmaker, Barron's, Provan's, McConkey's, and Meech, the butcher's. Mother made these visits interesting for me for it was fascinating to see her doing something she knew all about and doing it quickly and well. I didn't know what it was all about, of course, but she did and that was all that mattered.

The biggest and best part of my world was Uncle Walter's farm. It wasn't in Toronto then, though the site is part of the city now. I had the happiest times there I ever had "in all my life," as Mr. Pepys would say. It wasn't an outpost or a sphere of influence. I really belonged there. Uncle Walter had told me so.

That is about the size of my world in the years mother was there. It was quite big when you included Uncle Walter's farm. There were a good many people and animals in it.

At 519 there were Van, our coachman; James O'Neill, the aged groom; Jennie Richardson ("Miss Dick"), my nurse; Mr. Seldon; May Crammond; Annie Shields (the maids); Emma, our cook; Aunt Fanny, my pony; Mike, Van's pug dog; Barney and Dolly, the horses; and my brother Vincent, a future Governor-General of Canada, who was thirteen at this time and ten years older than I. On every August 30th I would gain a year on Vincent and until his birthday in February there would only be nine years between us. He was still at the Model School and would go to St. Andrew's the following year. I have nearly forgotten Dr. Algernon Temple, a dear old horse-and-buggy doctor who looked like the picture of the Earl of Dorincourt in *Little Lord Fauntleroy* that mother used to read to me.

Then there were the people at grandma's house — "Euclid Hall," as Aunt Lillie had named it for no known reason. Besides grandma, my principal friend there was Mrs. Amos, the cook, who was magic at gingerbread, cookies and pumpkin pie. All these delicacies were forbidden me by doctor's orders, but frequent and what I believed to be secret visits to Mrs. Amos' kitchen always were satisfying. There were also grandma's only daughter, aged about fifty, my Aunt Lillie, a confirmed hypochondriac and dietary faddist, and her husband, John Treble, a sort of John Bull type who ran a big haberdashery. I never knew quite where I stood with these two. It was often in hot water. I didn't like them.

Mr. Pragnell was grandma's gardener, and small boys are anathema to gardeners. Mr. White, grandma's coachman, had the distinction of being Georgina White's father. Georgie was a year

9

older than I and had very good freckles and when she was seven could throw overhand. I had to admit to Mr. Seldon that Georgie wasn't too bad a sort. It was the nicest thing I ever said about a girl until I was much older. There was a cousin of grandma's whose name was Margaret Phelps living with grandma. Cousin Maggie used to run the house for grandma. I liked her.

That's quite a lengthy cast for a curtain raiser. And I haven't included the two leads who were, of course, my mother and my father.

I knew my mother only when I was very young. She was there for three years only after I first remembered her when I was just four. For most of that time I was sick (I do not know the diagnosis) and must have been a nuisance to mother, and to father, too, although I didn't know it. Mother made me feel I was having a really good time. And I guess I was.

Mother was lovely to look at and to be with. She was small but she stood very straight and had a beautiful figure so that if she was standing alone she looked tall. When she was close to father, where she liked to be, mother came up to the height of his handkerchief pocket. Her eyes were big and dark brown and her hair black. She wore it mostly at the back to show her ears which were very pretty. She loved hats with big bows and feathers. She liked veils, too, and tight lace collars. She was beautiful.

Mother's voice was soft and low pitched and her laugh was like singing. She was mostly a happy person. There were times, though, when mother could be awfully firm. Then her voice would be very low and she would look right through me with her eyes not blinking. It was scary.

Father was tall, about six-foot-two, and broad shouldered. He had a trimmed, redding beard which he said he grew to hide a scar. I used to try to find the scar under his whiskers but I never could. The funny thing about father was that he looked longer lying down than standing up though he stood straight and not bent. He had to lie down a lot. I did not know why.

Father was about fifty when I first remember him, and it was only when I was much older myself that he stopped being like a grandfather and I really got to know him. My real grandfather, Hart Almerrin Massey, had died a few months before I was born.

I realize now, perhaps I knew way back when mother was alive, how different she was from father in so many ways. But they had strong bonds of common interests and each completely understood the other. What is certain is that even as a very little boy I knew mother and father did truly love each other.

Mother was of Huguenot stock and at the time of her marriage her branch of the Vincent family lived in Erie, Pennsylvania. She was a graduate of Smith College at a time when women with a college degree were few. She had a good mind, was quick witted, vivacious and gregarious, a bit impulsive but not rash. She had radiant good health.

Father was reticent, quiet and very shy. "I can only obey impulse after due consideration," he would say. He was in delicate health most of his life. If one word could describe my father, it would be "gentle."

Despite his sombre aspect, father was always ready to laugh. Mother was the one who could bring out a lusty chuckle or a great roar. "By George," he would say — his one concession to profanity — "that's comical!"

Father came of seven generations of pioneers, rugged farmers all of them. It was religious persecution which led Geoffrey Massey to the New World in 1630 and his Puritan convictions had been inherited by most of his descendants. Geoffrey had been born in Knutsford in the County of Cheshire in 1591, just three years after the bonfires were lit to signal the defeat of the Armada. It has always astonished me that only eight generations separate mine from this man who grew up in England while Shakespeare wrote his plays and the scholars translated the Bible into the poetry of the King James version. Geoffrey Massey and Ellen Fox had been married in 1625 by a dissenting minister, rebelling against the rigid Anglican conformity demanded by Archbishop Laud. What is more, they had received the Communion sitting instead of "reverently kneeling atte there owne churche." For this "fornication and blasphemy" Geoffrey had spent a deal of time in the stocks.

Perhaps that is why three hundred years later, father would kneel only on one knee at family prayers.

A graduate of Victoria College, then in Cobourg, Ontario, he was a good scholar; his mind was thorough rather than quick, and he was careful to think everything through before he acted or spoke. I can see him still at his desk in the library on the days he didn't go to the office and Tom Robertson, his secretary, would hand him cheques or letters to sign. The letter would be read and pondered over for five minutes and then would come the windup for his beautiful Spencerian signature. The hand would revolve in a clockwise circular sweep which would end in a feat of calligraphic perfection with flourishes that rivalled those of Elizabeth I.

Nearly all my early memories have to do with mother. One of the earliest is back in 1900. Mother is sitting in a buggy which had small wheels and hard rubber tires. I am in her lap. There is a sort of box with a handle or crank coming out of it; Uncle Walter is holding a rod that goes through the floor of the buggy. He too is sitting on the buggy seat. There is no horse!

The picture fades. I remember a man turning the crank. There is a lot of noise and the buggy is jerking forward all by itself. Uncle Walter is cheering himself as he steers the buggy; mother is laughing and cheering, too. We go round by the big barn. There is a terrific bang. The buggy stops. All three of us are laughing. I remember wanting to cry but I copied mother instead.

It was at Uncle Walter's farm. Mother told me afterwards that the buggy was the first gasoline-driven automobile in Toronto.

Another early memory. It is the first part of 1901. At home in Toronto, a grey winter morning, it is snowing with big dry flakes.

The streets were already well packed with snow and the sleighs ran easily. (That was one good thing about the horse-drawn age. It wasn't necessary to clear the streets of snow. The street railway plowed the tracks but that only meant more for the sleighs.) The sound of the sleigh bells was lovely, especially when it burst through the strange silence that falling snow brings. Barney and Dolly, the horses, carried clusters of silver bells on their harnesses over the smart blue loin blankets. We were in the big Victoria bob-sleigh, just mother and I in the back seat and Van, our coachman, way up on the box with his musk-ox fur cape and enormous bear-skin hat with a velvet peak. Mother and I were covered in fur rugs; the one we sat on hung out over the back.

I asked mother where we were going and she said, "To Queen's Park, darling, to the Queen's funeral."

We drove along Carlton Street over to College and turned up University Avenue. It was snowing hard now. But we could see the big crowd around a lot of soldiers lined up in a sort of square. There were hundreds of bandsmen at one side. In front, facing away from the soldiers, there were cannon with the gunners standing by.

We pulled up quite a distance off but we could see what was going on. The bands started to play a very sad tune, slow and booming. There was a shout way off and the soldiers all seized their guns and rotated them slowly. They pointed the guns downwards and gazed at their feet.

Long afterwards, a soldier myself, I knew that the beautiful movements of "Rest on your arms reversed" had been carried out. Then the cannon started to fire, great puffs of white smoke, one after the other every few seconds, many times. Barney and Dolly were startled and jingled their bells but then they were as still as could be.

Every man in the crowd had taken his hat off. Van, sitting on the box, held his big hat in his hand. I pulled my own hat off, but mother put her muff over my head.

The cannon stopped firing, some soldiers blew trumpets. That was sad, too, but the bands struck up a very happy tune, the soldiers shouldered their guns and marched off.

I looked at Van and as he put his hat on I saw that his head was covered with snow. Then I looked at mother. There were tears in her eyes. She said, "They have buried Queen Victoria across the sea at Windsor — just now."

Her arm around me, mother told me, "Raymond, you can always say, 'For four years I was a subject of the Queen.'" The snow was still falling and the bells were pleasant to hear as we drove home.

Mother was American but she had lived in Canada for a long

time and was as sad about the Queen as Canadians were. She said to father when we got home that it was the end of the Empire — it would never be the same again.

I thought mother might have been wrong about the funeral being the end of the Empire and all that, because at school later on we still kept May 24th as a holiday. That was the old Queen's birthday. It was one of two firecracker days and much the better. The other was Dominion Day, on July 1st, a holiday anyway because school was out for the summer.

Father was sick that day of the funeral, stretched out on a sofa in the library. His sofa, of hideous blue plush, had a mahogany frame with two arms the same height as the back; at the bottom of each arm there was a carved lion's head. When father stretched out, his head was against one arm and his ankles were on the lion's head at the other end. The sofa looked terribly uncomfortable but nobody, not even mother, could persuade him to change it.

He spent hours lying there with terrible aches in his back and blinding headaches. The attacks didn't come too often when mother was there and almost every day he went to the office. Later the aches got worse. Nobody was certain what caused them; though some doctors thought they resulted from the typhoid fever he had had years ago.

I knew nothing about this at the time. I found out about it long afterwards from Mr. Seldon and Vincent. The most interesting stuff always came from Mr. Seldon. I guess it's time to explain about Mr. Seldon, so far as I can, for he comes into almost everything in these years.

Walter Seldon's role in the life of the Massey family is almost indescribable. I don't know how he came to us. I think probably Uncle Walter produced him. Mr. Seldon was, I believe, primarily a photographer and in the days of the wet plate, the dark room, the big bellows box and the black cloth, he was as good as Brady. He looked like Brady, too, with a short, trimmed Imperial and moustache and longish hair. But he was much more than a photographer. An expert cabinet-maker, electrician, telephonist, carpenter, surveyor, historian, detective, psychologist, fisherman, from me he

14

deserves Pope's often quoted tribute, "Thou wert my guide, philosopher, and friend."

Father's office was in "the works," on King Street West near the Exhibition grounds — the Toronto factory and offices of the farm implement business founded by my great-grandfather, Daniel Massey, in 1847. By 1901, it had become a world-wide operation called the Massey-Harris Company. It was still a family business, but only just, since family firms tend to run out of family. On the sudden death of my beloved Uncle Walter, who had been President of Massey-Harris for five years, my father was the sole surviving son of Hart A. Massey, who had built the company to its present stature. Three Masseys, Hart, my grandfather, and two of my uncles, Charles and Walter, had been presidents. They had all been active factory men, vigorous and aggressive. Chester Daniel Massey, my father, could hardly be so described. The board of directors faced a puzzling decision.

Long afterwards, Mr. Seldon told me, "Your father didn't want the job. Your mother hated the thought of what such work could do to his health. There was a lot of opposition to having another Massey head the company, especially a Massey who didn't really know much about making binders and mowers and reapers. The Harris people and the Verity Plough men and the Bain Wagon lot, who had all joined the company while your Uncle Walter was in charge — they had their own ideas about who should be the top man. But your father, who always let his conscience make the decisions, accepted the post and your mother was desperately worried. Your illness didn't make it any easier for her."

My illness had been a nearly fatal attack of dysentery that struck me in Atlantic City, where mother had taken father for a brief visit to build him up for the new job. Why I was brought along I never knew; nor do I remember anything about the illness except that I was in a room seemingly forever in a hotel called Haddon Hall. Mother was there all the time although there were nurses, too, but mother did all the work. There was a nice young man called Dr. Bennett and I had a knitted woollen dog which mother gave me. I guess I was very sick but I don't remember about that. The woollen dog who had no name came back to Toronto with us.

Just about fifty years afterwards I was touring in a stage presentation of Stephen Vincent Benet's poem, "John Brown's Body," with Tyrone Power and Judith Anderson. After a performance in Philadelphia Dr. Bennett was announced at my dressing room. A tall, elderly man entered with a program in his hand. He looked at me and then at his program. I didn't know him and there was a silence before he spoke.

"Raymond, it says here that you were born in Toronto in 1896 and that makes me sure that you were my little, skinny patient at Haddon Hall over half a century ago. I am Dr. Bennett."

Suddenly the years fell away and I remembered my young doctor. I thanked him for his skill in pulling me safely through the illness.

"An actor must have a good stomach," he said. "But I think you owe more to your beautiful mother's devotion than to my ministrations."

When we got home, mother's burdens seemed very heavy for her. Her husband was in far from robust health and about to take on a job for which he was admittedly unsuited. Her younger son seemed likely to remain a sickly child for a long time. But the burdens turned out lighter than she feared.

Father proved he could fill the office of president admirably. His three years in the post turned out the most progressive and prosperous the company had ever enjoyed. Knowing what he could do best and what he could not do, father made no attempt to be an active, energetic executive like his predecessors. He quite consciously made the president function in the fashion of a chairman of the board. He was detached from management and this gave him added power in controlling the policies of the firm. It also helped him conserve his none-too-plentiful energy.

While father was delighting mother with his triumphs at the company, I remained sickly. A trained nurse became a permanent member of the household — a lusty, cheerful member but still a nurse — and although I loved her dearly, I rebelled constantly. Her name was Jennie Richardson — to us, "Miss Dick." I never knew what was the matter with me, but looking back from the vantage point of lengthy experience as a television doctor (as Dr. Gillespie, in the "Dr. Kildare" series) I think nine-tenths of the trouble came from the pharmacopoeia of Dr. Temple, who had deep faith in the efficacy of calomel. Dr. Temple was, for his times, a good doctor, but his confidence in this vile mercury powder, now considered potentially lethal, was tenacious. When I was at last freed of the calomel (mother read in a magazine that the drug had been declared unsuitable for children by the British Medical Association in 1800), I became almost at once a normally boisterous youngster. But before that I had to endure a long stretch of invalidism.

Both my parents were deeply religious members of the Methodist Church. Mother's elder half-brother was Bishop John H. Vincent of the Methodist Episcopal Church in the United States and a cousin was Boyd Vincent, a bishop in the regular Episcopal Church there.

Father was fond of his brother-in-law, my Uncle John. A Methodist bishop was all right and had nothing to do with that bunch of tyrants in England who had driven our ancestor to migrate to America. But bishops in the Episcopal Church were different.

Father was a Puritan. He liked Bishop Boyd Vincent but he had the suspicion of the liturgical order of Rome (that graven image commandment was pretty definite) which had persisted through seven generations of Masseys. Mother was not quite a Puritan, neither was my Uncle John. They were both touched with the new liberalism that would soon make such substantial changes in Methodist ethics, notably as to the theatre, which mother secretly loved. Father knew this but wisely disregarded it.

Mother had been reading me *Stories from the Bible* by Jesse Lyman Hurlbut. I was a little over five. It was a beautifully illustrated book and I knew many of the Bible heroes by sight. The night mother read me that story about the prophet Elijah being fed by the ravens, I was so enchanted by the comforting story that she read it to me three times. I memorized that bearded face in the picture as she read.

The next day in the late afternoon Bishop John Vincent arrived at our house for a short visit. I at once recognized the bearded gentleman in the black, tight-fitting frock coat who took my hand and kissed me as Elijah, the Tishbite. There was no doubt in my mind. The clothes weren't the same but that didn't matter. The prophet was here in our house. Tongue-tied, after a few bewildered minutes I ran back to the nursery. Miss Dick had put my supper on the table but it didn't look very nice. I was still on an awful diet. I went over to the window and looked out on the back lawn. I could hardly believe my eyes. There on the grass were two big black birds. I knew at once they were there to look after Elijah. If the food he got was like the stuff waiting for me on the table, the ravens would feed him. I wanted to see how they did it.

I finally ate my supper, keeping a sharp eye on the crows. Suddenly, as if dismissed from duty, the two birds flew off, much to my disappointment.

When I was sent for to say good-night, I must have puzzled Uncle John by asking him, "Did you get anything good to eat? The ravens have gone!"

The Bishop was a quick-witted old gentleman. Without hesitation he replied, "I had a very good dinner, Raymond, and the ravens were not needed."

Uncle John was by way of being a real prophet. He had co-founded Chautauqua Institution way back in the seventies, an adult education place where I got my first taste of theatre when I was about nine. Uncle John had been the first Methodist minister to approve of the theatre. He was advanced in a lot of ways. Father used to tell about what happened when Uncle John ran up against my grandfather, Hart A. Massey.

In the early nineties an electric trolley car system had been introduced in Toronto. It did not operate on Sunday, but in 1895 a proposition was put before the voters to permit the cars to run on the Sabbath. There was strong opposition from several church groups. My grandfather was a leader in opposing what he considered to be a violation of the Fourth Commandment.

On the Sunday preceding the referendum on the Sabbath trolley cars, my father and mother and Uncle John, who was visiting them, dined at my grandfather's house. Uncle John had preached that morning in our church. Grandpa held forth at length and with increasing vehemence about the proposed desecration of the Sabbath. He finally came to a close, exhausted by his own eloquence. There was an ominous silence.

As father told it, "Then your Uncle John spoke ever so quietly and there was a twinkle in his eye. He said, 'That's a fine pair of horses you have, Mr. Massey. They were looking their Sunday best outside the church this morning. I suppose your coachman drove you to church and home?'

" 'Yes, of course,' from my grandfather.

" 'Have you ever considered,' said the bishop, 'that the motorman of the trolley car is the coachman of a great many people?' "

The question was in the tradition of the prophets. I don't think Uncle John ever saw my grandfather again or that he convinced him about the Sunday cars, but I do know that the townsfolk got their Sunday coachman by the referendum.

I had another Uncle John. His name was John Treble but I never called him uncle although he asked me to. He was quite old and he had married my Aunt Lillie, who was nearly as old, about a year after my grandfather had died. Mr. Seldon told me he had been after her for a long time because she had a lot of money but grandfather had always chased him off. I always called him Mr. Treble or "he" or "him." He had a store called the Great Shirt House downtown at the corner of King and Bay. He had white mutton-chop whiskers and a moustache and tried to look like an Englishman. He was pretty fat.

Vincent told me that Mr. Treble got an invitation one time to the Lieutenant-Governor's reception on New Year's Day. Aunt Lillie didn't go, being "sick," as she often was. At the door "he" said in a low voice to the man who announced everybody, "John Mill Treble." The fellow didn't seem to hear. Mr. Treble explained, "Made your shirts." The man shouted, "Major Schurz!" and "he" went in.

I was always having trouble with Mr. Treble, usually at Sunday dinner at grandma's. I say grandma's, but you would think it was Mr. Treble's and Aunt Lillie's, the way "he" talked. Maybe it was because Mr. Seldon told me long afterwards that grandfather had made one of those, what Mr. Seldon called "Victorian," wills where Aunt Lillie got the house and some money and grandma stayed on as a sort of guest. Mr. Seldon said father was the executor and had done everything as best he could for grandma. I know that when grandfather died Aunt Lillie changed the whole house and made it into all sorts of styles — Moorish and French and what Vincent called "neo-bloody." Grandma had her great big bedroom in the front and her sitting room downstairs, which was lovely and Victorian. She never used to go into the rest of the house except, on occasion, the dining room. As Aunt Lillie used to be sick in bed a good deal, Mr. Treble had it to himself. Cousin Maggie Phelps used to look after grandma.

At Sunday dinner Mr. Treble would say the longest grace I ever heard. He used to shut his eyes but I finally did get caught sneaking salted almonds and "he" sent me out to the kitchen to finish my dinner, which was fine because Mrs. Amos looked after me and I had finished with the diet.

"He" was a very good carver and fairly quick too, and proud of it. One Thanksgiving dinner, all my cousins were there and Vincent and our household and grandma and there was a wowzer of a turkey. Grace had been very long but I had grabbed a handful of almonds and the soup business was over. Mr. Treble, going great guns, had served all the grownups and all the kids but me. "He" was having a little trouble with a wing when his carving knife slipped. The big turkey wing landed back of the cowl of a light over one of the paintings which hung on the dining-room wall. Everybody gasped but I laughed right out because it was my helping that was on the picture light. Mr. Treble gave me the dirtiest look I can remember, but he couldn't do anything worse because everybody else was laughing, too, including grandma. Father stopped it all when he said, "John, that was a fine niblick shot. Maybe you can make this chandelier in one next Christmas."

My first school was the kindergarten of a large girls' school called Havergal College, just down Jarvis Street on the west side. The building now houses studios of the Canadian Broadcasting Corporation, but the school lives on elsewhere. It was named after Frances Ridley Havergal, a Victorian hymn-writer of saintly character whose principles were staunchly adhered to by Miss Knox, the headmistress, and her chief of staff, Miss Kent. Miss Knox was a startling replica of Queen Victoria. As a boy of five, I was impressed to the extent that I sometimes had a feeling that those guns in Queen's Park might have boomed in error. I had a treasured picture of the Queen Empress. After attending two sessions of morning prayers at Havergal, I took out the portrait from its retirement in a box full of chestnuts, snails and the like, and examined it carefully. Miss Knox's gold pince-nez on a spring chain and her reticule at her ample waist seemed to merge into the jewels and the diamond George of my coloured print. The voice that read the collects that morning seemed just the kind that could have declared wars or frightened courtiers.

I showed the print to mother. "Miss Knox does look like the Queen, darling," she said, "but the Queen did die, and she went to Heaven three years ago!"

Among the one hundred and sixty young women at Havergal College in 1902, there were only two male members, both of us aged five. My co-mate and brother in exile was one Terence Sheard, comely, gay and debonair. As the stronger of the pair of us, I leaned upon him in our adversity. From the start we both hated the world of women into which we had been thrust. Terry lived just a few doors from the school and was allowed to walk there by himself; whereas I, two streets north on Jarvis Street, was considered incapable of making the journey alone. "Jarvis Street is a race track!" father said. So I made the quarter-mile trip back and forth each day in the pony cart with Van or on foot escorted by Miss Dick. Terry kept this humiliation alive by daily comments, but on the whole he was loyal.

Like all minorities, we were treated with mawkish solicitude and condescension or resentment. The bigger girls, who didn't see much of us except at prayers when "Queen Victoria" was present, fawned on us. Terry was able to conceal his resentment of these blandishments but not I. At prayers on the second morning, I heard a big, bloomered Amazon whisper to her neighbour, "What a sweet little boy!" I turned and stuck out my tongue at the offender, only to find her gazing rapturously at Terry. I was disillusioned to find him smirking; but later he reassured me that he considered all girls to be loony.

My first period of schooling at Havergal was short, just six months, but it was my only experience of co-education and I've never since been in favour of it. I acquired an awe of women *en masse* which even now attacks me in the pit of my stomach before matinees and theatre lunches; my mind wanders back to all those little beavers at their tables with the straw mats so neatly completed, the cat so triumphantly coloured with crayon and my own wretched effort botched and unfinished. And nowadays I haven't a beautiful agate or a conker in my pocket to give me courage.

Of the blurred mass of nameless little girls in that kindergarten, I would see one again in clear and tragic focus thirty-two years later when, as Alma Rattenbury, she was tried with her chauffeur at the Old Bailey in London for the murder of her husband.

2

The driveways from the stables of our house and grandma's joined up opposite Mrs. Amos' kitchen and then after a bit divided and went to the two front doors. They weren't too wide at any point but when we got back after a summer at Uncle Walter's farm we found that shrubbery had been planted where the driveways joined. Van complained to father that it was hard to drive a carriage and pair through because the shrubs were crowding the drive on our side. Mr. White said it was just as bad for him. Mr. Pragnell told father he had been ordered to plant the shrubs by Mr. Treble. Father did nothing although some of the shrubs were on our property. Nobody knew where the property line was anyway.

Mother said the main annoyance was that the shrubs were hydrangeas, which she didn't like. So everybody was bothered, but principally Van and Mr. White. Van was a good friend to me and I wanted to help him.

In the spring of 1902, Van used to drive me down to the school by way of Church Street, where there were some interesting stores. In the window of one of them, a couple of weeks before the 24th of May (the firecracker day for Queen Victoria's birthday), I spotted the biggest firecracker I had ever seen. Van stopped. I got out and looked again and it was a whopper, high enough to reach above my knee and very big around. I went in and asked the price. The man said it was $1.50! I don't think Van had noticed the firecracker but it did give me an idea.

The previous year, Mr. Seldon had exploded some little firecrackers on the "24th" and fired some pinwheels and Roman candles and little rockets in our back yard. They didn't amount to much, but a big cracker like the one I had seen might upset at least one of the hydrangeas and show Mr. Treble how wrong he had been to have them planted. By the time I went to bed that night, I had convinced myself that this demonstration would be worthwhile.

There were two serious difficulties to be overcome. One was the cost and a second was the transportation of the firecracker. I needed an accomplice. All grownups including Mr. Seldon were ruled out and there remained only one possible person to help me and that was Georgie White, the daughter of Mr. White, grandma's coachman. She wasn't "like a girl." She was strong and had those dandy freckles and was eight years old. She could read and play baseball with boys. When I told her about my idea with the firecracker, she wanted to be in on it right away. She produced a great plan for getting the firecracker from the store to our house.

It had been grandma's custom to give Christmas presents to everybody in her house. Mr. Seldon bought the presents for her. Last Christmas Mr. Seldon had goofed badly and Georgie had got a doll carriage instead of the catcher's mitt she had hankered after. This vehicle had been consigned to the loft of grandma's stables but Georgie took me over and showed it to me. It was a wicker contraption which she thought would just about hold what she called the bomb as I had described it to her.

She wasn't as helpful about the money. On my sixth birthday, father had started a weekly allowance of one dime and in the ensuing eight months I had managed to squirrel away a good proportion of it in a china dog bank. We counted out about $1.10, which left 40 cents for me to raise. Georgie had the same weekly dime as I did but said it was all going toward the catcher's mitt. That left only Vincent to touch — not a good prospect. He got a terrific allowance from father, something like a dollar a week, but according to him it all went on books. I went up to his room when he was doing his homework and told him I wanted him to lend me 40 cents. He said, "What for?" I said, "To buy candy." He said, "You aren't allowed candy. What do you want 40 cents for?"

"To buy books."

"You can't read. Go to bed. I've got to work."

"To have them read to me, then."

There was a pause and he produced four 10-cent pieces.

"Go to bed. You're a pest."

Now I had the $1.50 and the transportation and the sturdiest of confederates. It had taken about a week to accomplish this and the next afternoon, being the day before the 24th, we were to pick up the firecracker after Georgie's school was out.

We went down to the store by way of Jarvis Street. It didn't look right from the start. Georgie was too big for a doll carriage and she looked queer pushing it along. She had been playing baseball on the boys' side at the Model School and had scratched her face sliding. That day Miss Dick had put a sissy sailor suit on me and I didn't dare ask her to change it because I didn't want her to know why. We got to the store on Carlton Street all right. The firecracker was still there and I bought it. The man gave me a stick of punk for free.

The cracker fitted into the doll carriage — almost; there was a red cloth to cover it and a canopy that sort of hid it. We started back up Church on the west side. This time I walked in front, not wanting to be seen near the doll carriage. I remembered, too late, that we would be passing close to the fire station. The firemen were sitting out front on chairs. As we passed, one of them called out, "What you got in the cart, Georgie? Firecrackers?"

Georgie pushed the cart straight on.

Along Wellesley, Mrs. Warren, who lived at the corner, tried to look at Georgie's "dolly" in the cart, but Georgie didn't stop. It was lucky she didn't because when we got home there was a whole lot of fuse hanging over the blanket. We put the firecracker in our croquet box in the back yard inside the fence.

The next morning we had really good luck. There was a time about ten when all the horses were in the stables. Van and Mr. White were both in their apartments. James O'Neill didn't come in

25

because it was a holiday; father and mother were in the house and everybody in grandma's house was indoors. I sneaked out with the firecracker and set it up in the middle of the hydrangeas. Then Georgie lit the punk because she knew how to handle matches. She came out and we lit the fuse. Then we dived back through the gate into the back yard and shut it and waited and waited. Nothing happened. I thought the fuse had gone out. So did Georgie. We were going to go out and see if it had when there was a terrible bang and a whole hydrangea bush came over the fence and landed just beside us.

The driveway was covered with bits of the firecracker and hydrangeas, and a window of Mrs. Amos' kitchen was cracked. It was much more than I had intended. Instead of hurting one or two of the hydrangeas, the whole bed had been wiped out. There was a hole where they had been.

Mr. Seldon's "24th" fireworks planned for that evening were cancelled.

Georgie got a spanking but she said it didn't hurt much. "Daddy was laughing so much he couldn't find my bottom," she reported. I got a long lecture from father. I was forbidden to go away from the house except to kindergarten. I lost my allowance for two months. I also had to apologize to Mr. Pragnell, who said it was all right, and to Mr. Treble, who said it was wicked to destroy God's flowers.

Mother was very firm about it but I thought she really didn't mind too much. I heard Vincent say, "He did show some gumption." He said it was the first time he had ever financed an anarchist.

There were prayers at our house weekdays after breakfast before father went to the office. Everybody in the house came. Sometimes Van and Mr. Seldon were there. James O'Neill didn't come because he was a Roman Catholic. Father would read from the Bible and then he would pray. Everybody else sat and bowed their heads. Father didn't read the prayers but made them up. There were phrases and words that he used pretty often but the prayers were really new each time. One sentence I remember after

26

all these years — "Make bare thine arm throughout all the earth" — which was the same as asking God to roll up His sleeves and do something.

The morning after the firecracker business, everybody was at prayers. Father thanked God for sparing the lives of Raymond and Georgina and asked forgiveness for their senseless act. I thought it was fair to blame me for the firecracker but I didn't see why Georgie should go equal shares in it. What really burned father up was my telling Vincent that I wanted 40 cents to buy books. He asked God to forgive Raymond for lying to his brother.

I thought then and think now that it couldn't have put much of a strain on the Lord's forgiveness to overlook a 40-cent cadge from my big brother for a result so satisfying to friends who had proved incompetent to deal with those hydrangeas. Still, never since did I borrow a cent from Vincent, for evil or for good.

3

Walter Vanderlip, "Van," was, is and ever shall be to me the best coachman in the entire world. I can see him, clear as ever, on the box of the Victoria in his dark green livery, white breeches and top boots and top hat with the cockade. Barney and Dolly have been groomed till they shine. The best harness has been polished to perfection. Their hooves glisten with oil. James O'Neill stands clear, Dolly does a little dance and the two big bays clear the stable doors. Away they go down Jarvis Street and west on Wellesley as James and I shout "Good luck, Van!"

It was Dominion Day, July 1st, 1903, and Van and the horses were off to the Horse Parade in Queen's Park. We had been entered in the class for "carriages drawn by pairs." There were classes for heavy draft horses, light delivery, heavy delivery, a fire department class, single harness, every kind of horse, even ponies. After the judging, the winners — red, blue, yellow and white ribbons — would drive down University over to St. George Street, north to Bloor Street, east to Jarvis, then south to College and break up in the park. Father and mother and James and the rest of us could watch the parade as it passed. Father was sure we'd be "reserve" — which was the white. Van had asked me to tell father he had put the cockade on because the coachman's appearance counted. Usually father wouldn't let Van wear the cockade because he said we didn't have the right to it. (I never knew what you had to do to rate a cockade.) Mr. Rinehardt, the brewer with the iron deer and dwarves on his lawn, let his coachman wear a cockade. Mother used to say he was a vulgar man.

I gave father Van's message.

He said, "By George, are my wishes of no account?"

"What nonsense, Chester!" mother said. "It's Van's big day — let him wear his Orangeman's regalia if he wants to!"

Van was an Orangeman, a member of the Irish Protestant fraternal order. As a Lutheran Protestant he was much against the Ancient Order of Hibernians. Father approved and when Van came home a bit drunk after lodge nights, father would say, "If Nelson put his telescope to his blind eye, so can I!"

Van's big day was July 12th, anniversary of the Battle of the Boyne when King Billy beat the Irish Jacobites. Oh, I knew it all, small as I was. Van had told me many times about the valour of Dutch William. Poor old James O'Neill was always very silent on July 12; come to think of it, he wasn't too exuberant on St. Patrick's Day either. The Hibernians in those days were much outnumbered by the Orangemen.

About eleven o'clock James and I went out to watch for the parade. Soon I could see it turn down Jarvis way up at Bloor. I ran and called father and mother. They all came out, Annie Shields, May Crammond, Miss Dick and Mrs. Van. There was quite a crowd from grandma's house next door, and lots of other people.

First came six mounted policemen followed by two squadrons of the permanent force cavalry, the Royal Canadian Dragoons from Stanley Barracks. They looked wonderful — beautiful horses and troopers in scarlet tunics, white gauntlets and shining helmets with white plumes. There was the band of the 48th Highlanders, the drum major with his mace, the swirling kilts, the drummer in the leopard skin with the head hanging down his back. The brass band was playing as it passed our house, the pipers just marching. Then came some saddle horses and — I could hardly stand it, waiting to know — the carriage pairs!

Old James spotted it first. "Mr. Massey," he cried, "your horses have won! Barney on the near side wears the red ribbon — look at him step like an Irish King!''

"They *are* stepping high," said father. "Are they shod with heavy shoes, James?''

"Sorr, maybe they are but the darlin's would tread high if they was barefoot!''

As he came close, Van gathered his horses and they both showed off, thinking they were going to turn into their own driveway. Van touched his hat with the long-lashed whip and Barney and Dolly curvetted for grandma's benefit.

A light delivery class came next. This time it was father who broke the news. "I can't believe it!" he moaned. "They have given First Prize to that menace of our streets, Meech's delivery boy!'' There he was perched on his high, two-wheeled cart: R. MEECH FINE MEATS AND POULTRY, driving the trotter which so often had raised father's dander.

"We get our meat on time,'' mother pointed out.

There was no need to urge our band of spectators to see the rest of the parade.

After ever so many classes — the big dray horses, the two fine horse classes, heavy engine horses and the lighter hose-wagon ones — came the ponies. This was a great moment for me. Of the four ponies who had won ribbons, two were biggish Shetlands driven by young boys, maybe a little older than I, but boys all the same. I thought my own Aunt Fanny could beat any of them. I didn't say anything but mother could read my mind.

"You'd like to show Aunt Fanny next year, Raymond?''

Somehow the words wouldn't come.

"You may, darling!'' she said.

Next year, sure enough, I drove Aunt Fanny down Jarvis Street with the red ribbon. Mother wasn't there to see it.

It was a fine stable back of 519 with four big stalls and a loose box. Barney and Dolly had two of the stalls and Aunt Fanny another and when Vincent kept a horse from time to time, he had the loose box. There was a hayloft above, a big tackroom, a carriage house and wash rack. Van and Mrs. Van lived upstairs in an apartment. Van, unlike many coachmen, knew a lot about horses. He and James kept the pair in beautiful shape. James would hiss while he brushed away. I asked him why. He didn't know. He had been in a British cavalry regiment when he was young, I think the Royal Irish Lancers, and had fought in the Crimean War. He said all the soldiers hissed when they groomed.

Barney and Dolly were replaced occasionally, particularly Dolly, but the names remained the same regardless of gender.

I spent a lot of time with Van and James and the horses. Even when I was sick, mother would always let me go back to the stables. Aunt Fanny, like all Shetlands, had a real dislike for small boys but I wasn't in the least afraid of her. She would pretend to bite or would push me against the side of the stall but she never overdid it. We played a game when I was grooming her. It was James who invented it. Van would pretend to be the squadron commander, James was the troop sergeant-major and I was a trooper.

"Glory be to God, trooper Raymond, are you playing patty-cake with that horse?"

"No, sergeant," I would say, trying to be Irish.

Van would laugh like anything.

"Then give her the brush, trooper, or the major will have you ten days confined to barracks!"

I would brush away and hiss manfully. I almost believed it all. James would stand up straight and shout "Stables, 'shun! Sorr!" And Van in his white cotton driving gloves would rub Aunt Fanny's rump and look at his glove and say, "Parade this man at squadron orderly room tomorrow morning, sergeant-major."

"Very good, sorr!"

"Go in for your supper, trooper!" Van said.

Van had been in the Militia. In about eleven years I would be playing that scene for real.

It had to come, sad as it is to look back on. In 1910 father bought a Packard automobile and hired a chauffeur, a brash young fellow named Ayers. Van and James were still with us and the horses, but it wasn't fun anymore. I was away at boarding school but when I came home for the summer holidays there was uneasiness in the stables. Ayers would occupy the wash rack for the big touring car so there was no room for the carriages to be washed. Ayers was rude to Van and poor old James who was nearly eighty now. Father didn't like Ayers either, but he didn't know how to get rid of him.

We drove to Chautauqua that summer for two weeks and Ayers ran over a dog. Father practically bought the farm of the dog's owner. Ayers also drove forty miles an hour against father's orders and father really let him have it.

"Come to a dead stop, Ayers. By George, I will not be disobeyed. You have travelled at an outrageous speed and if it happens again I shall be very angry indeed!"

It happened again and father was very angry indeed this time. We drove home in an atmosphere like a Toronto winter. At breakfast next morning, father said he was through with automobiles and would sell the Packard. He called the stables on the house telephone.

"Good morning, Van. I want to speak to Ayers. . . . What? . . . Come in to the house. I can't understand you on this contraption."

In a few minutes, Van came in.

"Where is Ayers?"

"He's resigned, Mr. Massey. I've paid him off. He's gone."

"You paid him . . . . With what, may I ask?"

"My money, sir. He's gone."

With a certain hint of admiration, father said, "Gone . . . well . . . . You mean he's gone?"

"Yes, sir. I told him if he didn't go I'd break every bone in his body!"

"Well, well . . . every bone! . . . By George, that's comical! What am I going to do about the car?"

"I'll drive it around to the front door, sir."

"You? You can't drive!" Father, having driven the Ivanhoe electric, spoke with the authority of Barney Oldfield or Ralph de Palma.

"Oh yes I can, sir. Mr. Kennedy at the Packard place had me taught while you were away!"

In a few minutes the touring car was at the door with Van at the wheel in a white duster and chauffeur's cap. Van drove father's car until his death in 1916 while I was in France. The horses stayed two more years and James went home to his daughter in Ireland.

Another hero of my childhood was Mr. Seldon. I have already tried to explain Mr. Seldon's role in the Massey family. There is no label for Mr. Seldon.

Whenever father or any of the family carried out any building operations, Mr. Seldon was a sort of extra clerk of the works and no contractor ever ducked any of the fine print while he was around. He knew the mason's job, the painter's, the plumber's, the carpenter's or the electrician's as well as they did. When father finally remodelled our house, Mr. Seldon saw to it that a good workshop was in the plan. Consequently I can still make passably good furniture, am competent with most tools and a pretty fair hand on the lathe. I was taught by a master.

Father never got around to enlightening me about the mysteries of sex, though he did make a stumbling attempt to bring up the subject the night before I went overseas in the First World War. However, Mr. Seldon proved pretty well up to the job. Information came my way by bits depending on how fast fish were biting.

An ardent naturalist and wily fisherman, he was with us on Lake Joseph in Muskoka for part of the summer of 1907. We stayed at the Elgin House which father liked because Mr. Love, who ran it, had a chapel with services every Sunday and, as father said, he kept the young people in hand.

One day, Mr. Seldon and I were fishing for muskellunge in a rowboat — that is, I was rowing and Mr. Seldon was trolling. I asked him a question, wondering how muskrats got little muskrats. That was Mr. Seldon's cue. The answer took the remaining two weeks at Elgin House.

Mr. Seldon said muskrats mated in the water and had their young on land.

"The male muskrat doesn't . . . I've got a strike! Row as hard as you can, Raymond!" He played his fish while I nearly pulled my skinny arms off. After about ten minutes we pulled in a whopper of a muskie. Mr. Seldon banged him on the head and he was dead. Then he threw the troll out again and continued:

33

"The male muskrat, like all rodents, just hangs around until the young ones are ready to forage for themselves and then he's off chasing other muskrats."

There was a pause. "Your cousin Winnie has been married three times and that's what burned up your grandfather." He reeled in his line and stowed his tackle in a neat tin box. "We'd better row in to the dock, it's time for dinner." We weighed the fish and it was twenty-four pounds! Mr. Seldon photographed it. "I like Winnie," he reflected. "She's all right."

We did more fishing and this time I caught a muskellunge, a pound bigger. Mr. Seldon talked about the Cree Indians, about animals being in season, and human beings not having seasons, and anatomy and divorce. He covered a lot of ground. He sure could fish!

Thirty-two years after this I was on tour in *Abe Lincoln in Illinois*. During our Broadway run I had been married to Dorothy Ludington, a Connecticut lady, and she was with me when we played the Royal Alex in Toronto. This marriage in 1939 was and is my third. The first two lacked durability.

The day after *Abe* opened in Toronto, Dorothy and I went to see Mr. Seldon at 99 Howard Street where he had always lived. I particularly wanted Mr. Seldon to meet Dorothy. A very old man by then, eighty-six, he was too feeble to come to the theatre. But his mind was clear as ever.

Mr. Seldon's house was full of wonderful old photographs and gadgets. There was the telephone that father had shouted over and father's collection of trowels from laying cornerstones. It was a family museum.

Over tea, Mr. Seldon asked Dorothy if I had a workshop at home. She said no.

"He should have one," my old friend said. "You see, Raymond is a working Massey; he needs to work with his hands, no matter if he's an actor or whatever. His father wasn't handy, nor is his brother. Raymond is like his grandfather, old Hart, a tool man. That's what brought Hart Massey back to Toronto from Cleveland. There was a big workshop he could be part of. You'll

34

find him a lot easier to live with when there's a workshop in your house. You'll get some good furniture, too."

That was the last time I saw Mr. Seldon. I did get the workshop. Dorothy received some passable oak and walnut furniture. She stopped me from cabinet-making when I was about seventy. I had lost the tip of a finger with a new-fangled sabre saw Mr. Seldon would never have touched. Now I just tinker about.

4

It had been decided for quite some time that we would go to Europe in the summer of 1903 — father, mother, Vincent (then sixteen) and I.

After father's three years as president of the company, he had been made honorary president, a relief to him, since it was a much easier job. The trip abroad was to celebrate what mother called father's emancipation.

Preparations for the trip were in full swing. Mr. Seldon was rushing here and there, arranging tickets, hotel accommodations in New York, London, Paris; and the London office of the company was to confirm that Evian water was available at all points to be visited. Ample supplies of Walker-Gordon pasteurized milk were to be shipped to the boat and to Europe. The family was understandably scared of typhoid.

Bilton Brothers, the tailors, finished a new set of three overcoats for father, to fit one over the other. He would wear them in varying combinations, depending on the weather. The overcoats were fitted, mother observing. She laughed until she nearly cried. Father did, too. He said he was thinking of patenting the idea.

"Chester," mother said, "if you wear the top one alone, everyone will think I've starved you!"

Father said that just now nobody was using "Ceres," the company's private railroad car, and we were going to take it to New York. I never saw him or mother as happy as they were that night on the way to New York.

We crossed the Atlantic in a White Star liner, the old *Majestic* — not the big *Majestic* which was the former German *Vaterland*, yielded to the British after the First World War. The old *Majestic* was small, typical of her times. She took over eight days for the voyage from New York to Liverpool and she smelled of rubber and soup. One whiff and you could be seasick at the dock if you were as susceptible as mother. We ran into a storm almost before we dropped the pilot and all of us, including Miss Dick, were flattened for two days. This was the first of my sixty Atlantic crossings by ship, and one of only two on which I suffered seasickness.

In London we stayed at the Cecil Hotel in the Strand. To me it seemed like a fairy palace. The night after our arrival a first cousin of father's, Frederick Isaiah Massey, came to dinner. We called him "Fred Eye" and he was the European manager of the Massey-Harris Company. A big, handsome man who spoke very quietly, he had the most courtly manners. He was very nice to me. I had been allowed to stay up for dinner, and he told stories of the American Civil War. As a captain in the Union Army, Fred Eye had been wounded at the Battle of Gettysburg.

The trip proceeded with much pleasure for father, mother and Vincent. They revelled in the cathedrals, palaces, museums and chateaux as we progressed through England, Scotland, the Low Countries, France and Germany. But I missed the joys of my Uncle Walter's farm and longed for my wicked old Aunt Fanny. Still, there were compensations. In Belgium there were the dogs pulling milk carts; in London, Hamley's toy store; in Edinburgh, Rizzio's blood on the floor outside the Mary Stuart room at Holyrood Palace.

One particular memory I cherish. It is my tiny mother confronting what to me seemed a formidable contingent of the German army. Mother in a long, flared skirt with a tight-waisted jacket is wearing a jaunty hat with two birds' feathers on it. She carries a handbag with a chain, and a small umbrella. Half turned from us, she is facing a number of German officers sitting at a nearby table.

It was at some town on the Rhine, it may have been Bingen. We four had stopped at a café and were drinking hot chocolate. Across the café were five or six men in uniform at a table with big steins of beer which they were emptying with a great deal of noise and laughter. Vincent said they were officers. There was no one else in the café.

"Chester," mother said, "I can't stand this din. Pay your bill and let's go on." She stood and pulled her jacket down at the back.

One of the Germans stood up — a very tall man with a monocle. He mimicked mother, pulling his tunic down. The others laughed loudly.

At once mother picked up her bag and umbrella and walked over to the officers. She started to talk to them in a quiet voice. We couldn't hear what she was saying; she was speaking in English so I don't suppose the officers understood her but from the moment she started to speak they were quite still. This much I heard her say, "I have always thought German officers were gentlemen . . . . I have been mistaken — you have much to learn!" As she turned away, they stood, clicked their heels and the tall officer saluted.

Father and Vincent made the worst exit imaginable, father in his haste leaving as a tip a 20-mark piece. I looked back and saw a broken monocle on the marble-topped table of the German officers.

We went to Switzerland before going back to London. In Zurich we saw mother's brother, my uncle John Vincent, who had been made Bishop of the Methodist Church in Europe. Uncle John thought father should take mother to the opera in London.

"After all, Chester, you have all the great opera stars singing at Massey Hall. The only difference is that at Covent Garden they have scenery and costumes. You should see some Shakespeare in London, too."

Father did not seem convinced.

Back in London, Vincent and mother added their persuasive powers to Uncle John's. Father reluctantly agreed to let them attend a matinee of *Richard II* at His Majesty's Theatre. A matinee seemed less abandoned than a night performance. Riding her wave of success mother obtained father's surprisingly willing agreement to accompany her to the opera as well. Two tickets for *Romeo and Juliet* at Covent Garden (for a night performance!) arrived as if by magic.

Mother and her elder son left the hotel in high spirits next afternoon to see Beerbohm Tree play the hapless King Richard, while father, with an audible sigh, summoned a hansom cab in which he and I set out for the zoo. On our way to Regent's Park, we passed His Majesty's Theatre where the play had just started. Father looked at the theatre longingly. As we jogged up the Haymarket, he smiled as he said, "There is a sign over a door: 'TO THE PIT.' They're quite honest!"

Next night was the opera. Father and mother got themselves up splendidly. Father had gone out on his own and bought one of the new white waistcoats to go with his swallowtails. Mother wore a new dress she had bought in Paris. There was a big laugh from all of us when mother caught father in the dressing room admiring himself in the tall mirror with his "Gibus" hat on and the amethyst watch fob. Mother said she was afraid to go out with such a masher! Just before they left, mother caught father putting on the outside overcoat which was the loosest of the three. "Don't wear that outside one, Chester, I won't have you looking like an out-of-work magician."

Naturally, both of them loved the opera. One of the singers had sung at Massey Hall. Mother said the diva who played Juliet must have weighed about one hundred and eighty pounds but was wonderful if you shut your eyes. Father said that Romeo looked much like cousin Fred Eye, only a bit older. They couldn't stop laughing.

Next morning mother wasn't feeling well and said she had a bad pain way down in her stomach. Father looked very pale. Mother had never been ill. He got hold of Fred Eye, and in about an hour a doctor came to the hotel and diagnosed an inflamed appendix.

In 1903 this was shocking news. Acute appendicitis had almost invariably been fatal. In 1902 surgery had been introduced for removing the appendix; one of the earliest successful operations had been performed on King Edward VII. In the light of modern medical practice, there would have been immediate surgery. But the next day mother felt better. Dr. Brown told father it would be safe to sail home as arranged in two days' time. A relapse came. Instead of going home, mother was now terribly ill.

I will never understand why she was not taken to a nursing home. Father rented a house in Hampstead, 16 Frognal Lane; we moved in the same day mother took a turn for the worse. Fred Eye, that staunch friend, arranged for servants, nurses and a hospital bed.

For five days father watched in numb terror while two doctors did nothing.

All through that week, I was told to be quiet and I played by myself in the little garden at the back of the house.

At last, after eight days, surgery was decided on. A room was prepared for the operation. The surgeon, Mr. Dean, in frock coat and top hat, arrived at the house and performed an appendectomy.

After the operation I went out to the street which was covered over with straw to deaden the horses' hoof beats and watched the surgeon drive away. I felt sure he had cured mother. I went back to the garden and played a soldier game that had some shouting in it. Nurse Osman came down the iron staircase from mother's room. "Raymond, Raymond, remember your promise," she called out. "Be quiet!"

In a few minutes she reappeared on the steps. Tears were running down her face. She took me in her arms.

"Your mother says, 'Tell Raymond to play as loudly as he likes .... I want to hear him!'"

I knew then what was happening. I played as loudly as I could.

Mother died twenty-four hours later.

5

Cousin Kate, mother's cousin, and her daughter Nan came to live with us when we returned in 1903. Nan was to keep house and Cousin Kate was to occupy the two big rooms that had been mother's sitting room and dressing room. Father remained in the large front room in which I had been born.

His grief was endured with the reticence of consideration for his sons and family.

Cousin Kate was then an old lady. Born Katharine Byard of Mobile, Alabama, she had seen the American Civil War, in which her fiancé was killed fighting under command of Stonewall Jackson. She had suffered the horrors of Reconstruction and the carpetbaggers and was now the widow of James Warnock, a Scottish-Canadian who had had a tool-manufacturing business in Galt, Ontario. Galt was a long way from Mobile. In the thirty years she had lived in Canada, I don't think Cousin Kate had ever been warm in winter but she said our house was hotter than her own in Galt.

I never saw grandma's house as it was in grandfather's time. After he died, Aunt Lillie removed what must have been its Victorian charm, leaving a mass of mahogany, parquet and Oriental rugs. One room, grandmother's sitting room, was left untouched, with her own pictures, furniture and knick-knacks. It was enchanting and grandma never went elsewhere downstairs except to walk slowly through the hall to the dining room or the elevator.

This was an open-cage, hydraulic contraption which only Mr. Treble or Mr. Pragnell, the gardener, were supposed to operate. The elevator offered a venturesome trip but grandma, still a pioneer at heart, was a calm and willing passenger.

Aunt Lillie built a Moorish room next to grandma's conservatory, complete even to a hookah. It was fun to play in, as there were scimitars on the walls that could be taken down. Grandma let me carry them to her room.

On the top floor was an enormous room which was called the billiard room. There had never been a billiard table in it and certainly never would have been in grandfather's time, but the vast room was an everlasting delight to me. It had many alcoves, turrets, dormer windows, and at one end there was a platform with a lectern. I conducted my ministerial rehearsals up there, knowing I would be alone. Nobody ever came up. I practised sermons in the manner of the ministers at the Metropolitan Church we attended. There was Dr. Sparling, who cried when he preached; and the Reverend Dinsdale T. Young, who liked to bang the Bible with his fist. I thumped on a big dictionary because I thought the Reverend Young was too rough with the Bible. I liked doing the Reverend Solomon Cleaver. It wasn't exactly a sermon, it was more of a lecture about somebody called "Jeen Val Jeen" and it sounded the way I thought theatre was.

A large cupboard along one end of the billiard room was filled with the curios that Uncle Walter and Uncle Fred had brought from the Holy Land and Egypt and California.

And there was Uncle Fred's flute. It was a fine instrument with an ivory mouthpiece and two other pieces with the stops on them. I could make noises through it and I finally went to grandma and asked if I could have it and take lessons. Certainly, she said, she would love me to have the flute. I took it home and father said he would ask Professor Hartman, who had been leader of the Massey band, to be my teacher.

Next day, father told grandma I would be taking lessons on

Uncle Fred's flute. "Chester, how can you let that boy have Fred's flute?" Aunt Lillie broke in. "He died of galloping consumption!"

"That was fifteen years ago!" father objected.

Later, though, he suggested I try the banjo, and the next day he bought me one. I started lessons with Mr. Newton who lived out on Dovercourt Road near the Massey works. I was learning pretty well, until Mr. Newton scared me by confiding that he was an atheist. One day he said you could get arrested for sending the Bible through the mail because some of it was "something" graphic. Then he said there was no God, and that really frightened me. Clutching my banjo, I hurried out to Van who was waiting in the pony cart. There were such things as thunderbolts! When I told father, that was the end of the banjo.

Aunt Lillie had an organ, with pipes. It was in the drawing room at grandma's house, so that Mr. Wheeldon, the organist at the Metropolitan Church, could come up and play for her. It was fitted with a pianola arrangement, like a player piano, and there was a big collection of rolls of all kinds of music. The actual notes and harmonies were pierced on the rolls, but you could supplement these on the two manuals or the pedals and the choice of stops was entirely up to the performer. In the belief that I possessed a musical talent, I was encouraged to "play" the organ. After several vicious discords caused by my supplementing the recorded rolls, I was dissuaded from "improving" the records. My choice of stops was also limited after I cut in the full diapasons and bourdons and doppelflötes in a spirited rendition of "William Tell." These huge pipes, the big bourdons, were great boxes, next to the furnace room below the library. Mr. Pragnell complained that his clay pipe was shattered by the vibration while he was stoking the furnace. I had the tremolo on but it wasn't that which broke his pipe; it was cutting in the big stops that made him spit his pipe out on the floor. Mr. Pragnell was in a difficult position. He couldn't press the case as he shouldn't have been smoking in the cellar so he settled for a warning, "It's a good thing your grandfer can't catch up with you!"

6

After mother died I used to go over to grandma's house pretty often. She knew I was lonely, and looking back grandma was probably lonely, too. She was always ready to talk with me in her sitting room crowded with pictures, knick-knacks and the precious clutter of a long life.

On the table beside her chair was a big family Bible with pages of the "family tree" in front. Grandma said it had been started by my great-grandfather, Daniel Massey, and she had brought it up to date after he died. There were the usual notations of births, marriages and deaths but grandma had added her innovation — what each man had done for a living.

This family tree fascinated me — probably because I found my name on it. Grandma hadn't written what I or Vincent — who was then over seventeen — were going to do for a living, but there were spaces after our names and my cousins' names, too. Grandma would tell what she remembered about our ancestors and the family stories she had heard about those she hadn't known. There were tales of Indian massacres and land clearings, rowdy barn raisings with somebody getting killed on one occasion, eight-year-old sons doing a man's work on the land, and exciting drives in blizzards across the frozen St. Lawrence River.

Later research by my brother, Vincent, into the Massey doings,

44

talks with father and Mr. Seldon and, more recently, some prompting from Mollie Gillen in her excellent book, *The Masseys*, confirm that grandma was fairly accurate in her facts.

One ancestor on the tree always caught my eye. His name was Jonathan Massey and his twelve children took up a whole branch of the tree. Grandma said that Jonathan, who was my great-great-great-grandfather, was the fourth in line from Geoffrey Massey who came to America from England in 1630. Jonathan had been a lieutenant in the Continental Army in the Revolutionary War. He founded a place called Watertown in northeast New York State after the war. I thought he could have done it with just his twelve children. According to grandma, Watertown was a nest of Masseys after that, and the Canadian Masseys kept in close touch with them.

There were only two ancestors on grandma's tree who weren't labelled "farmers." They were my great-grandfather, Daniel Massey, and my grandfather, Hart Almerrin Massey. She had called them "manufacturers." I asked her to explain why she had done this and she said both of them belonged to the Machine Age and made things rather than grew them.

Daniel Massey had come to Canada with his family from Watertown in 1802 when he was four years old, and forty years later he owned a farm of over four hundred acres at Grafton near Cobourg in Canada West, with a large house, barns and cattle. Daniel and his father had paid for it by clearing land for sale.

He and my great-grandmother, Lucina, had seven children, the second of whom was my grandfather, Hart Massey, who was seventeen at this time. It was 1840. From the time he was able to walk, Daniel had worked like a man on the farm and Hart was the same way.

Daniel could look at his land, his house and barns and be satisfied. But he wasn't. He knew the agonizing labour that farming demanded; he knew that clearing land for sale was the reason he owned his beautiful farm. Grandma said that over the years Daniel Massey had cleared more than two thousand acres. He had the vision to fear that with the prehistoric farming methods of the time, he might well lose that farm. Great-grandfather was a successful, disillusioned and worn-out man just forty-two years old in 1840. He was a pioneer but he belonged to the Machine Age.

Grandma said that my grandfather did, too. But he did not know it then. By this time he was working on the farm just as hard as Daniel had at the same age. There was a difference, grandma said, for right from the start he went to school and later he put himself through Victoria College in Cobourg, a very good college that the Methodists had founded. She would say she never understood how a boy in his teens could practically run the four-hundred acre farm at Grafton, manage a logging business of his own with twenty-five men working for him, organize a new Methodist church and serve as steward, act as a volunteer fireman, and get a good education at the same time.

As Hart grew up, he heard more and more outcries from his father about primitive farming methods. Grandma once showed me an article which Daniel had written in the Cobourg paper: "The tools in use on the farms all over the world in 1840 are the same as those used in the days of the Pharaohs. There has been a small, metal share added to the plough and some smart Scot has put a long handle on the sickle a few years ago and we have the scythe, but the back-breaking chores of sowing, reaping, threshing and cultivating are still nightmares to most farmers."

Daniel and Hart had made several trips to Watertown around 1840 and they had found on the farms of relatives several new-fangled machines for harvesting and cultivating. They were clumsy and seemed impractical but Daniel imported some of these to experiment with at Grafton.

According to grandma, Daniel wasn't an inventor but he was a born machine man.

A big barn at Grafton became a workshop. One of the imports from Watertown was a huge behemoth of a contraption about the size of the first Massey log cabin. Grandma showed me an engraving of it. It was the first threshing machine to be used in Canada. My great-grandfather wrestled with the monster for two years and

46

made it work for the harvest of 1842. It still needed eleven men to work it but threshing with flails required double that number.

According to grandma, in about 1845 Daniel said to his son, Hart, "If only I had a factory instead of a farm."

Grandma was Eliza Ann Phelps of Gloversville in northeast New York State. She was a beauty, even in her eighties, and grandpa was "smitten all of a heap" on a visit to the Massey clan in Watertown, where she was a guest. It was an arduous courtship. Grandpa could be spared from his farm work in Grafton only in the winter, so over the frozen St. Lawrence River he would go. He made two drives in a bob-sleigh from Grafton to Gloversville. It was three hundred miles each way. He may have lacked time for subtle persuasion but in those two six-hundred-mile trips he got his girl.

Grandma married Hart Almerrin Massey in 1846 and she took her honeymoon ride to Grafton wrapped in a couple of big musk-ox robes behind the best light draft team in the Grafton stable. In the big sleigh, among other new wedding possessions, were the beautiful store of household linen made from cloth spun and woven by great-grandmother Phelps and the kitchen utensils made by my great-grandfather Phelps, who besides being a good farmer was an even better tinsmith.

Grandma remembered that drive. It took the full six days to Grafton. She said it was so cold during the last seventy miles that even her new husband admitted it was a mite chilly. I remember asking what the hotels were like along the way. In my eight or nine years of living, when one left home on a journey one stayed at hotels. This query caused amusement. She explained that there were no hotels. They stayed at "suitable Methodist farmhouses," carefully chosen in advance by Hart. She said, "We Methodists may not play cards and dance, nor attend theatres nor countenance frivolity, Raymond, but always remember we are given to hospitality."

As Hart drove the sleigh up to the Grafton farmhouse, grandma knew nothing of her new father-in-law's desire to abandon the farm for the factory. She had expected to wait for her own

47

home. Hardly had the sleigh been unloaded and the horses watered and fed, when Daniel read a poem welcoming Eliza Ann Massey to Canada. Then with the excitement of a schoolboy who had won a prize, my great-grandfather announced that he had found a two-storey building for sale with a machine shop, a six-horsepower steam engine, two lathes and a two-ton-capacity cupola furnace. Grandma said she could still remember all these things although she had no notion of what they meant.

This factory was at Newcastle, seventeen miles west of Cobourg on the Kingston road, and it was going cheap. Daniel wanted to buy it but he didn't have the cash. He had the farm, and Hart had the cash from his logging business. If Hart would buy the farm for cash, Daniel could buy his longed-for machine shop.

Next day Daniel talked it over with Hart. Grandma hadn't heard the discussion, though she wished she had. She said they were two hard-headed men and there was no sentiment involved, just a practical business deal. After it was settled, grandfather owned the Grafton farm, Eliza Ann Massey was its mistress, and great-grandfather Daniel owned a factory at Newcastle which would shortly become the property of "The Massey Manufacturing Company," making farm implements with two employees. One hundred and thirty years later, this firm would have another name, "Massey-Ferguson Limited," and a great many more employees.

About four years later, my grandfather received a call from great-grandfather Daniel, asking him to take control of the Newcastle business. Daniel was only fifty-two but he was tired. Though he had been a good farmer at Grafton, Hart knew where he belonged and the move to Newcastle was eagerly made. My uncle Charles and my father were too young to remember the farm so there were no regrets for Grafton. If grandma had any, she never let anybody know. Father always said that the Newcastle years — there were twenty of them — were grandma's happiest. Like most people of pioneer stock, she liked small towns where living was close to the country.

Uncle Charles and father were not placid or docile boys. They seemed to have been a couple of young hellions whose favourite playgrounds were the factory or their grandfather's workshop. They were given to practical jokes and to the incessant torment of two young aunts who were only a few years older but who could fortunately give as well as take in combat. On occasion there would be an unholy alliance of the four and their evil efforts would be directed at old Daniel, who in his retirement liked nothing better than to be pestered by the kids. He seemed to delight in having his tools hidden or his workshop invaded by a small fife-and-drum band. I would have loved to see my father tooling a fife.

Father had had a teacher in first grade at Newcastle grammar school whom grandma remembered happily. Father, with his flaming red hair, arrived at school for the first time with two small Negro boys. Before seating the newcomers, the teacher presented them to the class.

"These are three new pupils, Chester Massey and the Johnson boys," she said. "You must all remember to be kind to coloured children and red-headed boys."

"Your Uncle Charles had to stand in the corner for laughing," grandma said. "And your father was roughed up a bit on general principles after school, although the Johnson boys escaped."

Grandfather died in 1896 after a short illness. He had driven himself with merciless disregard for his health to the end of his seventy-three years. At the time of his death, Hart Massey was a national figure, who in slightly less than fifty years had built a small, village smithy in one of Britain's colonies into one of the largest and most successful manufactories in the Empire.

He died a wealthy man by Canadian standards, but he could have left a much larger fortune had he chosen a different manufacturing code. He clung to the principle of making the best machines for a just profit. Quality set his price.

In the final decade of his life, my grandfather engaged in a number of philanthropic projects but remained oblivious to social life. Most of his benefactions were connected with the Methodist Church but some were for the whole community.

Hart Massey personally received scant recognition from his

contemporaries, nor has his memory fared better in subsequent comment. The picture of the man remains a Victorian stereotype — a domineering patriarch, a ruthless, penny-pinching, slave-driving employer.

The truth is that Hart Massey was no worse and in many ways far better as an employer than many of his contemporaries in business. He believed in a reasonable wage for a reasonable day's work. All through his life, Hart Massey remained a Puritan, guided by the Ten Commandments, as my father said, not one of which he ever broke. Such a record does not lead to popularity but he was one of the founders and makers of modern Canada.

The winter of 1907-1908 was long and bitter. Father had told me that grandma had always dreaded the Canadian winters. I knew this was so, not that she talked about it, but she was always so glad to see the sun.

In 1908 grandma was eighty-five, and she was still beautiful. She had lived in Canada for sixty-two years. She had had much joy and too much sorrow. Only two of her six children had survived. Four of her sons had died with shocking suddenness — one in infancy, one at twenty-three, and two others in the prime of life. Grandfather too had died unexpectedly. Now grandma was tired and almost bedridden. Just when the end of March was showing signs of a final thaw and nearly all the snow had gone, a blizzard blew up overnight covering the city with a foot of snow.

In the morning, as every morning before he went to work, my father went to see grandma.

"There's more snow, Chester!" she almost complained. "Is it never going away?"

Father sat down at grandma's level to estimate what she could see from her bedroom windows that looked out on Jarvis Street. Then he went to the office. During the day he made certain arrangements. Mr. Housser and the Reverend Dr. Burns who lived opposite were delighted to co-operate, as was the Baptist Church on the corner of Wellesley. Then my father telephoned the Fred

Victor Mission (a memorial to my uncle, grandma's son Fred Victor). There was a skid-row department at the Mission and the men could make some money on emergency work like snow shovelling. That was what father was going to have done; remove all the snow that grandma could see from her windows.

At six o'clock, when it was dark, the skid-row men marched up Jarvis from the Mission with snow shovels and brooms and two big snow carts. Van, James, Mr. White, Mr. Pragnell and I went to work, too. Everybody was told to be absolutely quiet. We started at seven and by three o'clock in the morning there wasn't a snowflake visible from grandma's windows. The men from the Mission had made a sign which they placed on the lawn:

SPRING IS HERE,
MRS. HART MASSEY

In the morning father and I went to see grandma.

"Chester, it's so like you to do that!" She seemed very happy. "Were they the poor men from the Fred Victor Mission?"

"Why, Mother, did you hear anything?"

"Hear anything?" she laughed. "I tiptoed to the window and counted them. There were twenty-five or thirty men with shovels and when that many men try to be quiet it's like those barn raisings in the Newcastle days! Did they get a good supper?"

"Oh, yes, half at your house and half at mine. And they were paid, don't worry, Mother."

"I'm so glad the Fred Victor men did the work. That sign was so dear, Chester."

She was suddenly asleep. It had been a tiring night for the old lady.

Grandma, the last pioneer in the family, lived to see the spring and part of the summer.

7

Uncle Walter's farm was near East Toronto, then a village about seven miles from the city. It was started in 1897, but before Uncle Walter died in 1901, it was already the most beautiful farm I have ever seen. He called it Dentonia Park after his wife Susan Denton of Boston. Its two hundred and fifty acres included every kind of land; more than seventy acres of rolling, arable fields; the same amount of ravines and hills for pasturage; the remainder, small lakes and woods. Today the property is part of the big city, vanished in streets and housing.

Father had built a house on a knoll that overlooked fish ponds in a valley. Uncle Walter's house was on another small hill with a ravine between us. Both were big, Victorian, shingled houses with enormous verandahs. Inside, the floors were covered with grass matting that smelled like hay. The furniture was mostly wicker and our house was full of alcoves and turrets and great fireplaces where we burned big logs at night.

That summer of 1904 we moved out to Dentonia after the Dominion Day Horse Parade. Aunt Fanny had won First Prize in the harnessed pony class and I had driven her — just as mother had said I might. I had just finished my first term at the Model School. It was good to see the farm again.

All the same, it was sad without mother. Miss Dick had left, as I had recovered from whatever had plagued me. May Crammond, the Scottish housemaid, was supposed to ride herd on me as to the remaining medicines. Since she didn't believe I needed any, the "physicking" had stopped. My natural health had won out over the doctors. May kept the bottles lying around the bathroom anyway and I kept quiet. Let "them" credit bottles — May and I didn't care.

Cousin Kate and Nan drove to Dentonia this time with Barney and Dolly in the "extension top" — a double buggy with a top that extended from the rear seat to two notches by the box seat.

The "extension top" always provoked Vincent; he said it was a farmer's cart. Maybe it was a bit like a surrey but mother had always liked it. A couple of years later Vincent, then nineteen, persuaded father to buy a four-wheeled conveyance called a "T-cart." It was a high contraption seating four or six passengers, with long steps on curved steel rods to let one climb in. Van took an immediate dislike to the T-cart. I overheard a conversation in the stable.

"It's loike a shootin' brake," James defended the vehicle. "Our Currnel of The Royal Irish had one when we was on the Curragh years ago. Ah, the Currnel was a great man with the ladies!"

"Well, I can see you could get a woman into the thing, but in all decency you ought to marry her first!"

The T-cart was not used very often.

I drove in the pony cart with James. Van had already made a trip with May Crammond, Annie Shields and Mary, the cook. Father would come from the office in the Ivanhoe electric which, on a full charge all day at the factory, could just make the round trip to the farm and back. You could always tell father's arrival because the planks of the bridge over the ravine rumbled but there were no hoof beats.

After seven miles of bumping on the Danforth Road, and passing the smell of the glue factory, it was a thrill to turn north on the Dawes Road and see the wide-opened farm gates on the right and a quarter-mile sweep of smooth gravel road lined with hydrangeas and young maple trees just beckoning you to come in. Even surly old Aunt Fanny perked up, as she had in the Horse Parade the day

53

before, and trotted along between the two huge fields of young corn. Soon we came to a dip in the road and the plank bridge that rumbled under the wheels. On the right I could see the powerhouse with its tall chimney and greenhouses. We passed the wooded enclosure with its deer and in a few minutes were on the long planked bridge over the second ravine. And there was our house. In front of it, across the road, stood the great water tank, a hundred feet up on a steel tower topped by a flagpole. I knew that one day my masculine pride would force me to climb it — probably this summer for I was nearly eight — but I was very much afraid. Its narrow iron ladder went right to the top of the big wooden tank that held thousands of gallons of water. Early one morning that summer of 1904 I climbed it. Nobody saw me.

Beyond the tower, across a broad lawn, stood the big barn. The rambling, four-storey building was perched on a steep slope that gave access for cattle at each of its four levels.

For me there has never been a place of such enchantment as Dentonia. How I had looked forward to returning to it! I would explore the mysteries of its hills and valleys — the bull barn, the piggery, the dizzy trolleys on high poles for the buckets to haul manure from the cattle levels to the great fertilizer tower across the valley, the fish ponds, the powerhouse with the big Corliss engine and the dozens of other excitements that invited rediscovery each year.

The old witch Aunt Fanny would once again be my companion, my boss, and sometimes, I would pretend, my war horse. Due to illness, I had been forbidden so many childhood pleasures, but here at Dentonia I was entrusted to the old Shetland pony. True, I had known Aunt Fanny since my earliest memories, but it was a surprising privilege all the same. It must have been because father knew I could ride well — about the only thing I could do well — and because he knew I wasn't afraid of my pony.

In retrospect it seems hard to believe that, in less than four years, Uncle Walter made Dentonia into a practical farming operation. Still more astonishing was the formation of one of the finest Jersey herds on the continent, together with a smaller herd of Ayrshire dairy cattle. But this was my uncle's achievement. His farm was part of a larger project of Walter Massey to supply pure milk to the city of Toronto. For this he had founded the City Dairy Company. The farm was to be a model for the company's participating farmers. The milk supply of the city was appallingly bad, pasteurization almost unknown, as it was elsewhere in Canada and the United States. It was a bitter irony that Uncle Walter, in the midst of his campaign for milk purification, had died in 1901 of typhoid, caught by drinking contaminated water on a railway car. He was only thirty-seven.

My uncle had taken over as president of the Massey-Harris Company on grandfather's death in 1896. He inherited Hart Massey's craving for activity and kept as many projects running as a juggler keeps bottles in the air. His farm was his favourite enterprise and when he died, his widow, Aunt Susie, who knew everything about the farm, completed all his unfinished projects.

That summer I had plenty to do. I hadn't been to Dentonia the previous year and there were many things to be investigated — new buildings, animals and men. I scarcely knew where to begin, so I settled for a second breakfast over the ravine at Aunt Susie's house. Four cousins were there: Ruth, who was my brother's age and almost grown-up; Madeline, a month or two older than I; Dorothy, six; and Denton, four or, as he kept proclaiming, almost five.

Breakfast was in full swing when I arrived. I found myself able to tackle a plate of pancakes and sausages. I arranged to play with the cousins that afternoon and walked to our stable near the Dawes Road about half a mile away. Aunt Fanny did her old trick of blowing herself up with a deep breath when I tried to tighten the girth.

"Just give her a tap of the knee, trooper, as you girth up, like this," said James, who had been watching.

He applied his knee to the pony's inflated barrel as he gave the girth a good tug. Aunt Fanny grunted and bared her teeth.

Off we went down the road to the powerhouse. Aunt Fanny deliberately walked off and brushed my knee against a tree trunk. As soon as I got her back on the road with crop and heels, I beat her into a canter. It wasn't ever easy but once you did, she would go galumphing along with the grace of a runaway hippopotamus. Soon we were at the powerhouse. Tethering the pony, I went in. There was Mr. Steen, nursing his big steam engine that drove the dynamos for hundreds of batteries, the switchboard and the great furnace. Mr. Steen was not only the farm engineer, but he did the carpentering and ran the trout hatcheries by the stream and ponds below our house. He also knew all the farm news.

"Why, you missed the whole of last year at Dentonia, didn't you, Raymond?"

I nodded and sat down.

"Well, we got a new superintendent, Mr. Morrison, and he's quite a fellow for changes. Good man, though. We have two Walker-Gordon cow barns over beyond the horse barn and the Jersey herd's now near the two hundred your uncle was aiming at. Last year we got four red ribbons at the 'Ex'. Now there's a heifer that'll do better than Miss Nellie if she don't blow herself up with those crab apples!"

Mr. Steen was recalling a disaster of 1902 when Miss Nellie of Dentonia, the champion Jersey cow of North America with more ribbons than you could count, had broken into the orchard along Pharmacy Avenue and gobbled windfalls until she burst her stomach. She had been named for Aunt Nellie Perrin, sister of Aunt Susie. It was lucky for the real Aunt Nellie that she had a good figure. As it was, she endured plenty of ribald jokes about apples.

"How about Lord of Dentonia, Mr. Steen?"

This was the Jersey bull, the head one, who two years ago had gored a herdsman.

"He still has his job, Raymond, and there's been no more trouble. That fellow got gored in the seat of his pants. Proves he was either running away or not paying attention."

"How are the trout, Mr. Steen?"

"Never better. You'll catch bigger ones than ever this year. Your aunt is going to make the little pond into a swimmin' pool . . . Oh, there's Pengilly — you'll want to say hello to him!"

I rushed out to greet my friend the head gardener, a Cornishman.

"How's Richie, Mr. Pengilly?"

"He's well, Raymond, and looks forward to your coming."

"And George?"

"Getting old, but he does his work well. Come and see my flowers."

The greenhouses and forcing house were just across the road by the powerhouse furnace. George was the old farm horse who pulled the gang of three lawn mowers. To protect the lawns, George wore huge leather boots, of which he was proud. He would lift his big hooves high and delicately when he wore boots.

Richie, Mr. Pengilly's son, used to play with my cousins and me. He was mentally retarded and spastic, but one of the kindest human beings I ever knew. He'd participate in our games with eagerness and enjoyment, though mostly as an onlooker. Richie was a happy part of the childhood of the four of us — Madeline, Dorothy, Denton and myself.

I thought I would take in the bull barn before I saw my cousins that afternoon. I had to be braver than the girls and the kid Denton. I parted from Mr. Steen and Mr. Pengilly with a casual announcement that I would have a look at Lord of Dentonia. Aunt Fanny ambled off carrying her extremely trepid master.

Madeline had frightened me a previous summer with her stories of "leaf men" and "yellow men," "feather men" and "iron men," in a game called "Adventures" which we all played. I wanted some exploit of my own to counter her scary tales. As I rode past the deer woods, I was rapidly reaching a decision to do more than just look at the bull barn from the outside. We were now on the plank bridge. As we passed the farm hands' boarding house and the horse barn, my mind was made up. I rode by the new Walker-Gordon cow barns, hardly noticing them.

About a quarter of a mile ahead was the castle of the Lord of Dentonia. I rode up to the drawbridge which, I saw to my dismay, was down. There was no retreat. I tied my war horse to a small tree and walked forward to the huge door of the fearful beast's lair. With a sinking heart I saw that there were no guards to keep me out. My sword had turned back into the light riding crop that had been mother's. I leaned against the door, too frozen to do anything.

There was a bellow from inside. I jumped into a ditch by the side of the barn. The door opened. A herdsman came out and walked away. He hadn't seen me, and he hadn't shut the door. Something invisible pushed me through — and I was in the bull barn with four ferocious beasts glaring at me from their cages. Three were Jersey bulls, black with tawny bellies. The fourth was an Ayrshire, large and mottled. I recognized one Jersey as His Lordship. He started to paw the straw, snort and toss his head. Suddenly there was a blood-curdling bellow. The two other Jerseys joined in a wicked chorus. Right where I stood I vomited. The bulls were silent. I looked at them with hatred. They stared back. My fear gone, I sneaked away, hoping the bulls didn't know of my humiliation.

That afternoon I joined Richie Pengilly and my cousins at their tennis court. "I went over to the bull barn to see Lord of Dentonia this morning," I told Madeline. "He seems to be tamer than he was two years ago."

"Maybe you're older, Raymond," she said. The remark cut deeply. Of course, she didn't know what had happened in front of the bulls.

Madeline invented the game "Adventures," which we were to play that afternoon. Unidentified Flying Objects played an important part in her games. She called them "Sky Wagons." What made Madeline's game remarkable was that the inventor was an eight-year-old girl who had never read *The Wizard of Oz*, had never heard of Jules Verne and would have to wait forty years to read Bradbury's science fiction. In 1903, she imagined aeroplanes, radio, even television.

"The Leaf Men have landed near the Powerhouse. They've come in Sky Wagons and they are now in the wood where the deer are. Leaf Men can glide like leaves, you know. They have some weapons we don't know anything about, except they can kill you just by your breathing! Raymond, go and explore the deer wood, then come back and tell us what's happening there. Take Richie with you, and be careful how you breathe!"

Twelve years later, in 1915, when the 1st Canadian Division

58

suffered a German gas attack at St. Julien, they learned that Germans could kill you just by your breathing.

Aunt Susie's sister Nellie and her husband, Willard Perrin, arrived the next week for the summer. "Uncle" Willard, a Methodist minister from Boston, was a born athlete. In his sixties and somewhat portly, he still moved with the grace of a cat. There was nothing in the way of sports that he could not do well: golf, tennis, fishing, even ping-pong. He taught us how to "snap" apples from the far knoll back of Aunt Susie's house right into the middle pond, which was as far as driving a golf ball. First he cut willow stalks the length of a fishing pole; then he stuck an apple on the thin end and, just like cracking a whip, sent the apple for miles!

Uncle Willard's knuckles were thick and some were bent because in his youth he had caught bare handed on the Harvard baseball team. That was when Abner Doubleday was codifying the rules for baseball, the greatest game played by men. I could see why they wore gloves when I looked at Uncle Willard's knuckles. He didn't have a mask either. I asked why he never had his nose broken and he said yes, he had broken it twice.

In the valley below the tennis court, providing about thirty acres of pasture for the cows, Uncle Walter had laid out a nine-hole golf course. There was more grazing land along Pharmacy Avenue so that the greens and much of the fairways could be roped off without constricting the dietary requirements of the herd. But Jersey cows have the agility of gazelles and the golf course, always incorrectly referred to by my father as a links, often presented a spotty appearance.

"Willard," I heard him say as he surveyed the fairway, "judging by what Walter has invested in this Jersey herd, he has the most expensive layout of hazards of any golf links in North America!"

Whereupon he put his tee shot right in the middle of a cow pat on the green.

"By George, a hole in one!" he cried. It pleased him more than any shot he made that summer.

Father was left-handed, at least his clubs were left-handed, and, without regard to what my natural dexterity might be, I was given a sawed-off cleek of his. For twenty-five years I played left-handed with a consistent and vicious slice, which Archie Compston, the great English pro, told me was because I was naturally a right-handed man. So I changed over and had a consistent and vicious hook, but did lower my handicap three strokes.

I was fairly young when Uncle Walter died and I don't remember much about him except the gasoline-buggy episode. I remember the pasteurizing machinery in the big barn, the first such equipment to be installed in Canada. My uncle was very proud of it. The dairy was lined with tile. In addition to pasteurizing, the milk went through a modification process, which was supposed to make it more digestible. The men working in the lab, as Uncle Walter called the dairy, wore long white coats, as did the milk hands in the barns.

I also remember well my Uncle Walter's Bible class, which he held at his house every Sunday afternoon. Seventy or eighty people would arrive — farm hands and their families and all of us Masseys. After my uncle died, Uncle Willard conducted the class. When cousin Denton grew up, he held a large Bible class in Toronto, which was also broadcast. At sixty, he was ordained as an Anglican priest and having had a parish in Waterloo in Ontario, became assistant to the Bishop of Arizona.

On Saturdays and holidays, people used to come out from Toronto to see the farm. They would be met at the Street Railway terminus at De La Plante's lumber yard in East Toronto with a tallyho and four horses, and be driven the few miles to Dentonia. There they would be shown around the farm buildings by some of the farm hands.

It occurred to me that this might be a profitable and entertaining undertaking. I once managed to entice a few unsuspecting victims and show them where Richard the Lion-Hearted had been imprisoned and held to ransom on his return from the Crusade; where John Wesley had preached and where Cornwallis had surrendered to General Washington. For these points of interest, I used the manure tower, the bull barn and the upper loft of the main barn. But my enterprise was ended by May Crammond, who had spotted my guided tour from our kitchen window. My audience was reluctant to dispense with my services. When father heard about it, he wanted me to take him over the rest of my tour. He could tease better than I could.

In August there was a Coaching Parade. All the family took part, and so did the farm employees. A great many people came from the city.

There were about fourteen entries. Uncle Willard was a sort of Uncle Sam on a hay wagon draped with Union Jacks, drawn by Clydesdales. Aunt Susie's niece, Grace Carter, drove a big rake so wide it carried away three hydrangea bushes from Aunt Susie's driveway and dropped them by the main barn. Mr. Pengilly said he was going to replant them right there. "She has an uncanny planting sense," he said. Just the same, she didn't move hydrangeas as thoroughly as Georgie and I had with the firecracker.

Madeline drove a champion Berkshire hog, or rather the hog drove Madeline and one of the farm boys. The hog had a wonderful time and ate a bed of flowers. It wasn't Mr. Pengilly's afternoon. I was an old farmer with Aunt Fanny in spectacles, a mob cap and apron. We won the prize for the funniest entry. As we waited in line for the judging, Aunt Fanny deliberately bit a hole in her apron and held the piece of cloth in her mouth. Angry, I could not help crying. It was not the last time I failed to understand the feminine mind.

8

I went to school in the fall. Mine was the Model School, a boys' public school attached to the provincial teachers' college. There were some girls among us but their playing field was behind a high fence. No boy would admit that the old Model wasn't a regular all-male place and that the squeals and giggles from beyond weren't imaginary. The building was of dingy grey brick and considered outmoded and overcrowded in 1904. On a recent visit to Toronto I saw that, apparently unaltered, it was still in full use sixty-five years later. I would back it against any of these southern exposure, sun-glass factories we're taxed for today.

Our playground, about three-quarters of a proper football field, presented a glutinous surface of clay with patches of gravel. A hard tackle could leave permanent scars. The Model was no place for sissies. Recreation for the younger boys consisted of fighting (all seasons), "bully-up" in the fall and marbles in spring and summer. The fighting was not conducted by the Marquis of Queensberry's rules. Bully-up or "conking" was a fine old Canadian sport based on the toughness of a dried horse chestnut. There were several theories as to the best method of drying the chestnut — the "bully" or "conker." Some favoured the "back-of-the-furnace-for-a-week" technique; others, the quickie way of getting their mothers to bake it in the oven for an hour. But it was agreed that nothing could better a year's seasoning in the attic. Once properly dried, the bully was pierced or drilled, a process comparable to cutting a fifty-carat diamond. The hole had to be in the right place. Then a strong shoelace was run through the hole, knotted, and with eighteen inches play the bully was ready for contest. Its owner would offer battle by holding out the bully at string's length and crying "bully-up!" A challenger was always forthcoming. The game was simply to smash the opposing bully by alternate "conks" or swings. The winner's bully gained all the previous victories of the loser. These were known as "lives." There were titanic contests between veterans of a hundred lives or more. Records of lives were scrupulously honest, recorded by knots on the shoelace, each knot denoting ten lives.

Marbles were the spring pastime. In addition to conventional methods of play, some of us made pinball contraptions by which great fortunes were won. Some of us may have been dullards at arithmetic but in exploiting our cigar-box drops and obstacle slides, the odds we demanded gave us a good ten-percent edge.

Two dark spectres haunted my early weeks at the Model. One was my past at a girls' school and the other was that, although now seven-going-on-eight, I still had to be escorted to school. It seemed to me that Havergal might remain secret. But the pony cart that brought me to the Model School couldn't be hidden. Father still thought Jarvis Street dangerous. In addition to whirlwind two-wheel butcher carts, there now was the menace of Cawthra Mulock's huge French automobile. Father claimed it frequently exceeded the speed of the fastest horse. But the Darracq rarely completed its brief journey down to King Street without a prolonged breakdown. I suspect that father, who drove his own electric buggy at an inflexible speed of ten miles an hour, considered himself the main threat to any user of Toronto streets. Anyway, in October, when the electric was put up for the winter, I was allowed to go to school alone.

The tingling freedom that was now mine allowed me to walk to the Model by way of Church Street and this would take me past the firehouse. It was an engine company with a hose reel and a small ladder truck. There were seven horses, two each for the vehicles and a spare. The two trucks had good-looking bay teams, and the engine as beautiful a pair of grey Percherons as you could dream of.

I knew all the horses. Every day they passed our house on their exercise rides and were shod, like our own, at Mr. Crow's blacksmith shop over on Isabella Street. It was a pretty sight to see the driver in uniform riding the near horse bareback. I often wondered what happened if there was a fire during the ride.

The first time I passed the firehouse on my walk to school, the captain said, "Come back home this way and we'll do the alarm drill for you about half-past three. Bring some of your friends."

I chose my friends with care — Willie Caven, Doug Ellis and the Warren boys, Harold and Eric.

This was not the first time or the last that I was to watch the alarm drill but I think it was the best I ever saw. The fireman with his red shirt and handle-bar moustache needed skill with hose, hooks and ladders, but he had to be a bit of a horseman as well. It took two or three men to handle the harnessing, and the drivers had to be understudied. In the Church Street station the stables were in the rear, the horses in small boxstalls whose doors could be opened by a single lever near the brass descent poles. Two large doors, also spring-loaded to fly open, gave access from the stables to the engine park and were released by a second lever. The horses were always unhaltered. Harnessing for action involved lowering the complete assembly onto the eager pair, releasing the two suspension lines and snapping shut the collar and hames, fastening a belly-band with breast strap attachment, and putting on the bridles. The whole breeching unit, traces already attached to swingletrees, neckyoke with breast straps, even the reins looped round the whip in its socket, were all hung ready to be lowered with the pole.

The men slid down the brass pole to the clanging of the alarm bell that also excited the horses. Stable doors and box-stall doors sprung open. Six unbridled and eager horses emerged and trotted unguided to their stations. There was no stamping and snorting as the partners exchanged dignified bows of greeting. The drivers

64

harnessed up, climbed to the boxes, the grooms standing by, and all was ready.

They were off and back in a few minutes. It was a pleasure to see the men steer the heavy vehicles into their places. We all helped to water the horses and bed them down, praying for the real alarm to ring.

About three months later, Doug Ellis and I were walking home when we saw, at the corner of Carlton and Church, clouds of smoke billowing out of Carnahan's Drug Store and the windows above it. The Company was in action. The engine smoke stack was throwing out sparks that threatened the house next door. Firemen were smashing up Mr. Carnahan's stock with axes and drenching his store. Nearby, the horses were tied up and blanketed, munching in their nose-bags. I went over to the huge pair, Gog and Magog, seventeen hands high. They nodded and lazily chewed away.

Winter brought new delights. All of us wore moccasins or shoe-packs, which were good for sliding on the icy sidewalks. Long stretches of smooth ice could be made by shuffling and tramping. The fact that none of the good Toronto citizens cleaned sidewalks adequately gave us some grand runs.

The equipment of the old Model School may have left something to be desired. We used slates for what were called "sums" and were frequently tested on a blatantly competitive basis. We were well disciplined with punitive measures, such as extra sums and lines of copy-book to be written and even Mr. MacIntosh's cane. But all our teachers were patient, understanding and determined.

There were five divisions or classes corresponding roughly to American grades. I was in the first division two and a half years. This was not as shameful as it might seem. The class was divided into junior and senior sections equivalent to present-day first and second grades. The whole division had one teacher. She had over fifty savages in her charge and two distinct classes to direct. Miss Taylor was tall, her voice was soft and deep, and I thought her beautiful. Her clear blue eyes saw everything, and she made each one of us feel that her undivided attention was on him.

My first report, dated September 4th, 1904, was not promising.

"Greatest number of credit marks obtainable: 126; obtained by this pupil: 26; number of pupils in this section: 27." The ample spaces for Teacher's Remarks and Parent's Remarks were ominously blank. I also have to confess that number 27 had been persistently absent following a bout of scarlet fever. But the future did become brighter. By March 23rd, 1906, I stood number 5 in the senior section of thirty-one boys; and not only that, I scored a possible 60 in arithmetic.

My teacher in second division was Mr. Sorceliel, a burly, ebullient moustachioed French-Canadian. A stern disciplinarian with a sense of fun, he was a gifted teacher. When things went well "Sorcy" would read us poetry — Scott, Tennyson, Macaulay and the like. This we enjoyed almost as much as he did. He was a genuine Romantic, Victorian and sentimental.

We had a healthy young rebel in the second form, Gawn Clemes, a realist slightly ahead of his time. Smart and articulate, his collisions with Sorcy were frequent and violent. Sorcy, in one of his expansive moods, was defining beauty. He asked what we had seen recently that was beautiful.

"I saw a lovely wax dummy wearing a new dress in Simpsons' window," Gawn Clemes said.

"Clemes, I can do nothing with you!" I thought Sorcy was going to bust. "Remember this, all of you! The ugliest living thing created by God is far more beautiful than anything that man has made. Life is beauty!"

The drawing master, Ernie Casselman, taught all the divisions. He looked like Groucho Marx, only he wasn't funny. He was a big man with a voice like a bullfrog. He certainly could draw and he had no patience with those who couldn't. He would put up a vase or other object and we would have to copy it. If he didn't like the work, we'd get a crack on the knuckles from his heavy pencil.

One day, soon after Sorcy's debate about beauty, Ernie had the form. He set a pot on Sorcy's table, telling us it was a copy of a famous urn, perhaps one of the most beautiful things in the world. Gawn Clemes' hand went up at once.

"Mr. Casselman, if the urn isn't alive, how can it be one of the most beautiful things in the world?"

66

Ernie said that it didn't need to be alive to be beautiful. "Just keep quiet and draw it."

Just then Sorcy came back; Gawn was still on his feet. Sorcy asked Ernie what Gawn had been doing. Gawn burst right out and told him. Sorcy grunted and hemmed. At last he conceded that there could be different kinds of beauty . . . the urn was very beautiful of its kind.

9

Father married again in 1907, over three years after mother's death. His second wife was Margaret Phelps, a cousin, and grandma's great-niece from Gloversville, New York. I was glad about the marriage. Nobody could ever take mother's place; but Cousin Maggie, as I called her, was different. Father was a lonely and aging man, and the marriage was a blessing for him and for me, as it turned out.

Cousin Maggie had lived with grandma for several years and kept house as Aunt Lillie was in poor health, or thought she was. The wedding was to take place in the drawing room of grandma's house where the organ was. Mr. Wheeldon from the Metropolitan Church was to play it.

Mr Wheeldon was a swarthy Englishman of great vanity, who owned an assortment of buttoned boots with various coloured uppers, fawn, grey, cream, in which his small feet literally danced on the organ pedals. At church these displays — and the beauty of his Bachelor of Music (Oxon.) hood — were hidden from view by a carved oak screen displaying the hymn numbers. But the wedding at grandma's house would give him a chance to tap-dance his way through some of the more esoteric works of Bach, Handel, Haydn and Mozart, exposed to a select group of music-lovers.

Mr. Wheeldon discussed the matter with father, who quietly

but firmly informed him that the primary purpose of the gathering was to be a marriage and not a concert. Mr. Wheeldon demurred. Mrs. Treble, he felt (that was Aunt Lillie), would like a great deal of music. Father wondered what Mrs. Treble had to do with it, though he did not say so. He suggested that after the ceremony Mr. Wheeldon could play anything he liked. With a hundred or so close relatives of the family in the spacious rooms of Euclid Hall, even the double bourdons, the diapasons and the doppelflötes of the Aeolian organ could not top the mighty unison of feminine tongues wagging in praise of Mrs. Amos' wedding cake.

On the day of the wedding, grandma came downstairs in the elevator and the relatives were all there. All, that is, but Vincent who didn't attend. My stepmother looked very nice. She was, I think, about the same age as my mother. She was a shy, self-effacing and gentle lady, and I was devoted to her, and remained so until her death twelve years later.

Vincent, who was now twenty and in his third year at the University of Toronto, still lived at home though we did not see much of him. The two back rooms were his bedroom and study. The latter, recently panelled in black pine, was a strange mixture of Oxford sophistication and juvenile Americana. Vincent was warming up for Oxford. Coats of arms on tin shields of several Oxford colleges and Charles Dana Gibson drawings hung side by side. Gracing the wall next to an aquatint of Magdalen College were burnt leather pipe racks bearing such deathless verse as:

"Here's to the bliss that's found in a kiss,
When lip meets lip in rapture.
But sweeter far than others are,
Are those we get through capture!"

Two deep, upholstered wicker armchairs, such as were college issue at Oxford, faced the fireplace. There were many pipes and tins of tobacco lying around. It was my practice to smoke the heels of these pipes whenever I could. Sometimes, I would fill a pipe with fresh John Cotton mixture and enjoy a good smoke up the chimney. In spite of this precaution, I was detected by Vincent. He warned me of the dire consequences of what he described as my addiction. These included tuberculosis (which he emphasized had taken away Uncle Fred), stunted growth, jaundice, pimples, boils, bad breath and many other conditions and diseases. He did not try to account for his own immunity. Chastened as I was, I did not pursue the subject.

In spite of my stepmother's retiring nature, she possessed a strong will. Her determined effort when she became the mistress of 519 was to get me to a boarding school. It was certainly not because she wanted to get me out of the way. I never for a moment had such a thought. She had realized long before her marriage that I was becoming spoiled and pampered by everyone in father's household as well as grandma's, where I went constantly. Although I had two close friends at the Model School — Willie Caven and Doug Ellis — I was mostly on my own except for school hours. My stepmother rightly considered that I should be exposed to the rigours of school sports — there were none for the younger boys at the Model.

In this boarding-school project my stepmother was strongly supported by Vincent, ostensibly for my own interests but in reality to safeguard his tobacco and pipes.

Father finally gave in. I was enrolled in the Preparatory School of Upper Canada College for the ensuing fall term.

I rather looked forward to leaving home. After all, I was ten years old. But I knew nothing of the pangs of homesickness. At last the day arrived and my foot locker was packed. I decided it would be best for me to drive to the school alone in the pony cart with Van rather than in the carriage with a parent.

It was early afternoon, and as we went north on Jarvis towards the top of Avenue Road where Upper Canada College was, I began to feel awful. It would be one of my last trips with Aunt Fanny. I was now too old for a pony and she was going to a new post in the country to look after two children.

My spirits were low by the time we reached the school. Van drove off, while I lugged my trunk up the steps into a hallway with classrooms opening off it. I sat down on the trunk. I could hear boys' voices but couldn't see anyone. I waited. I tried to remember that I was nearly eleven, but it didn't help. I felt sick.

70

"Are you a new boy? You're rather early. What's your name?"

Two enormous, heavily booted feet were close by. I looked up to see a tall, florid man with a close-cropped small head. I stood up.

"R. H. Massey, sir."

He consulted a list on the clipboard he carried.

"Ah, yes. You're in 'D' dormitory. That's on the second floor. Ah, Scherer, give this new boy a hand with his box to 'D' dormitory."

"Yes, sir, yes indeed, sir!" Scherer, a dark, handsome boy about twelve years old, grasped one end of the trunk and we climbed the stairs with it. 'D' dormitory was on the top floor, a long room lined with cubicles, each with a bed and chest of drawers. The dormitory was empty. We set the trunk down at the foot of a bed. Scherer looked "down" at me, though I was a good head taller. "You're Canadian, aren't you?" There was a faint foreign accent.

"Yes."

"Then you're probably poor."

This assumption seemed unreasonable. I had thirty-two cents in my pocket, my allowance for the current week plus seven cents saved from the previous one.

"I'm quite rich," he said. "See this?" Scherer took a bill from his pocket. Unfamiliar with paper money, I couldn't detect its denomination. With his other hand he extracted a kitchen match, struck it on my trunk and lit the bill. "We own thousands and thousands of acres in the Argentine and great herds of cattle!"

Scherer dropped the unburnt end of the bill on the floor and walked away.

My grandfather's genes pulled themselves together. I shouted, "You're wicked — very wicked!"

Suddenly there was pandemonium. Eight or nine boys were dragging their trunks and bags into the dorm and putting them by their cubicles. Most of the noise came from two Americans from Fresno, California, officially known as Saunders I and II. They had the two cubicles with windows. Mine was near theirs, on the inside row. I sat at the end of my bed in abject misery.

Saunders I spotted me.

"Are you a nigger?"

71

He seemed to mean it kindly. Dark eyed and dark haired, I considered his question reasonable.

"I don't think so."

"Hawaiian?"

I denied this angrily. I wanted no part of Hawaiians. They had killed Captain Cook, hadn't they?

"Well, he's awful dark looking," was Saunders I's final assessment.

Crowded with new arrivals, the dorm was now like a railway station. For the next seven years, at three different schools, I would be known as "Nigger" Massey, "Nig" for short.

A boy who had not joined in the chatter came over to me. A year or so younger than I, he was a freckled-faced boy with a crest on his reddish-brown head.

"Are you a new boy?" he asked.

"Yes. Are you?"

"Yes." A pause. "What's your name?"

"Raymond Hart Massey. My grandfather's name is in the middle. What's yours?"

"John Marshal Harlan. That's the whole of *my* grandfather's name." There was another pause. "What time do we eat here?"

A raucous bell sounded. A woman in a white uniform came in and, spying us, advanced aggressively. She read my name on the cubicle post.

"Well, Massey, why haven't you unpacked? Waiting for someone to do it for you?"

I made a move.

"Not now. Both of you go and wash your hands."

As she left, the man with the big feet and small head came in. "Come along! Didn't you hear the bell for supper?" He hurried out.

"How can we keep the rules if we don't know what they are?" was John Harlan's comment. A fitting one for a future Justice of the Supreme Court of the United States. We went downstairs unwashed.

"Gimper" Guest, J. S. H. Guest, the head of the Preparatory School of Upper Canada College, was a Cambridge man, and in

72

almost every way the opposite of the traditional schoolmaster. He was invariably in formal clothes, immaculately tailored. No Mr. Chips, he. There was nothing tweedy about him. He didn't believe in the new intimacy between masters and boys. He thought the proper relationship was that of the regimental officer with his men.

I was with Mr. Guest three years at the Prep and another three years at a new school he started near Toronto. He was a fine teacher and a superb headmaster but I never really knew him as a man. Not that I didn't have a deep respect for him.

I found myself shoved into the lowest form, I-B, with boys mostly a year or more younger than I. As I had never heard of Latin at the Model, I had to start at the bottom. It was a humiliation I hadn't expected. John Harlan was put in I-A and permanently seated at another table in hall.

What with a continuing effort throughout the day to keep my ears clean (an obsession of Gimper's) and a fierce determination to master the first declension of Latin nouns, there was hardly a moment to brood over the loss of home comforts. Homesickness came on in the evenings and lasted all night. I retired with my stiff clean copy of *Elements of Latin* by Benjamin Hall Kennedy, late Fellow of Caius College, Cambridge. In the fifteen minutes before our private prayers I learned to decline *mensa*, a table, and to conjugate *amo*, I love. I was going to make I-A by half-term or bust. During private prayers I fervently sought divine assistance.

My prayers were answered: at half-term I was rewarded with promotion to form I-A. In my third year at the Prep School I took the Latin Prize. I still believe it was won on my knees when I was trying to make it out of Form I-B.

The classes, or forms, were larger than at the Model. The "A" forms, I, II and III, had about forty-five boys each. The "B's," for boys who were slower learners, were much smaller. Five or six masters divided up the subjects and taught them in all three forms. There were Gimper Guest himself, and the two Colley brothers, T. B. and J. N. B., who were Englishmen from Oxford. They were the permanent teachers, professionals and very good. There were always two or three Canadian masters who came and went. One, Mr. Rossiter, stayed for most of my three years. He was writing a thesis.

You couldn't get away with much in his classes. But the others were lots of fun, particularly Mr. C. E. Luce, an Anglican clergyman and a very prissy one. We gave him a rough time. He lasted only two terms and went to Africa as a missionary. He said he was quite certain to have an easier time in Africa than with us in II-A.

Mr. Luce succeeded in ruining our handwriting. He used to hand out "impositions" by handfuls. These "impots" were enormous multiplication sums, ten figures by ten figures, or fifty or a hundred lines. They would be done after school hours. We would have to write a sentence a hundred times. For throwing bread in the hall, Mr. Luce gave me two hundred lines: "A piece of bread thrown in jest blinded Prescott the historian." Just writing the line once was a stifling bore.

"T. B." Colley kept good discipline. He hardly ever gave "impots" but he could be so sarcastic that you wanted to sink through the floor. He could also throw a piece of chalk with the perfect control of a good baseball pitcher.

The cane was reserved for offences out of the classroom and was not too frequently used. I got it for mimicking Mr. Sage, the dancing master.

T. B. Colley told me to go to his study.

It was a big room with pictures of cricket and rugger teams and some cups. On the desk was a glass with coloured water. Sniffing it, I guessed it was whiskey. Anyway, I finished it and put it back. T. B.'s canes were in a tub by his desk. I took one and tapped my fingers with it. It sure hurt. I had hardly put it back when T. B. came in.

I got four strokes on each hand. T. B. wasn't as good with the cane as he was with the chalk. His second stroke, meant for my right hand, caught my wrist. I didn't let a squeak out but I couldn't write too well for a day or so. T. B. wrote "Conduct excellent" on my half-term report. It was the only caning I had at the Prep.

One of the major vexations of life at U.C.C. Prep was the Eton collar. All males in the first decade of the twentieth century were victims of stiffly starched neckwear. My father wore a rigid stand-up collar even when playing golf, although he removed his detach-able cuffs. But adult collars were blissfully comfortable compared with the Eton collar. We had to wear it all the time except on the playing field. Designed by some sadist to be a constant irritation, it had a narrow neckband that came adrift of the back stud immedi-ately on tightening the tie. Then the collar would ride up at the back and the sides, suggesting a garroting. After the school laundry had done its worst, it would have a serrated edge like a crosscut saw.

As for sports, or "games" as they were called, I was hopeless at them. Consequently, my social status was low. In addition, my shyness made me a "loner."

The caning I got for mimicking Mr. Sage gave me a temporary social lift. I was elected to "The Wanderers," a somewhat exclu-sive club, requiring the digestive powers of a goat. "The Wander-ers" had a gilt tie-pin stamped with a "W"; and the sole activity of the club, which was limited to ten members, was the holding of "bean feasts" and "weenie roasts." The president was Edgar McConkey, a gourmet who disdained school food. These feasts were enjoyed at midnight in the third-floor bathroom, the farthest place we could find from both the Colleys' rooms, and virtually soundproofed by a blanket hung over the door. At my first meeting I won much prestige by consuming a 10-cent can of beans in three and three-quarter minutes, a club record never broken. The 10-cent can was twice the size of the present 69-cent one. Evidently my gastric trouble had vanished.

My three years at Upper Canada Preparatory School had been satisfactory in the classroom where I finished top of my form of thirty-two, though I had been a dismal failure on the playing field. I cannot understand why my father did not send me on to the Upper School.

10

I was transferred to another large private school, St. Andrews College, then in north Rosedale.

Like Upper Canada College, it was modelled on the English public school. My brother had graduated from St. Andrews a few years previously and had not liked it much.

I missed the fall term. I had gone to England with my father and my stepmother to be with Vincent who was seriously ill with typhoid.

I arrived at the new school at the beginning of the winter term, a bad time to start.

My record at St. Andrews was like that at U.C.C. — good scholastically and dismal otherwise. In my two terms in the upper school, I did not make the acquaintance of any boy I really remember. I do recall one of my three roommates for a peculiar reason. During the time I was rooming with him, he was buried in a ten-volume encyclopedia which he read at every possible moment. His father had given him the books with the promise of a considerable sum of money if he finished reading the whole set before he matriculated. He was halfway through the letter "C" when I left St. Andrews. If ever I saw anyone with mental indigestion, it was that poor fellow.

I was nagged incessantly by my roommates because of my

skinny frame. I really hated going to the room. At this time I was 5'8" and weighed only a hundred and eighteen pounds, so I was fair game. Luckily all three of them were in the IV form and so I didn't see them except in the hall and in the room at night. The discipline in the "corridors", as the floors were called, was supposedly in the hands of prefects who were VI form boys. But I never saw a sign of supervision except by masters.

Canings were administered by the headmaster, Dr. MacDonald, and by the housemasters; and for classroom offences detention was meted out in quarter-hour units. You could accumulate as many as a hundred quarters which meant twenty-five days of detention. Only an hour could be worked off in any one day. But when a hundred quarters had been accumulated, you could have them caned off at ten quarters a stroke — on the tail. I got rid of two sets of a hundred quarters at this discount rate. As I took the precaution of wearing heavy corduroy pants, it was cheap at the price.

From the start I was out of step with all but one of five or six masters. An Englishman named T. B. D. Tudball was my arch enemy. He taught arithmetic and algebra to the III-A form. The only really unfair master I ever had, he would begin a class by saying, "Massey Primus, you had better stand in the corner." (I was Primus, my cousin Denton, Secundus.) With my height, it was an extra humiliation to stand in the corner, a provocation to do something to earn the unmerited punishment.

Disciplinary action by the boys was as bad as lynch law. At Upper Canada Prep the boys would often send a wretched schoolmate to coventry — a kind of total boycotting. Trivial or serious, whatever the offence, the self-appointed Kangaroo Court was invariably unfit to decide questions of guilt or punishment.

At St. Andrews I saw two or three such instances of mob discipline, one of them quite frightening. A IV-form fifteen-year-old in our corridor had been the victim of a good deal of ragging. A loner, who came from a mining town in northern Ontario, he was a rough fellow — and luckily for him, extremely strong. One night in the common room the teasing went too far; the victim could take it no

77

longer. He pulled a switch-blade. Cursing his tormentors, he challenged them to a finish fight. All of us saw him goaded to it. Still, nothing could justify the brutality that followed.

The boy was disarmed by treachery and an immediate "trial" held. The whole corridor, some forty teenagers in all, constituted the jury. There was no defence and no judge. Worst of all, there was no charge. It was mob sadism at its worst. The sentence: five minutes of the "sweats." Some of us did not know what this punishment meant, but there was no holding back.

The victim was not allowed to speak for himself but immediately pinioned with some lengths of sash-cord. A bed was stripped, he was thrown on the mattress and five other mattresses were piled on top of him. Six of the bigger boys climbed on top of the pile.

In silence, the boy who had acted as principal accuser daubed the sufferer's face with shoe blacking. Perhaps two minutes went by. It seemed an hour.

A fourteen-year-old of frail build suddenly shouted, "Stop this, he'll suffocate!"

He hurled himself at the six louts on top of the mattresses, struggling to pull them off. With that frightening turn-around that typifies the mob, he was at once joined by a number of us. After a short fight the victim was freed. Half-conscious, he had managed to hold his breath for the first minute and he rapidly came round. A ghastly silence followed.

I took the boy into our room and cleaned his face. He said, "I don't think they're going to rag me anymore!"

Mr. Tudball's detentions prevented my taking part in hockey and cricket. I liked hockey. At U.C.C. I had been in every sense a painstaking goalie, but throughout my schooling I detested cricket. Both were closed to me at St. Andrews.

I obtained a certain amount of exercise and experience in agility by riding the frequent east-bound freight trains on the C.P.R. to the junction at Leaside and catching a west-bound back. About 4:15 P.M. there was an eighty-car freight to Montreal usually with about twenty coal cars that were easy to ride. The upgrade passing the College slowed all freight to ten or fifteen m.p.h., and since the track was on a curve you could jump the train without being seen from the caboose. It was about six or seven miles to Leaside, where there was almost always a train waiting on the west-bound siding. Once or twice when there wasn't a train at Leaside, I walked back and made 6:30 P.M. roll call. It was fun "riding the rails." I usually did it alone but I had a friend named Hickey who sometimes went with me.

I was in the cadet corps. I may not have been the tallest male to wear the kilt (our corps was affiliated with the 48th Highlanders) but at a hundred and eighteen pounds I was the skinniest. In answer to the inevitable question, I wore a bathing suit under my uniform, plus a heavy sweater to help fill the scarlet tunic.

St. Andrews was not my finest hour as a schoolboy. It was, with the exception of classroom marks, another failure. Hearing of my refractory behaviour from the headmaster, Vincent excoriated me for being what he called a "village cut-up." I showed him my report. He was impressed, but he still insisted I was a cut-up.

He cross-examined me as to smoking. The John Cotton tobacco and misuse of his pipes still rankled.

I said I had smoked up the ventilator of our room but had never been caught. I told him I didn't like it and had smoked only because it was risky.

Vincent wanted to know what I had smoked.

I said, Melachrinos. And, no, I had not been sick.

This impressed Vincent: for his part, Melachrinos had made him sick. He thought I deserved credit for smoking such an awful cigarette and surviving, so he went to father and told him it would be best for me to go to another school.

"Why?" father said. "The boy seems to be doing very well. Have you seen the report?"

Vincent was in a difficult position. He couldn't say I was driving a master to a nervous breakdown or that I was smoking the wrong brand of cigarettes. But he had, I am sure, been asked by the headmaster of St. Andrews to get that boy out of here. So he took a middle course and told half of the truth.

"I think Raymond should be at a school in the country," he said to father. "He'll get lots of good air to breathe."

"What's the matter with the air in Rosedale?"

"I mean the real country. You know Guest, who has been head of U.C.C. Prep, is starting a new school in Oakville next fall. He married Gladys Walker a few years ago. She's Sir Edmund Walker's elder daughter and he's financing the school. I think it would be fine for Raymond. He got along pretty well at U.C.C."

Sir Edmund was a friend of father's and head of one of the big Canadian banks. Both men had for years collected the same kind of pictures. There was mutual respect for each other's taste for the Barbizon and the Dutch schools of painting. Besides, Sir Edmund had once backed grandfather with a big loan. Anything Sir Edmund had in mind was propitious. I was set for Mr. Guest's new school.

11

On a morning in early September, 1911, I found myself one of some thirty boys travelling the twenty-six miles to Oakville on the 9:15 train of the Toronto, Hamilton and Buffalo Railways.

Some of us knew each other from U.C.C. days. John Harlan was one of these, so were Jack and Alec Gillespie, Andrew MacLean, E. V. Brown and several others.

It wasn't like starting an ordinary term, though. There was a feeling of setting out on an adventure, even that we were part of it. For the three years I was at Appleby School, I never lost that feeling.

We were met at Oakville by Mr. Blythe, a master in an Anglican dog-collar, with two tallyhos from Hillmer's Livery Stable. We drove through the sleepy village with its tree-lined, unpaved streets and boardwalks, out the Lake Shore Road about two miles to two white-washed stone gateposts, one bearing a bronze plaque that said APPLEBY SCHOOL.

Gimper and Mrs. Guest greeted us. We met Mr. Powell, an Englishman, and found Mr. Rossiter who had come from the Prep. We stowed our boxes and looked over the school. There were still workmen around. Another contingent would arrive that afternoon, making us about fifty-five boys. That was all we would have room for that first year. While I was at Appleby, there were never more than a hundred boys.

The new masters were first-rate. Mr. Powell was from Keble College, Oxford. I soon learned that he had just finished three years as tutor to the sons of a Russian prince. He had recently recovered from digestive trouble caused by a love potion fed to him by the French governess. He thought she was mixed up in her potions and had overdone the "entente cordiale." He had a lot of wonderful stories about the old Prince who lived in medieval conditions with dogs and rush-strewn floors and serfs doing all the work.

The Prince had asthma very badly. He would make Mr. Powell tell him stories that made him laugh. That brought on his asthma, and then he would nearly die. This, Mr. Powell said, annoyed the Prince, so he fired the story-teller.

I asked Mr. Powell why the French governess wanted to give him a love potion. He said that if I had seen her I would understand. Thinking it over, he wasn't sure that just seeing the French governess hadn't given him the indigestion. The Prince lived in Georgia in southeast Russia and Mr. Powell said the Georgians were like the Irish and the Hungarians.

Mr. Powell had also lived in Ireland, where he had been tutor to the sons of a lord. He told the best ghost stories I ever heard. Two or three of us older boys would get really scared listening to them. They were horrible yet believable. Several were about the castle in Ireland where he had worked.

Then there was Mr. Blythe, a cherubic clergyman of low church persuasion and a good master. He coached the football team for two years. Mr. Price and Mr. Whittington came in the second year. They both passed their tests with the boys and no master had anything like the trouble I had seen in other schools. The discipline in classrooms was good because it was not enforced by wholesale penalties. Impositions were sparingly dealt out.

The school property was a piece of land about fifty acres on the lake shore spread over a valley with two gentle hills on each side. In the valley were the playing fields and at one side a stream flowed to Lake Ontario.

Oakville was a lovely town about a mile and a half east of the school toward Toronto. Mazo de la Roche had patterned the town in her Whiteoaks and Jalna novels on Oakville. In 1911 there was nothing suburban about it. A visit to Toronto meant a train journey; as yet there were very few automobiles.

The squire of Oakville was Cecil Marlatt, a genial, bearded gentleman straight out of Trollope, who lived in a rambling, verandahed house, loved horses and yachts and had three attractive daughters and a hard-riding son. He and his charming wife were kindly patrons of Appleby. Often we boys were entertained at their house and aboard the big schooner that was Mr. Marlatt's pride. Once, the V form disgraced his hospitality: eleven of us were seasick in the schooner, though the Marlatt daughters tended us with the devotion of Florence Nightingale at Scutari.

There were stables at Appleby in the care of a Gaelic-speaking farmer we knew as Mac, and Mr. Guest allowed four or five of us to keep horses during term time. We were responsible for the grooming, exercising and feeding, all of which took time out of a day crammed with the classroom and football, hockey or that cursed cricket.

Mr. Powell was a fine horseman, a bond between us. He bought a rangy, seventeen-hand hunter, whom he named "Yeoman." Yeoman was not much to look at, with a long back and a tendency to cow-hocks, but he was a whale of a jumper. He was also a kicker. Mr. Powell had to tie the red ribbon round his dock as a warning when he went hunting. Mr. Powell was proud of a horse-shoe mark on his thigh that Yeoman had given him in the stable. Ken Marlatt said it was the only time he had ever heard of a horse branding his owner.

Mr. Powell, Geoff Machell and I kept our horses in the barn across the road. Mr. Powell was now housemaster of what was called "Powell's House" with about twenty-five boys in it. The house was near the stable, under the gym, where Mr. Guest's horses were kept.

About a week after Thanksgiving, while on duty as prefect and making midnight rounds of the third-floor dormitory, I looked out of the window and saw the roof of the gym in flames. I rushed downstairs to our floor, hollered out to the IV and V formers to get to the gym, and pulled on a pair of pants. I thought of the horses and grabbed a couple of towels for blindfolds. When I got to the gym, Mr. Powell was running down the road from the other side with some of his boys. Wilson, the ex-R.N. petty officer who was physical training instructor, had just got out of the gym, now completely in flames. I ran round to the stable door and rushed in. There was a lot of smoke but the fire hadn't reached down to that level. I tried to get one of Mr. Guest's Percherons out but paralysis of fear had set in. Mr. Powell was trying to move the other Percheron. We blindfolded both, struggling to back them out of their stalls. They would not budge. The smoke was now stifling. Huntly Christie could do nothing with his horse. The three were immovable.

The horse's instinctive refusal of safety in the face of fire is inexplicable. All other animals flee from danger. It is as though the horse alone among mammals is determined to perish by fire.

By this time the floor of the gym overhead was ablaze. We could see flames at the far end of the stable. Several other boys and Mr. Blythe had joined us. We were still frantically pulling at the terrified horses to get them out when Mr. Guest appeared.

"Get out of this stable!" He was trembling with anger. "Are you all mad? The roof will fall at any moment! Get out of this place! I order you!"

There was a crash above us as burning rafters fell. We left the horses. Almost as we came out the door, from which smoke was now pouring, the roof of the barn came down and the stable became an inferno.

We could hear the screams of the horses through the roar of the fire, and we could see the three wretched beasts, standing motionless, literally aflame.

Mac, the Scots farmer, appeared naked except for a meagre shirt, and tried to run into the burning barn. We had to overpower him. We kept him from destruction but I can still see him, mad with grief, screaming curses in Gaelic.

There was no way to shoot the poor beasts. The horror had to go its slow, agonizing way. Then the screams stopped and almost at the same moment the bodies toppled over. The fire was still raging. The Oakville fire department arrived at the trot, powerless to do anything but drink coffee.

A few hours later a tallyho carried the football team to catch a 7:30 A.M. train for Woodstock, where we were scheduled to play a Woodstock College team that afternoon. As we passed the still-smouldering remains of the gym, the stench was sickening. We were beaten 48-0.

In the holidays I saw a good many plays.

There were two theatres in Toronto that booked the Shubert and Klaw and Erlanger touring shows from New York. These bookings also included tours of English stars direct from London. The Princess and the recently built Royal Alexandra would both be open for continuous seasons of nine months and more, with the best plays of Broadway and the West End of London with the top stars playing in them. In one year, I saw Otis Skinner, Nat Goodwin, David Warfield, Nazimova, Holbrook Blinn, Martin Harvey, John Drew, Ethel Barrymore, George Arliss, William Faversham and Tyrone Power, the elder. It was the heyday of the "road." There was no indigenous professional theatre in Canada at that time. Although father didn't go to the theatre and my stepmother didn't want to, he staked me to quite a few plays when I was home.

In one miraculous week during the Christmas holidays of 1913, I saw E.H. Sothern and Julia Marlowe at the Princess Theatre in *Hamlet, Romeo and Juliet,* and *Macbeth*; and at the Royal Alexandra, Forbes-Robertson and Gertrude Elliott in *Hamlet, The Passing of the Third Floor Back* and *Caesar and Cleopatra*. Both Hamlets were wonderful and the prince was played with full poetic values by men with voices like violoncellos. Each star was in his sixties but that didn't trouble anyone. The new style, a youthful Hamlet with the psychological gimmicks and the Freudian overtones — such as perhaps my own performance — was still in the future. Sothern and Marlowe certainly would not have satisfied current demands that Shakespeare's ill-starred lovers, Romeo and Juliet, be played by naked children, but they gave delight to audiences of 1913.

I was riding on a cloud that week. My father had seen *The*

Passing of the Third Floor Back in Toronto years before with mother. It was the only stage play he had ever seen, and he had loved it. It was a contemporary morality play by Jerome K. Jerome, who also wrote *Three Men in a Boat*. Nowadays such a play would be laughed off the stage but I shared father's enthusiasm. He made me tell him all about it when I got home from the matinee. I think he couldn't bear to see it again, or any play for that matter. If mother had lived, it might have been different.

Sir Johnston Forbes-Robertson and his wife, Gertrude Elliott, had just completed a short season of nine of their great successes at the Shubert Theatre on Broadway and the repertoire had been reduced to three plays for the road. Lady Forbes-Robertson retained the role of Ophelia rather than that of Gertrude which she would have played magnificently but Sir Johnston wisely thought his Ophelia must have a balanced maturity. After all, when Hamlet is in the mid-sixties, he can't address such lines as "Nymph, in thy orisons, be all my sins remembered" to a child with a lollipop! The third play in the road repertory was *Caesar and Cleopatra*, which Bernard Shaw had written for the Forbes-Robertsons a decade previously. In this revival the stars were superb. Shaw had supplied them both with fresh characters which they played with astonishing skill. This play made a deep impression on me.

Fourteen years later, my first starring engagement was with their daughter, Jean Forbes-Robertson, in a revival of *The Constant Nymph* in London.

Sitting in the balcony of the Royal Alex, watching the Shaw play, I hoped the future would hold many more such enchantments. I lay awake that night hoping that while I would be busy making and selling binders, mowers, harrows, plows, cream separators and the like, there would be plays I could see like *Caesar and Cleopatra*, *Romeo and Juliet* and *Hamlet*. But I didn't think of acting in them. I was going to try and be like my grandfather, an implement man.

There were two burlesque theatres in town. The Gaiety played the Columbia Circuit shows. Father did not include the Gaiety in his program of drama for me but for 40 cents I would surreptitiously pursue my studies of the burlesque art form. I was well rewarded for my clandestine patronage. Burlesque in those pre-war days was lusty and honest bawdry at its comic best, before the strip-teasers ruined it and replaced laughs with leers.

Burlesque bore no comparison to any other form of entertainment anywhere. It was really "only in America"; it was unique. It died because it lost its honesty. But what fun it was while it lasted! Vaudeville too was at its zenith then. At Shea's Theatre twice daily there were ten good acts, with headliners like Nora Bayes and Houdini and often "legit" stars such as David Warfield slumming in a dramatic sketch for ten weeks of variety. In a scant ten years the movies would obliterate live vaudeville.

Then there was the old Grand Theatre which always seemed to be showing an Irish musical with Chauncey Olcott. It also booked the great magic shows such as Thurston's and the good old melodramas. I doubt if any melodrama ever offered at the Grand could top the case of its manager, Ambrose Small, the charred remains of whose body were found in the furnace of the theatre. The crime was never solved.

For a city of about three hundred thousand, there was good theatre of every kind in Toronto.

The theatre wasn't exactly forgotten at school. Beside horses, Mr. Powell and I had another common interest. He was as stage-struck as I. But whereas I was merely a fanatical theatre-goer, he had ambitions for a stage career. He had confided to me in June, 1914, that he thought he would give schoolmastering one more year and then try his luck as an actor in England. He knew a number of people in the English theatre, actors and producers, and he was a talented amateur actor himself. It wouldn't be too risky a venture. But he never made the attempt for he died of wounds in 1918 after four years of active service with the Gunners.

In my last winter term at Appleby, Mr. Powell staged an ambitious production of Goldsmith's *She Stoops to Conquer*. The new gymnasium, to replace the old one destroyed by the fire, was not yet complete and we performed the play in the Oakville Town Hall to two capacity houses of paying customers. This was the second production of the Appleby Dramatic Society, the first having been an attempt at a Victorian farce called *Ici On Parle Français* in the old gym, which nearly put an end to theatre at Appleby. Even doting parents admitted that not only was our effort bad, it was "godawful." Like some other minor disasters in my past, the production of *Ici On Parle Français* left me in a state of shock. A merciful amnesia has blocked all memory of what was in truth my first encounter with the theatre.

She Stoops to Conquer was a much different experience. I knew the play, having seen Annie Russell and Oswald Yorke act the Hardcastles, father and daughter, in their repertory of the two Sheridan comedies and Oliver Goldsmith's play which had come to Toronto the previous year. When Mr. Powell had suggested *She Stoops* for our winter term production of 1914, it seemed a perfect selection. Mr. Powell worked with his cast for the entire term and although the majority approached the production with some reluctance, suspecting that the project was an English class in disguise, Mr. P's enthusiasm was so infectious, and his skill as a director so effective, that all misgivings were soon dispelled. He himself played Squire Hardcastle to perfection, supported by another master, Mr. Price, in the part of the Squire's crony. A boy named Aubrey Turquand gave a comic performance of Tony Lumpkin which character can easily become an egregious bore. The rest of the cast was adequate. The female parts were played by boys on the assumption that the eighteenth-century belles of Goldsmith's comedy had very large feet and spoke in husky contralto tones.

It happened that the McKenna Costume Company of Toronto possessed the wardrobe of a company that had been marooned at the Grand while touring in an Irish light opera. As it was an eighteenth-century period piece, we were at least properly garbed.

I cannot say that my first stage appearance (I refuse to count *Ici On Parle Français*) fired me with any theatrical ambition. I played Young Marlow and I wasn't good. I loved the theatre but I preferred to be out front. I couldn't stand not being a "pro." This feeling lasted through my subsequent amateur stage experience.

It was June, 1914, and suddenly my schooldays were over. The last cricket match had been played, the last prefect's meeting had been

88

held in Mr. Guest's study, and John Harlan was chosen to succeed me as head prefect.

I had been in Toronto three days writing my Honour Matriculation exams and then in Cobourg for a day where I had been invited to ride an entry in one of the jumping classes of the Horse Show. The owner of my mount was a horsey old lady, a friend of my brother's. To console me for a poor performance (I had a fall), she took me to tea at a nearby farm with some friends of hers.

"Their name is Tracy and they won't have been at the horse show. They only like working horses. You'll meet a perfectly lovely girl who's staying with them. She's from Buffalo."

The young lady from Buffalo was the most beautiful creature I had ever seen. She had a musical voice. Tall and dark, she had eyes like my mother's, big and far apart.

Her name was Katharine Cornell. All my life I have automatically forgotten the names of people I meet but hers was an exception. Miss Cornell, at Mrs. Tracy's request, took me to see the cow barns that housed the Guernsey herd, the pride of the Tracy farm. Miss Cornell and the cows evinced a mutual disdain.

Miss Cornell asked me what I was going to be.

"I think I'll make farming machinery or something."

She looked through and beyond the cows. "I'm going to New York next fall. I shall become a professional actress. On the stage."

With that pronouncement, so calm and determined, I knew that the cows and grandfather and the family business were not for me, not for the long pull anyway. Somehow, somewhere, sometime, I would be a professional actor and act with Katharine Cornell . . . on Broadway.

That dream remained my secret for a long time. Twenty-six years later I starred with Kit Cornell on Broadway in the first of three plays.

12

One morning in June, 1914, under my napkin ring at breakfast I found an official envelope containing the joyful news that I had passed my Honour Matriculation. I had also accomplished a successful retake of an algebra flunk in the previous year's junior matric.

As a reward, father agreed that I could spend the holidays touring in France with Vincent. He hoped (vainly, as it turned out) I would return with a command of the language.

Late in June I boarded *R.M.S. Compania* at New York for a nine-day voyage to Glasgow. Vincent was already in London. We were to travel to the Loire country by automobile.

Nobody had ever called the *Compania* a luxury liner. She had sailed out of Glasgow under the old Anchor line most of her life and she was a dour old ship.

This was my eleventh Atlantic crossing.

I shared an inside, lower-deck cabin with two other men, a taciturn Scot and a garrulous Hungarian. I saw little of either, the Scot being determined to walk his way to Glasgow and the other intent on the conquest of two pretty schoolteachers from Ohio.

Our first morning out I woke at eleven, feeling wretched. I looked in the mirror and scared myself. I was completely yellow. I asked the steward to find Dr. Caven, a friend who was a fellow passenger. His brilliant diagnostic powers were not overtaxed. The first week of my jaundice was spent in that heaving cabin as the ship weathered a series of midsummer gales. Only an old jaundice victim knows the discomfort and depression that disease can cause. I was grateful for the presence of Dr. Caven. He ran interference on the ship's surgeon whose therapeutic resource for all ailments was a powerful cathartic pill called "Number 9."

The first night I was ill the Hungarian came in to change for dinner. He was highly excited and voluble about an archduke who had been assassinated in Bosnia. He had read the news on the ship's wireless bulletin. He said it would mean very bad trouble.

When I arrived in London, Vincent got me into a nursing home straight from the train. My doctor was the same one who had attended mother ten years before. Frock coat, top hat, florid face, Dr. Brown looked just as I remembered him. I hated him, for he brought back all the sadness of mother's illness.

He poked avidly at my swollen liver. His fat, moustached face gleamed.

"I think we're going to snip out a little stone!"

"The hell you are," I said. "If there's any snipping to be done, it'll be in Canada!"

I don't think Dr. Brown's heart was in my case after that. Another doctor — and nature — took over.

Three weeks later nature had done a fair job. I left the nursing home, still yellow but in high spirits. Things were moving again. Vincent had bought a second-hand, somewhat decrepit Hupmobile touring car for the trip. I went straight from the house to take my international driving test. I felt too weak for even a short walk, let alone driving a strange car in London's left-hand traffic. The Hup was very low and the horses — hauling buses, hansoms, vans, carriages — seemed about to step in beside me.

But all I had to do for the licence was start and stop and do a little steering.

That night we stayed at Vincent's lodgings in Cambridge Terrace. It was the night of July 30th. We had dined at his club, the Saville.

I'd heard much talk of mobilization, "The Belgian Treaty,"

"The Russians can deal with 'em — just numbers, old boy!" There had been warnings: "You might have some trouble moving about France. Take a few sovereigns, old fellow, nothing a sovereign can't do!" One thing mattered: nothing was to stop our going to France in the morning. My brother had made a plan: that we should spend two months at a language crammer's house near Orleans. It would take more than the Kaiser to make him change it, at least without a proper demonstration of force. That wouldn't come for another two days and by then we would be in the depths of France.

The morning of July 31st brought one of those miraculous, soft, shining days that make up for all the murk and mist that plague London. We loaded up the Hup as we breathed in that summer air. The engine fired first crank with an ear-splitting report; a greasy black cloud shot out of the exhaust. As the shaking motor roared in defiance, the gases of the petroleum age filled our nostrils. The gentle summer air odour was now a memory.

Though I've spent a great deal of my life with horses, am fond of them and understand them, I was eager for the motor car as a faster means of travel and as a mechanical toy.

In those days everybody who drove a car had to administer first aid and change tires. I had a fairly good diagnostic sense. Vincent had none. At the coughing, sputtering stall which obviously betrayed carburetor trouble, Vincent would insist on stripping the distributor. From there he would go on until the entire motor lay piece by piece on the pavement. Then we had to reassemble it. There was no pathological instinct in Vincent's operations, no clinical sensitivity, no therapeutic scheme, just wildly extravagant surgical curiosity.

I had discovered my brother's absence of disciplined thinking about automobiles the previous summer on a hundred-mile trip in a Packard. I was prepared to back my theories against his. The opportunity came near Reigate when the Hup missed a few beats, then went dead.

Vincent managed to glide to the side of the road. "Blocked feed-pipe!" he snapped as he leapt out. He raised the bonnet.

"Ignition," I murmured softly and repeatedly.

92

My brother deftly removed countless vitals and strewed them on the ground. He was noisily blowing through a length of tubing he had pulled from the engine with great difficulty when I pointed to an unattached wire near the magneto.

"What's this?"

"Oh, that!" Vincent said. "Glad I found it — a loose terminal. It's probably the trouble. Now I'll attach it and you put all this junk back."

We reached Newhaven about 6 o'clock with no further trouble except a puncture. Mending this, we discovered an advanced state of decay in the inner tube. Had my brother bought four other decayed tires? We were soon to find out he had. Meanwhile, we got the Hup slung aboard the packet boat for Dieppe and went to a Newhaven inn for supper. A London evening paper carried alarming headlines about war within a few hours between Germany and Russia — not shocking enough, though, to deter us from our trip. We boarded the packet about nine. The British Customs officer seemed surprised to see anybody with a car. Indeed, we were almost the only passengers of any kind.

It was a smooth crossing to Dieppe that night but there was a frigid reception for us at the French Customs. It was now August 1st and Russia had partially mobilized. Within a few hours Germany would declare war on Russia; and France, as Russia's ally, was sure to be the next target for the Kaiser. Frenchmen are naturally suspicious, and England was only bound by treaty to defend Belgian neutrality, not France. The "Entente Cordiale" meant just about what it said when the chips were down. In French eyes, Vincent and I were English: the douanier could detect "la perfidie" oozing out of our pores. Still, there was nothing he could do but let us and the Hup proceed.

We chugged gaily along toward Rouen, our objective for lunch. In the end we just made it for the night. The battle of the tires had begun. Two of the diseased inners went flat during the first forty kilometres. We had the repair kit with us but mending the two punctures took over two hours. There seemed plenty of gasoline for sale — a good thing, since the Hup proved mighty thirsty — but we met only stares and snorts when we tried for tubes. During the afternoon, my jaundiced stomach shuddered at its first encounter with rich French food.

At Rouen there was a tumultuous crowd outside l'Hotel de Ville. With a sickening thud the news hit us — Germany was now at war with Russia. French territory had already been violated by Germans. War against France would come any moment now.

What would we do, the two of us — go back? Or go on to our destination, Cour-Cheverny, three hundred kilometres farther south in Touraine? Vincent decided it would be better to go on. If England and the Dominions were involved (as it seemed certain they would be), it would be more sensible to sit out our delay in getting home in Touraine rather than in some seaport.

So we had dinner, at least Vincent did, looked at Ste. Ouen, one of the most beautiful churches in France, tried unsuccessfully to buy tires, and went to bed.

That must have been quite a night in the chancelleries of Europe as ultimatums were hurled back and forth. I didn't sleep much. My liver was to blame rather than the failure of diplomats. By morning France was at war.

That day we rumbled on toward the Loire; our objective, Orleans. But a leaky valve in one of the tires and a broken brake cable delayed us. Chartres was as far as we got before nightfall. In all the towns we passed, the "Mobilization Générale" posters were displayed. At Dreux, where the brake cable was repaired (for that was beyond our skill), our mechanic laid down his tools after he had done and left the garage to report to the local caserne for duty. As he departed he turned to us and saluted.

"Aux armes, mes alliés!"

It was the first kind word we had heard in France.

That night of August 2 we slept at Chartres. The news was confused and bad but it would have seemed worse if the Cathedral hadn't been there. It was comforting to have something transcendentally beautiful nearby. To me, Chartres is the most lovely cathedral in France. It was incongruous to see the call for "L'Armée de la Terre" and "L'Armée de la Mer" plastered on its walls. But that building would stand serene and blessed through two great wars.

We had hoped to reach Cour-Cheverny the next day, but overnight one of the "good" tubes had flattened out and disintegrated. This left us with no spare.

Gasoline was still unrestricted but the government was grabbing all the rubber it could find. After a morning's search of the garages of Chartres, we found a rugged individualist who took a dim view of trade restrictions. He sold us a Michelin casing and two tubes at a reasonable price. He also persuaded us to buy a spare fan belt, another rubber product. Later that afternoon we blessed him when clouds of steam from the radiator betrayed a severed fan belt.

At Chateaudun we learned that Belgium had been invaded. A small group of patriots told us, spitting, that Albion was more perfidious than ever. We holed up in a small hotel in Orleans after an anxious but mechanically successful trip of about two hundred kilometres. Rumours next day were wild and contradictory. Britain's foreign secretary, Sir Edward Grey, had persuaded King Albert of the Belgians to let Germans pass through his territory. Most of this lying scuttlebut was at Britain's expense. We were harassed near Orleans by an official who wanted to commandeer our new casing and tube. Somehow Vincent talked him out of it.

We didn't know much about our objective, still a hundred and fifty kilometres off. Vincent had been told that "Les Tourelles" was the house of a certain Vicomte De Seze. He took a select number of British candidates for service examinations and crammed them. Vincent had also heard that his food was pretty good.

We arrived late that night of August 4, 1914.

"Nous sommes alliés, mes amis," cried our host. "La Grande-Bretagne est en guerre! A bas les Allemands!"

M. le Vicomte was an impressive figure as he stood in his doorway making this tremendous announcement. Tall and heavy, he looked like the biggest of the Keystone Cops.

England was at war! Then Canada would at once be in it, too. It was shattering news, but I was not yet eighteen and still had dreams of glory.

The Vicomte, who scorned continental breakfasts, joined us over bacon and eggs and never stopped talking in a rapid, deep roar. He looked the way Bernard Shaw might have, had he eaten meat. His antecedents were splendid, but he was more interested in hunting and shooting than teaching. The title had been conferred on the present Vicomte's grandfather, one Raymond De Seze, who had had the courage to defend the hapless Louis XVI at his trial. Vincent and I enjoyed our stay with him, but our main desire now was to get back to England as soon as possible. "Les Tourelles" was a small, charming, seventeenth-century country house, and considering the effort we had made to get there it seemed a shame to desert it so soon. What's more, it wasn't going to be easy getting back. French authorities had just ordered the issuance of visitors' permits to all aliens. We could not leave without them. Obtaining ours took a merry three days. The identity of British and Canadian citizenship at that time was baffling to the French. Vincent didn't want to abandon the Hup and lose nearly all the money we had paid for her. On the other hand, we couldn't make the trip north without more tires.

In a preliminary search, we blew up one of our good tires in Cour-Cheverny, and there wasn't another to be found anywhere.

Suddenly Vincent had a bright idea — Paris! Mr. Duncan, the manager of the European office of Massey-Harris, was there: he would help us find two of the thousands of tires that must be crowding the garages! There was one snag. It was even harder to get to Paris than to the Coast and England. It was now August 10, the railways were glutted with troop trains, and to reach Paris by rail seemed out of the question. Vincent decided to try it by Hup even with our now desperate collection of pneumatic deathtraps.

On the morning of August 11, we clattered off on our trip. We got within two hundred yards of a garage in Orleans, nearly a hundred kilometres on our way.

A battalion of infantry was marching to the station, flowers in the muzzles of their Lebel rifles. They were singing lustily as we passed them.

Their song stopped at a terrific explosion. It was our one sound tire — on a front wheel.

I was driving. The blowout wrenched the wheel from my hand.

We rammed one of those cast-iron pissoirs. Luckily no one was using it.

The crowds cheering the troops turned to investigate. We were at once up to our necks in sympathy. We were "soldats Canadiens" trying to rejoin our regiment (true in spirit); and our voiture was considerably more bouleversed than the sanitary monument (true in fact). The pissoir still functioned, as two citizens at once obligingly proved. But the Hup would not go at all. There were no repair trucks, of course, and no horses.

"Au secours de vos alliés, mes amis!" I cried. I set my shoulder to the "tonneau" as Vincent leapt to the wheel. We shoved the Hup to the garage, two hundred yards away.

Now there was bad news. Repairs to the Hup would take at least two days.

But again luck smiled upon us. Wherever one goes in the world there is a fixer, a putter-to-rights; sure enough, there was one in Orleans. Even now, I can hear his raucous voice as he reassured us. He knew the station master. He would put us on a troop train for Paris. We were all friends and allies, bound for glory and victory.

Within thirty minutes we were standing in the corridor of a train carrying a battalion of infantry reservists toward Paris.

The troops sang "La Marseillaise" over and over. Since that trip I have never felt the same about it.

They wore the uniforms of 1870, the red pantaloons, the long dark blue with the tails buttoned back, the knapsack and kepi. They would wear these archaic red targets for nearly another year of fighting before the horizon blue would appear. But they were fully equipped. French mobilization had been a miracle of efficiency. Here was a battalion going into action five days after the call-up. And France already had eighty divisions in the field.

In Paris, Mr. Duncan quickly found us tubes and tires; next day we took a train back to Orleans.

All this time we knew nothing of the shattering struggle that was going on. During those six weeks of the Marne and the Aisne battles, news was so garbled that we were ignorant of the state of the fighting. Not till long after the sweeping series of battles, when the exhausted armies had settled down to face each other in three and a half terrible years of trench warfare, could the military meaning of the war's first six weeks be known.

Back in Orleans, we found the Hup far from recovered. Nevertheless, the patient was, in a mechanical sense, ambulatory. After one more night at "Les Tourelles," we bade goodbye to the Vicomte and his household, and set out for the most promising channel port.

We had learned at Rouen that it would be impossible to get through to Dieppe, Boulogne or Calais. It was rumoured that General von Kluck, a German forerunner of the immortal George S. Patton, had already reached the Channel. Havre seemed our best hope. We did not know that Havre was the main base for the five British divisions to land in France that third week of August. It now seems madness for two British civilians from Canada, with French papers and an American car, to try to enter Havre, let alone use the port for tourist travel on August 20, 1914. But enter we did. Our embarkation was simple enough — in an empty Channel steamer that regularly shuttled between Havre and Southampton.

In one short hour in Havre we had seen British infantry marching on French soil again after a century's absence. We had seen the guns of an eighteen-pounder battery being unloaded at a jetty, had watched countless horses, wagons, supplies and equipment entraining in the dock terminals. We saw a battery of horse artillery with their wicked snubbed thirteen-pounder guns trotting to another railhead. Everywhere khaki-uniformed soldiers were busy but calm. Even to my ignorant eyes, it seemed we were watching professionals at work. They were part of the first hundred thousand of the British Expeditionary Force, the men the Kaiser called "contemptible," though von Kluck, who fought them, called them "incomparable."

Outrageous as it now seems, while the British Expeditionary Force disembarked, our civilian Hup was slung aboard the packet boat for Southampton.

At Liphook, on the road to London, there was an ear-splitting bang in the engine of the Hup. A consultation with the proprietor of a nearby garage disclosed a broken big end. This was deemed a terminal condition and we proceeded by train. We didn't even put a bullet in the radiator as we had no gun.

Our return seemed to me a retreat. Privately I vowed that I would be back. It would take me just over a year to keep my word.

Back in London we caught up with the news. Canada was committed to sending several divisions overseas but they would do their initial training in Canada. It seemed essential to return as soon as possible.

We waited two weeks for passage. In spite of my fear that the war would be over before I could get into it, those weeks were fascinating. England was rubbing her eyes. For the first time in modern history she was going to fight a war with a people's army rather than professional soldiers. The people knew it, many of the politicians knew it; but the generals were slow to understand and the most hidebound professional of them all, Lord Kitchener, was now Secretary of State for War.

Towards the end of August, a new rumour swept England: Russian troops were moving to the French front by way of Scotland. Bearded men had been seen with snow on their boots. I almost believed I had heard the Volga boat song heartily rendered in a darkened train at Woking. A porter sadly informed me that the train was the disabled 5:37 from Waterloo.

About the second week in September, we were homeward bound in the fastest ship afloat — certainly the ship with the greatest vibration at speed — the new *Lusitania*, pride of the Cunard fleet. The voyage was uneventful. I don't remember that there was even a blackout. Little was known of the capabilities of submarines or of the intentions of the German Admiralty.

13

Although Canada had been at war for six weeks when I got home and units of the 1st Canadian Division were already in training at Valcartier, Quebec, there was little sign of warlike activity in late September, 1914. There were no symptoms of recruiting fever as in England, no troops marching to railroad stations and nothing like France's beflagged announcements of "Mobilization Générale de l'Armée de la Terre et l'Armée de la Mer." It was all much as usual, perhaps a little quieter.

My father, that gentle, peaceful man, probably gave me a clear picture of Canada's true state of mind. A few hours after I came home he told me, "The company will begin manufacturing shells in a few weeks. Fortunately, this won't entail extensive retooling. We can fulfil our government contract without seriously jeopardizing the output of regular machinery. You know, Raymond, it's strange that although the Russians are giving large orders in Canada for shells, our Russian representative says they don't want us to supply them. With us they want to increase their orders for binders and reapers. I fear they think it will go on for a long time. By the way, I see that cousin Victor Odlum is at Valcartier. He's commanding a group there; going overseas shortly. I hope you'll be in his outfit when you go."

Cousin Victor, then a lieutenant-colonel, later was promoted brigadier-general and took the 11th Infantry Brigade to France. He became famous for developing the deadly but successful daylight raids. That wasn't perhaps what father had in mind.

The University of Toronto, unlike the rest of my native city, seemed an armed camp. Faculty members and undergraduates were constantly drifting off for military duty. The head of the French Department, Professor de Champs, a massive man with a Toulouse-Lautrec boulevardier's beard, left to rejoin his regiment of Cuirassiers.

Like almost everybody else, I at once joined the Officers Training Corps, now at a strength of two battalions. As an institution of learning, the University marked time, but for some eighteen hundred would-be officers and non-commissioned officers, infantry training rolled along.

As Christmas approached, overseas service seemed for most of us farther away than ever. Strangely, in spite of bad war news and the enormous expansion of the British Army as planned, there was a lull in recruiting for overseas service in Canada toward the end of 1914. The 1st Canadian Division was on Salisbury Plain in England and the 2nd Division, up to strength, was training at various Canadian camps. There seemed no preparations for the reinforcements that would be needed.

I was enrolled in Victoria College which my grandfather and father had both attended. Victoria had been moved from Cobourg to Toronto, as a component college of the University. It retained its autonomy under the control of the Methodist Church. We had recruited a full company of the O.T.C., one platoon being almost entirely composed of future Methodist ministers from the Theological school. I won my corporal's stripes, as did Lester (Mike) Pearson, the future Prime Minister of Canada and winner of the Nobel Peace Prize. Our platoon, with its fledgling clergy, was known as "Cromwell's Own." Mike and I were secular members. Most of the platoon put their calling on ice for the duration and went into combatant service, several becoming signallers in the Field Artillery. When I got to France about a year later as a lieutenant, two of

101

the old Cromwell platoon were already seasoned trench warriors with my battery. Signallers, they accompanied me on a number of tours in the trenches and "O. Pips," or forward observation posts.

By the end of October it was obvious that the war would be a long one. The big battles of movement were over. The line had stabilized into the pattern it would hold for the next three years. The University tried to cool our martial ardour. There would be plenty of time to go overseas; in the meantime, the classrooms and lecture halls were open and were to be regarded as a place of learning. In our ill-fitting uniforms, we reluctantly took notes of the philosophy of Locke, the theories of John Stuart Mill, the tragedies of Racine, while we exchanged rumours as to the coming recruitment of the 3rd Division.

The usual fall schedule of the University football team was to be carried out. This was a popular decision in all circles, academic and otherwise, as the Varsity team was particularly strong in 1914. This would be the last season, war or no war, in which college football would be played under the Canadian rules. Henceforth the U.S. rules would prevail.

The team won the Rugby Football championship and was undefeated except for one ludicrous humiliation. As if to put the quietus on Rugby Football in Canada, an exhibition game was arranged between the Carlyle Indians, a great American team, and the University of Toronto. It was to be played under U.S. rules for the first half and the Canadian code for the second — an insane idea. Any team used to interference will pulverize a team inexperienced in such tactics. The Indians scored at will. Toronto rarely got possession of the ball and the great Jim Thorpe scored something like a dozen touchdowns. Under Canadian rules in the second half, the Varsity team was able to hold its own but it was a sad defeat for a grand game.

That 1914 team was perhaps the best Toronto ever had. The names of that season's players would eventually be found in the nominal rolls and casualty lists of the Canadian Corps — every one of them: Jack Newton (the Captain), Charlie Gage, "Bull" Ritchie, Smirle Lawson, Connie Smythe, Jack Maynard and the rest.

102

In December of 1914 I joined Kappa Alpha, one of the fraternities. Lunching in the Kap house, I found a British officer with a tense group around him. He was wearing the double-breasted tunic of the Royal Flying Corps, known as a "maternity jacket," but with no pilot's or observer's badge. His breezy account of life in the R.F.C. was attentively received. I have never seen a pitchman with a more eager crowd of suckers. A Great Portland Street motorcar salesman, he had obviously never been near an aircraft, but he painted a rosy picture of what the war in the air would be like. Six of us made an appointment to go to his office in the Armouries the following day.

Canada took no active interest in the air arm in the First World War. There was no Canadian Air Force. But Canadian pilots and observers were continuously recruited and by the end of the war nearly half of the Royal Air Force pilots were Canadian.

We turned up at the Armouries next day to find a Canadian medical officer with the Englishman. On the orderly room floor was a long, white chalk line. At one end a very high, rotating office chair had been placed. One by one we sat in the chair while the R.F.C. wallah vigorously spun it round. We were then invited to walk the line. Three of us could walk straight but the other three, including myself, staggered miserably. The successful three were blindfolded and put through the test again. Another was eliminated. Two out of six. The winners were given further tests, but the chair was the essential one. A sound one, I think. Years later, in the early 1930s, I failed to win a civilian pilot's licence because of my inability to tell which way was up when flying blind.

Three battalions and several field batteries of the 2nd Division, all up to strength, were training at the Exhibition grounds at Sunnyside. Soon they would be overseas. The O.T.C., meanwhile, seemed to offer no future. I visited the camp.

Vernon Powell, my schoolmaster from Appleby, was now a lieutenant with the 13th Battery. He had brought with him his own wicked old horse Yeoman. I wondered how many gunners, drivers and other horses Yeoman would kick while in the King's service. A mean old creature, but it was good to see him again. I thought soldiering would be more fun with a mounted unit.

Edward Johnson, a fraternity brother of mine, had by default become commanding officer of a militia artillery unit.

"Your troubles are over," Ed told me. "I'll put you up for a militia commission in the 9th Battery which will go through right away. Then I'll get you into the course at Kingston. You'll be ready to apply for one of the 3rd Division batteries that will be forming about the first of June."

Ed kept his promise. I was commissioned lieutenant in the 9th Battery of the Active Militia within two weeks. Ed informed me I was now "His Majesty's trusty and well beloved" and should purchase a uniform and accoutrements. I was to attend a number of drills at the Armouries, which closely resembled evensong services at a village church in England.

Once outfitted, I took my uniforms home. I was ashamed to appear on campus as an officer. My father, though as civilian-minded as anyone could be, was anxious about the authenticity of my commission, as indeed I was.

Ed Johnson didn't help by suggesting that (until the officers' course) I continue as a corporal by day and keep the militia commission as secret as possible. I gathered he wasn't sure of his own position.

About this time I played the part of Ferrand, a French drifter, in an amateur production of John Galsworthy's *The Pigeon.* It was staged in the big dining hall at Victoria College, most of the cast being faculty members. I never have been able to do a French accent or speak the language; looking back on that performance over the years, I can only confess it was just awful.

About the middle of February, Ed informed me that my application for the third course at the Royal School of Artillery, Horse and Field, had been approved and I was to report at Tête du Pont Barracks, Kingston, on a date in March. As I had requested service overseas, it would be necessary for me to have a physical examination at the Armouries. Discharged from the O.T.C., I had left the University. My brother, by the way, as adjutant of the O.T.C., had thoughtfully entered my date of birth on the discharge paper as August 30/06. The medical officer wondered about the propriety of sending eight-year-olds overseas. In the end I convinced him that the correct date of my birth was 1896 and I was honestly eighteen.

I passed. I did not have flat feet or a hernia; I could breathe. That was all the physical examination I ever had before I crossed the English Channel to France.

There were about fifty of us in the third course at Tête du Pont, Kingston. About two-thirds of us were completely new to artillery. During the First World War, everything in the artillery was different from other arms, even the foot drill, and the months of training in the C.O.T.C. had gone for nothing. Some fifteen of us were taking the course as a refresher, several field officers among them. But we all got the same treatment: foot drill, stables, section gun drill, the works. We all had comfortable quarters in the officers' mess.

The course was rugged. We worked nearly twelve hours a day.

Of the junior officers, half had never ridden a horse and few had more than a little riding experience. We knew nothing of gunnery and the science of artillery. What was worse, we raw ones had no sense of soldiering. Though some of us had had some military training at school, Canada had not felt war near for a hundred years and showed it.

Eight weeks later we might not have been the best gunners in the army, or the best horsemen, or the smartest officers, but we had learned something about discipline, about the duties and responsibilities of an officer. The man who had hammered these virtues into us was Captain Thomas Duncan John Ringwood, Royal Canadian Horse Artillery, acting commandant and gunnery instructor of the Royal School of Artillery, Horse and Field.

Ringwood was a bull of a man, a fine athlete and first-rate boxer, and having "won his jacket," as a commission in the Horse Gunner was termed, he had passed out of the Royal Military College near the top of his class. He was an excellent horseman, despite his weight, with hands as gentle as a woman's. The perfect regimental officer, Ringwood's misfortune was that, in a small regular force geared to supplying instructors at just such a time as this, he should be denied service in the field. Though a good instructor, he had no empathy with his trainees. He did not conceal his burning contempt for the young, would-be officers who came to the school. Later, Ringwood would have his wish for action. He was killed commanding a 4th Division battery in France in 1918.

Ringwood's chief concern was equitation. He said to us, "An officer can be a genius in gunnery and he can lose his guns if he can't ride a horse." We had two hours every afternoon either on the road or in the riding school and Ringwood was a very fine riding master. I had ridden all my life and I was in good shape but much of the riding was "strip saddle" (stirrups crossed over the withers) or on a folded blanket and surcingle. I felt the unused muscles crying out and the fellows who had never ridden were really suffering.

On our third day two or three were a few minutes late for C.O.'s parade. Just a minute or so but there was hell to pay and we got a dressing down, innocent and guilty, then and there from Ringwood. He finished his harangue by announcing that because of this breach of discipline the whole course would go on a punishment ride that afternoon. We didn't know, we young officers, what this meant. If we had, we would have brought a second pair of breeches. We also didn't know that such a ride was inevitable, regardless of our imperfections. Every course suffered at least one.

We paraded at 2:00 P.M. and were marched to the stables and given the order, "To your horses!" I had an idea that this would be what was called a "numnah" ride or the blanket and surcingle job. A numnah pad is a thickness of felt which is placed under an officer's saddle. We would use blankets only. I spotted a comfortable-looking horse and quickly moved to him.

"May I ask why you came over to this horse?" Ringwood asked.

"Sloping pasterns and low withers, sir," I answered with confidence.

"Oh, a smart ass, eh! I have just the horse for you . . . come with me." He pointed to a huge beast about seventeen hands high with cow hocks, perpendicular pasterns and withers like the Rockies. I found out later that he was used to pack the heavy reels of telephone wire.

"There," he said, "I think you will be quite happy . . . you and your goddamn pasterns!"

Jimmie Burns, who lived opposite our house in Toronto and

106

was the son of a Methodist minister, laughed at my discomfiture. He was promptly transferred to a mount with vicious vertebral malformation.

"We aim to please," murmured Ringwood.

We filed out of the stable and lined up.

"Ride, prepare to mount . . . . MOUNT!"

I never thought I'd make it all the way up but I did with a mighty effort. I was mounted on a gigantic razor-back hog!

"Half-sections right . . . . walk . . . . MAARCH!"

It had begun.

An hour later we were near Gananoque, twelve miles from Kingston, and had turned for home. We had trotted half the time. I could feel the blood soaking my breeches and could see the blood on Jimmy Burns' behind. Try as I would, I was unable to sit back, and Ringwood's repeated exhortation, "Sit back on your asses, gentlemen!" fell on unheeding ears.

"Ride, TURROT!"

The agony of the great clodding beast jolting my bleeding backside on the row of saw-toothed vertebrae was almost more than I could bear. The trotting seemed interminable but at last came some slight solace: "Ride . . . . WAALK!"

Two of the older officers had to dismount and walk in but the rest of us finished the ride. Ringwood walked us through the barrack gate, over to the stables and wheeled us into line.

"Ride, prepare to dismount . . . . DISMOUNT!"

What a blessing is gravity which makes dismounting relatively easy, that is if your legs don't give way on touching the ground!

"Dismiss to stables!"

Ringwood passed along the stable with acid comments as to our abilities with brush and currycomb. He came to me and as I stood to attention he rubbed a flank of old "Hog's Back" with his white-cotton-gloved hand. I thought of Van and James in the stable at "519." Apparently he was satisfied for he asked, "How are those pasterns?" I took a chance of dire penalties and replied, "Quite solidified, sir, thank you." Ringwood smiled.

There were more numnah rides but they were not for punishment; and muscles, hardened in the riding school, made them tolerable. For the next road ride, Captain Ringwood unobtrusively motioned me over to a smart little mare stabled among the battery headquarter party horses. I put her bridle on and a standing martingale which was hanging on her post, and as I cinched up the surcingle I wondered what was in store for me. Apparently Ringwood was making a peaceful gesture, for the mare gave me a beautiful ride. I saw the need for the martingale soon enough for she was a happy little thing and tried to throw her head all over the place but she rode like thistledown. I found out afterward that she was the first trumpeter's horse and in her exuberance she had recently removed two of his front teeth as he sounded "Prepare to mount" at a parade of "C" Battery.

The eight weeks came to an end quickly. It had been a bone-crushing experience but most of us finished it fit and eager and with caudal lesions healed. Thanks to Ringwood, we had a fairly good idea of elementary gunnery knocked into us. It was the only real instruction I would have before going to France.

Ours was the third course since the war had started. Eighteen months later, Ringwood was still grinding his teeth in frustration and conducting his tenth course. I don't know how many officers of the Canadian Field Artillery he qualified but it must have amounted to over half of those who were the junior gunner officers of the Canadian Corps in France. As far as I know, not one failed to acknowledge the debt he owed to Ringwood. At long last he got to France in command of a 4th Division Battery. Most of his fellow battery commanders had been taught by him at Kingston. Major Ringwood was killed in action in 1918, about the same time as Major James Burns, D.S. O., and Major Vernon Powell, M.C.

14

Back in Toronto, I had no choice but to await orders. The best I could hope for was to be attached to one of the 3rd Division batteries, already up to strength, for further training, with the possibility of going overseas with a reinforcement draft. In any event, these batteries would not be in active training for another two months. I had cut the painter with the University and anyway the O.T.C. was out for I was already commissioned. Father suggested I might work at making shells at "the works" in Toronto.

And so I made my acquaintance with factory life. It was not love at first sight.

Working conditions at Massey-Harris were, I think, no better and certainly no worse than at other factories of the period. Work began at 7 A.M. and went on until 6 P.M. with an hour off for lunch. Most of the work was of stifling monotony. My job was putting on the driving bands on eighteen-pounder shell cases, an operation that would not have taxed the powers of a half-wit. It consisted of inserting a flat copper band or ring in a channel near the base of the shell, fixing it with a lead hammer and pressing the band into the concave channel in a concentric steam press. You simply gave the band eighty pounds pressure and that was that. The foreman said, "Don't give her more than eighty. She won't take it and that live steam's a bugger." You could do about four shells a minute, but there was an extra routine that cut down the count quite a bit. Driving band setters had to stamp each shell with the company mark and a code number signifying the date of manufacture and identity of workman. An extra hand job, it cut the output of each press to about two thousand shells a day.

Some ten months later I was on duty at the guns near Dickebush in the Mount Kemmel sector in France. Inspecting the ammunition in the gun pits, I found five rounds of shrapnel stamped M-H B.X. This meant the shells had been made in May, 1915, by a workman called X. It was my own letter! Ammunition was rationed at the time, but I wanted to see what kind of work we had done at the factory. I had a couple of rounds fired at a suspected sniper's post.

The driving bands held. I may have been the only gunner officer in the Canadian Corps who fired ammunition he had actually helped to make.

About the middle of June, I received orders to report to the Commanding Officer, 8th Brigade, Canadian Expeditionary Force, at Caesar's Camp, Niagara-on-the-Lake. This officer was Major Austin Gillies, an affable fellow, a militia officer and successful lumberman in civilian life. His one concern was the training of his newly formed battery, the 30th, for active service. He was also acting C.O. of the brigade which consisted of the 31st and two other batteries in training elsewhere.

"I'm glad to have you with the 30th. The orders say you're attached for training. But I'm damned if I know what to do with you, what with a raw unit to train and my full complement of horses. Now I'm told that the brigade is getting a hundred and forty more remounts sometime this week. They're for some 4th Division battery, I think. How are you with horses?"

"I'm pretty good, sir."

"Good. You've had a course with Ringwood, I see. I'll give you twenty or so drivers I have supernumerary and you can take on these remounts."

"Will that interfere with my going overseas with a draft?"

"Don't worry . . . . I'll see that you get across the first chance."

I spent the summer breaking in remounts, most of them never

110

having had a bit in their mouths. I was assigned a "Corporal Roughrider" from the regular cavalry and two good N.C.O.'s, and the four of us took on the rabble of horses which were off-loaded at the railroad siding a couple of days later. We made six trips from the sidings to Caesar's Camp with twenty-five terrified, whinnying beasts, each time escorting them through miles of infantry lines. Twice only we had to round up errant animals but the second fugitive made quite a shambles of the officers' mess tent of a Western Ontario battalion. I eventually came to cues with this fellow. It wasn't a bad record for four amateur range riders.

The horse is a stupid but willing animal. It has a brain about the size of a polo ball but a will to please as great as the dog's. The horse is also an instinctive imitator. We always tried to have one or more trained horses in each group of trainees, about ten in number, and this brought excellent results. Initially, of course, the first bit and bridle, the first saddling, were individual achievements.

Most of the horses took readily to the bit and bridle. A few hours with one of us on a blanket in the riding ring we had built, and most of them had learned the feel of the aids, the touch of the reins on the neck, and the shifting of weight. In short, each remount was "bridle-wise" before we put a saddle on him and this encumbrance most of the class accepted without complaint. At the end of two months we had brought the mob of remounts to a stage of training which would allow them to be taken over by a newly formed battery.

There were, of course, recalcitrant horses who took longer to qualify, and one veritable outlaw who proved to be hopeless. Not surprisingly, he was the one who had entered the infantry mess without permission. A well-conformed, compact gelding, he looked a good ride but he was the only really savage horse I ever met, Vernon Powell's old hunter Yeoman being a playful gazelle by comparison. The horse's business end for defence is the hindquarters and he wants plenty of room for combative action. In general there is no impulse to attack anything in front, be it another horse or a human being. This limb of Satan, however, would bite and paw anyone who tried to feed or water him. He would use his forefeet to stamp on anyone who approached him. When his turn came for the first bit and bridle routine, we drew lots for the job of being "up" on the blanket. I lost. The corporal put a blindfold on him and we snapped a lunging line to the bit. I jumped aboard and the blindfold was yanked off. I expected a good few jolts but instead of the traditional straight-legged bucks the wretch went for my left foot with his teeth and then into a spin Nijinski couldn't have equalled. The lunging line swept me off and I lay still. Normally a horse, however enraged, once divested of his burden just forgets and forgives, but not my friend. Still spinning, he spied his erstwhile rider prostrate. With a surge of what we would now call "equine power," he jumped the few feet which separated us and, in a most unhorselike manner, proceeded to stomp me. Thank God, he wasn't shod for if he had been I wouldn't be telling about it sixty years later. The corporal and two drivers dragged the beast off me. I could not move. They took me into the hospital in an ambulance which was as rough as the horse had been. There was nothing broken and no real damage but the next day my body presented a chromatic scheme of blues, browns and yellows, which was quite beautiful, and the brigade was minus one "gelding br.," cast as unmanageable.

A bright moment came in late August when I was detailed with fifty "other ranks," who were also "supernumerary for training," for overseas inoculations, anti-typhoid and smallpox vaccination. Anti-typhoid injections were being given for the first time. Nowadays injections are a way of life, given for every conceivable purpose, from infancy to senility; but to all of us in 1915, the hypodermic needle was an unknown hazard, and apparently equally repellent to the young M.O. who was to administer the injections. He was fresh from medical school, his uniform hanging on him like a frock coat and his new Sam Browne belt a light, jaundiced beige. I knew him as a school friend of my brother. After the war he became a notable internist but at this time in his early days his professional powers had not reached their peak. I refer to him as "Ambrose." He was an endearing person and at this time a very nervous one.

112

With a casual disregard of sterilization procedure, he set up his clinical post in the loft above an old farm stable where some officers' horses were kept. Parading with my fifty men at the stables, we were ordered to strip to the waist. An issue folding table had been placed among the bales of hay. On it was a trough with a spirit lamp underneath with some hypo needles boiling in it. Bottles littered the table. A medical orderly stood by. I was first in line. Filling his large syringe from a rubber-capped bottle, Ambrose approached me in the familiar "this-is-going-to-hurt-me-much-more-than-you" manner. I could see that the needle seemed to have the calibre of a shotgun. Ambrose took hold of my meagre pectoral muscles and very gingerly inserted the weapon. He then extruded a tremendous dollop of the anti-toxin, intently examining the measurements on the syringe. I murmured, "Ambrose, that hurts like stink!" His reply, "Does it?" did not reassure me. He withdrew the needle. I expected to bleed to death. A husky sergeant was next and without hesitation Ambrose replenished the syringe and poked the same needle into his pectoral preserve.

"Goddamn!" the sergeant murmured and fainted, thus failing to receive his shot. The prostrate N.C.O. was placed on a pile of hay. The third victim bravely presented himself. The needle, or javelin, was poised for the third time as if to stab the heart, when I snapped, "Ambrose, may I speak to you?" With needle still poised he stepped over to me. I whispered, "Shouldn't you sterilize the needle?" "Oh, yes," he murmured, "thank you!"

We each had three shots and Ambrose gave each of us a clean needle after his attempt at communal service. Most of us were sick each time and the huskier the man the worse it was. Five or six passed out with shock in the first session. But the inoculation was successful. It took a world war to teach us that the scourge of typhoid fever could be licked.

Just before we broke camp for winter quarters in September, we were reviewed by the Governor-General.

In line for inspection with our two batteries and attached personnel on the right, the parade of seventeen thousand men stretched for well over a mile. The Governor-General was the Duke of Connaught, a regular soldier and a field marshal. A splendid figure on his horse, he really looked like a general. Instead of the usual tedious inspection, he rode along the whole line at a brisk canter, saluting each unit. Every unit cheered him as he passed.

Back at Exhibition Camp in Toronto, I at last got my sailing orders. I was to ship out from Montreal to England with a hundred men.

Expensively re-equipped for action, we embarked in the *Metagama* of the Allan Line. The old ship was jammed to the gunwales with some five thousand troops.

About midnight the gangways were hauled in and cables let go. The band on the wharf marched to a spot just below us.

We could hardly believe our eyes! There he was, with his white moustache, walking down to the dockside in his gold-peaked cap. The old Duke of Connaught, Queen Victoria's favourite son, had come to see us off. He stood there alone, as the band struck up "God Save the King." We broke King's Regulations and sang the words. We yelled our heads off; the band played "Rule Britannia"; the ship started to slide away. The Duke was still waving to us as we slipped into the darkness.

15

In England, the draft and I were sent to the Reserve Brigade of the Canadian Field Artillery at Ross Barracks, Shorncliffe Camp, near Folkestone on the coast of Kent. This was the depot brigade that supplied reinforcements to the Canadian Corps in France, consisting in 1915 of the 1st and 2nd Divisions.

Two other gunner subalterns had come over with me, Parke Cameron and Nolan Patterson, and we hoped that if immediate service in France was not forthcoming, in the short interval before it did we would at least undergo some useful training.

Our hopes were soon dashed. Our brigade of four batteries was fully equipped with eighteen-pounders and horses. But once again we were outside looking in, attached for training and denied the experience of regimental duties. It was clear now that we would arrive in France without experience in leading men.

The commanding officer of the Reserve Brigade was an elderly militia colonel named Rathbone, a spit-and-polish officer who believed victory would come through glistening buttons and boots and parade-ground discipline. Colonel Rathbone, since he wore a gold-rimmed monocle, was known as "Dead-Eye." He received ardent support in his disciplinary efforts from his brigade adjutant, a moon-faced dandy.

This Captain Bertie Biggar was a good fellow in the mess, an eager and indifferent poker player, which made him a source of income to impecunious brother officers. On parade, his "pink" breeches were cut with a perfect flair, his boots and belt had a mahogany sheen, the spurs with extra-long chains were ankle-high, and his buttons glittering through the November fog made him a sort of constellation.

Daily "C.O." parades were conducted with the utmost punctilio and there seemed to be a liturgical solemnity about them which turned Dead-Eye into a bishop as he blessed his adjutant and inspected the assembled congregation. The inspection over and "His Grace" satisfied that all the souls in his charge were in a high state of polish, the components of the brigade would be marched off to engage in preparations to meet an enemy, who seemed to become more remote each day. After about a week of these solemnities, I found myself softly singing "Nunc dimittis" as we trudged away to map-reading or some such class, in which anthem I was soon joined by several brother officers, similarly inspired. A German spy who heard a detachment of thirty officers marching off a parade ground softly chanting, "Lord, now lettest thou thy servant depart in peace . . . " would have been much puzzled!

The training to which we were marched was the old drill-book stuff with which most of us had been crammed at Kingston months before. We knew it had no relation to the trench warfare we would find in France.

The gunnery instructor at the Reserve Brigade was an elderly lieutenant-colonel named Battiscombe, a regular R.F.A. officer who had commanded a battery of 4.5 howitzers in the retreat from Mons. The fact that as a "half-colonel" he had held such a command — normally that of a major or even captain — is a comment on the promotion situation in the peacetime British Army in 1914. He was a kindly, gentle old fellow, much like a country vicar, and the retreat had been a ghastly experience for him. Never in the three months that I was at Shorncliffe did I hear Colonel Battiscombe speak of his service in France with the "Old Contemptibles."

One subject that could and should have been included in our

training was the care of horses in trench warfare. The winter of 1915-1916 was one of the coldest and wettest on record in Europe. Flanders in particular was a quagmire. Horses and men are vulnerable to continually wet feet, horses perhaps more so, and it was a problem to keep the poor creatures dry. There was plenty to learn in this respect.

But Equitation was in the charge of a warrant officer of the Household Cavalry, better qualified to lecture on the paving of the Mall and the tan-bark in the riding school at Knightsbridge Barracks. He knew nothing of Flanders' mud. This obnoxious fellow gave elementary riding instruction, apparently to humiliate us. He actually excelled Bertie Biggar in elegance of turnout, his rank denoted by a small royal coat of arms on his right sleeve. For all I knew, he could have been a field marshal except that he was too young. Our first day, he singled me out.

"May I remind you, SIR, that you are not in the hunting field but are now an officer on parade. You will arch your back and sit upright in the saddle!"

"Yes, sir."

"Do not address me as Sir, sir. I am only a warrant officer, class one, Royal Horse Guards, and far inferior in rank to you, sir. I am to be addressed as Mr. du Pledge. Resume your place in the ride, sir!"

I was, thank Heaven, well mounted on this occasion. Without a word, I wheeled away from Mr. du Pledge and gave my horse a dig with the spurs. The good beast obligingly deposited a spatter of tan-bark on the beautiful pink breeches of our instructor.

London leave was easy to obtain, although Bertie Biggar put up a show of reluctance at each request. On the fourth and, as it turned out, our last application, three of us were announced at brigade orderly room.

"Mr. Cameron, Mr. Patterson and Mr. Massey, Sir!"

Bertie looked up from his littered table.

"My God, I don't believe it! You three had leave last weekend."

I had been appointed initial spokesman.

"Yes, that is so true. But we are all three of us in the process of obtaining breeches like yours from tailors in London, and —"

"Boots like yours, too, Captain Biggar." This from Patterson.

"And a jacket as well," Parke Cameron put in. "We wish to do credit to the Canadian Field Artillery as you have done, Captain."

"Also, we thought," I went on, "that possibly we might find some fellow in London, returned from the wars, who could tell us what fighting with the guns in France is like!"

"Get the hell out of here and get your bloody breeches . . . I'm paying for them anyway!" Bertie was signing our leave warrants.

"You exaggerate your poker losses, dear Adjutant!"

We were on our way.

London leaves were made as pleasant for Canadians as British organization and hospitality permitted. Officers were put up at the Royal Automobile Club in Pall Mall and, if that palace was full, there were plenty of overflow billets. Theatre tickets could be had for any show and there were plenty to choose from. We hadn't seen many, but my aim this time was to see a Toronto girl who had just opened in a small revue called *Now's the Time.* Her name was Beatrice Lillie. I had heard she was very good but when I tried to get a ticket, I found the show had closed. So I took a seat in the Palace Theatre and saw enchanting Gertie Millar in *Bric-a-Brac* for the second time. I waited at the stage door to see her and, when she came out, she waved at me and threw me a kiss.

We got back to barracks about midnight on Sunday. The mess was deserted except for a sleeping officer who seemed to be a fixture. From the board where Daily Routine Orders were posted, Parke called to us to look at them. What I read was the most shattering disappointment I ever had. Twelve officers, all lieutenants, were posted "to proceed to Canadian Corps Headquarters in France for attachment to various batteries of the 1st and 2nd Divisions for two weeks' instruction commencing January 10th." It was now January 5, 1916. My name was not on the list.

Parke and Nolan were. Though both were safe on the list, they advised me to persuade the gunnery instructor to shove somebody off to make room for me. I had a good case, for I was senior to anybody on the list both by my date of commission and attachment to the 8th Brigade in Canada.

I was waiting outside the gunnery instructor's office when he arrived next morning.

"I know why you've called on me at this early hour, my boy. I can't alter the list."

"Sir, I am senior to every officer on that list. May I ask you why I am not included?"

"My dear boy, it's only a Cook's Tour, as we call it. They'll all be back after the two weeks. You're only nineteen, there's plenty of time."

There were tears in the elderly lieutenant-colonel's eyes. This maddened me.

"Sir, am I to understand that you are excluding me solely on the grounds of my age?"

"Yes, I think so."

"With all respect to you, sir, I don't think that is a valid reason for denying me the opportunity of active service. I wish to put this matter before Colonel Rathbone. Have I your permission, sir?"

"That is your right, Massey."

A few hours later, with the unexpected help of Bertie Biggar, I stood facing Dead-Eye at his orderly-room table.

In answer to his question why I was bothering him, I burst out, "I have every right to be one of the twelve subalterns to go on this next Cook's Tour, sir, by seniority and training, and I have been informed by Colonel Battiscombe that I'm too young. I know the list is subject to your approval, sir, and I'm asking you to include me."

"Well, I'm damned! I never heard of such impudence! What makes you think I haven't considered your age as the gunnery instructor has?"

"I'm quite certain you wouldn't allow such sentimentality to influence your judgement, sir."

"What did you say your name was?"

"Massey, sir."

"From Toronto?"

"Yes, sir."

"And your family used to be in Newcastle and Durham County.

Well, you know this is only a Cook's Tour — two weeks, they'll be back soon."

"On the last Cook's Tour, six of the officers stayed on with the batteries they were assigned to, sir. It's a genuine test and I've — I've got to go!"

There was a long pause. Dead-Eye fiddled with his papers. He looked up.

"All right. I'll talk to the gunnery instructor."

The following Friday, I was on a packet boat to Boulogne with eleven other Cook's Tourists.

16

Twelve hours later, we had arrived by truck and train and bus, and truck, at Canadian Corps H.Q. at Bailleul, in Belgium, forty-five miles from Boulogne.

It was ten o'clock in the morning; we were shaved and shining despite snow and sleet as we were herded into a farm kitchen that was the Artillery H.Q. General Burstall came in and briefly greeted us, leaving us in charge of Captain Norton, a young officer in hip-length fishing boots. Staff captain to the Commandant, Royal Artillery of the Canadian Corps, he later become the youngest divisional commander in the British Army.

"I take it you chaps have drawn your rations?" he said.

Luckily, we had also visited a couple of estaminets.

He read out our assignments. Mine was to the 13th Battery, 4th Brigade.

My heart almost stopped. It was Mr. Vernon Powell's battery.

The captain told me I was lucky.

I soon found the 13th Battery mess cart. The driver informed me that I was coming to the best battery in the Canadian Corps, and that meant in the whole British Army.

During the drive, I heard about Major George E. Vansittart, the Battery Commander, and how he loved horses. "He'd commit murder for those long-faced bastards!" the driver said.

We were passing battered farmhouses and barns, wagon lines and concealed heavy guns. The driver, a corporal, had praise for all the battery officers.

"Captain George Drew ('Uncle George'), Mr. Curtis and Mr. Powell," the corporal said, "there are three officers who really know their bloody jobs. Mr. Powell's an Englishman, but he's been in Canada quite a while. He's got his own horse, calls him Yeoman. A big son-of-a-bitch that can jump a five-foot wall but he needs riding!

"I'm at the horse lines, being a driver. I think if this Yeoman belonged to anyone else, he wouldn't be with the 13th, but Mr. Powell, he can have anything he wants."

We were among fields pocked with shell holes; most of the buildings we saw were badly damaged. The road continued through a large wood. Most of the trees were skeletons, water-filled shell holes pitted the ground. I knew this was the Ploegsteert area ("Plug Street" to all British troops) where some of the heaviest fighting had raged in the first and second battles of Ypres in 1914 and 1915.

Suddenly we left the road and, for a short distance, followed a rutted track past a group of half-ruined farm buildings, then across a field that looked as if it had recently been heavily shelled, to a group of dugouts and Nissen huts. Nearby were the remains of a grove of trees, now bare, shattered poles.

Only at close range could these splinter-proofs and gun pits be seen: camouflage, more skilful than anything I had seen on the drive from Bailleul, had been carried out.

I was shown to the Battery H.Q., a splinter-proof of corrugated iron sections, heavily sandbagged, with a gas blanket pulled back from the open entrance. Despite the winter cold, a brazier was keeping the dugout completely warm.

As I went in, a very tall major rose from the makeshift table. He was Major Vansittart, the reputed horse-lover who was the Battery Commander.

He introduced me to the battery sergeant-major and his brother, the orderly sergeant. Their name was Rimmer. "Thank God for the Rimmer brothers," the Major said.

I found I had been assigned a batman, Gunnor Anchor, a groom and two horses. Eager to see Mr. Powell again, I learned he was at the O. Pip and would be back next day.

While the Major was talking, we were interrupted by four shell bursts that seemed quite close. I followed the Major out of the dugout. There were the smoking craters just a hundred yards away on our right flank.

"Whizz-bangs," said the Major. "That's the German field gun. Hasn't the punch the eighteen-pounder has. They've been trying to find us for the last few days. The next salvo will be closer — about twenty-five yards and the same range. Fritz always sweeps the same pattern."

Again we heard the brief whine and the bursts, this time about twenty-five yards closer. One round came a lot closer. We were splashed with mud from the explosion.

"A careless gun-layer, but he nearly got results." The Major brushed mud off his breeches. "Next salvo will be plus twenty-five yards. Let's hope Fritz has corrected his line."

The third salvo burst exactly where the Major predicted. After six salvos, an empty area smaller than a football field had been neatly pocked with three-foot craters.

Large flakes of snow were falling, melting as they landed on the sticky mud.

Soon the snow turned to rain. I became acquainted with Flanders mud.

I spent the day settling in and discovering the way things worked at the guns. The Major told me that tomorrow I would relieve Mr. Powell at the O. Pip.

Next day, about two o'clock, I set out for the O. Pip with the signallers, Bill Wilkinson and Art Vokes, former comrades in the Victoria College O.T.C. It was a two-mile walk. It was pleasant to get Bill and Art alone for a good yarn about Victoria. Bill had been within a few months of graduating when he enlisted. A divinity student, his calling went into storage for the duration. Passing through "Plug Street" (the wrecked village of Ploegsteert), in full view of Fritz, Bill and Art led me cautiously into a little estaminet supposed to contain the original of a famous cartoon. The pub was a ruin, but on one wall, half blown down, was the Bruce Bairnsfather drawing of Old Bill and Alf looking over the edge of a crater. The caption was still intact: "If you knows of a better 'ole, go to it!" The artist's signature was clearly visible.

Through the village we entered a communication trench, little more than a ditch, with water covering its rotting duck boards. It led into a trench that Bill told me had been the old front line. Soon we came to a traverse. A splinter-proof shelter in the corner housed the telephone. There were a couple of chicken-wire bunks and a nice puddle with a brazier apparently floating in it. The two signallers were shivering with cold.

Mr. Powell had gone to Battalion H.Q.

The lookout was over the parapet, with a couple of sandbags shielding an aperture. You couldn't see much anyway. It was the worst O. Pip I remember. Our front line was about a hundred yards ahead. At this point, No Man's Land was barely seventy-five yards across. Since the Germans had chosen the line, their forward trench was a few feet higher and drained nicely into ours.

The rain slackened. I was trying to get my bearings when Vernon Powell returned. I found he was known now as de Buttes, his middle name.

We greeted each other happily.

"This is a quiet sector," he told me. "We've got a Bavarian Corps opposite, a fairly peaceable lot. As you know, we're covering the Highland Division. The problem is that Winston Churchill has just taken over a new battalion, the 6th Scots Fusiliers, and he's raising hell, calling up Division for retaliation all night. His lot were in the line last week and they'll be back in tomorrow. You won't have him . . . the Fusiliers will be the next on your right flank, but Winston will be wandering around in your battalion's area, trying to stir up a war. Probably stumping along the parapet in one of those new French tin hats."

The whole length of trench that the 13th was covering was about three hundred yards, and from the actual O. Pip you had a reasonably good view.

"While it's still daylight, show me the registrations, the targets and explain the drill to me. I'm green as hell and I only know F.A.T."

"Don't worry." He stood up on the firestep of the trench, his head and shoulders above the parapet. I joined him, ill at ease. I was a bit taller, unfortunately.

"Now here are your targets. The zero line is on that single tree trunk . . . . "

He went over the targets with me and I felt a lot more confident. As the light began to fade, the rifle- and machine-gun fire increased all along the line. "De Buttes," as I now called him, took me over to Company and Battalion H.Q.'s. In this particular situation, infantry liaison was combined with observing. The battalion was a regular Highland one, the 1st or 2nd Seaforths. It had started to rain again, a bitter, cold sleet. As we passed shivering, kilted figures huddled in shelters or standing in rigid silence on icy duck boards, de Buttes remarked, "There's nothing so depressing as a lot of Jocks in the rain!"

The Company Commander was wearing those hip-high fishing boots under his kilt and stood outside his dugout in a foot of water. He greeted us dourly, "Everything seems quiet but Winston comes in again tonight with his Fusiliers, so it is likely that the war will start up. If we had anything but complacent Wurtemburgers over there (he pointed at the German front line about a hundred yards away), there'd be one hell of a raid to try and bag him! He's done everything but yell 'come and get me!'"

We had a nip of Scotch with him and went back to our O. Pip, which had all the lure of a flooded chicken coop. De Buttes thought it would be a good idea if I checked on a few targets, particularly the German wire. So I "stood the battery to" and had a little shooting. The registrations seemed sound, but I made one or two corrections. The light was fading fast and the first star shell went up, looking hazy in the rain. A wet night was ahead.

Just the rattle of rifle- and machine-gun fire was heard and the popping of flares sent up by both sides. The signallers took three-hour turns on the phone. All three of us managed to get enough sleep in cat naps but it was horribly cold.

About two o'clock, artillery fire on our immediate right signalled that Lt.-Colonel Churchill was back in the line. Our battalion stood to about 4:00 A.M. as a sort of routine. Otherwise there was "peace."

I had a dream during one of my naps. I was in school again and we had a new headmaster who was very strict. He looked like Major Vansittart. I was trying hard to be made a prefect. Even now I remember that dream vividly. Awake again, I thought I was doing what I had wanted to do for so long. I was being told what to do and the decisions weren't difficult. It was much like school and I liked it.

About dawn, I was peeking through the observation aperture with my field glasses when I became aware of a figure standing on the firestep, head and shoulders above the parapet. I was scared stiff.

It was Lt.-Col. Winston Churchill, a couple of his officers with him.

"Good morning," he said. "Things seem very quiet."

"Yes, sir!" Privately, I was thinking, *Please go away before you warm up a sniper*! He did so, much to the relief of his escort. In some parts of the line, I had been told, anyone rash enough to peer over the parapet for longer than a couple of breaths would get a bullet through the skull.

17

There never was a man less military minded than my father. Not that he was a pacifist, far from it, but his idea of making war was based on the exploits of Joshua, Gideon, of Saul and David and the heroes of the Old Testament. Come to think of it, such thinking did not put him so very much out of date, at least in some aspects of trench warfare. Just before I left for overseas, father asked me if I had a good pair of field glasses. I said I had the regulation type which officers have "on repayment."

"They will only give you eight magnification, I suppose," he said. "I would like to see you have a telescope for looking at the enemy."

I thought the idea was ridiculous, but I thanked him, saying I didn't think it would be needed, and forgot about the telescope. But after a turn at O. Pip, this time in front of Messines on a hill with a much better view, I realized how valuable a telescope would be, giving three times the magnification of field glasses. I spoke to de Buttes about it and he thought it was a grand idea. Since his leave had just come through, I told him of father's offer and he agreed to buy a suitable telescope and charge it to the Massey-Harris Company in London. Off he rode to railhead with his groom who would bring Yeoman back to the horse lines.

It was now late in February and I was doing a stretch of duty

127

with the horses. The battery had just taken over a new position in the Messines sector and the horse lines which we inherited from a British battery were appalling. The weather had been terrible, rain and snow almost constantly, and the actual standings were a quagmire. Attempts had been made to soak up the water with straw and sawdust but this had become a sodden mess and the poor beasts were up to their fetlocks in mud and water. The tarpaulins covering the lines were torn to shreds and Major Vansittart had curtly ordered me to "put things right."

It looked to be a pretty tough assignment. The only bright spot was the men's quarters which were in Nissen huts and these were in fairly good shape and moderately dry. The previous occupants, one of the Lahore Division batteries, had certainly ignored the gunner credo, "Guns first, horses second, men last!"

The first thing was to shift the lines to some nearby turf which would remain comparatively dry until the horses stamped the ground into mud. This change was accomplished and the one hundred and forty horses were on "dry" land for maybe as much as two days. But we were in Belgium, a marsh at the driest of times. In winter, a new shell hole would have a foot of water in it within a few minutes. The water table in Flanders must be less than a foot below the surface! There was no alternative to stone or gravel standings. Thrush, a severe inflammation of the frog of a horse's hoof, would run through the battery, as it had with other units. Thrush was a menace to mounted units as much to be dreaded as trench feet in the infantry. But it was far more difficult to combat.

Just about one hundred yards away from our lines was a farm, the usual group of barns, sheds and house in a rectangle enclosing a midden. The house had been partly demolished by shellfire sometime previously, but the rest of the buildings were almost intact. The farmer had abandoned his property but visited it frequently, living in the village close by. All the buildings were of small stones — beautiful stones — including some fifty yards of wall. I looked at this attractive quarry from a distance with Sergeant Fryer. He was the senior N.C.O. at the horse lines, there for a "rest" from the guns.

"There's some good stone, Sergeant."

"Yes, sir . . . pity to see it going to waste."

"If only the Hun would drop a couple of 5.9s in that barn, we could get some good standings from the ruins."

"Yes, sir, but they haven't shelled here for some months."

"It's high time they did. Is that a sapper dump just down the road?"

"Yes, sir."

I shouted to the stable picket to have my horse saddled.

Fryer continued: "I think I'm ahead of you, sir. That wall alone would do half the job!"

"Have you any idea when this fellow visits his farm?"

"No, I haven't, but we can put a picket to watch for him?"

My groom brought my horse and I cantered over to the sapper depot. Never, in all my time in the army, had I found a sapper officer of any rank who wouldn't do twice as much as he was asked. The engineers are the housekeepers of the army and their spirit of "nothing is too much" is something to be experienced. The captain I talked to, a field company of our own 2nd Division, didn't know there was a negative in the language. He listened to my tale.

"The only fellow who could get a message through to the Boche heavies would be the farmer himself. Some of these bastards in the forward area who pretend to work their farms have their pockets lined with marks and get their reports back to the Hun all sorts of ways. Just two days ago, they picked up the man that farms this one where the dump is. But I don't know about your man and I daresay he'd be reluctant to ask the Hun to have a shot at his own farm. So you'd like to have the sappers knock it about a bit so it's fair game for horse-loving but predatory gunners?"

"That's the substance of my prayer," I answered.

"How many bursts do you want?"

I thought a moment: "I think three in the barn and a fourth crater say fifty yards short, just for local colour!"

"Right. They'd better simulate eight-inch . . . we're about two miles from the line here and that's stretching a 5.9 howitzer a bit. You're in a hurry for this bombardment?"

"I certainly am. Every hour counts! I'll have at least half of the battery horses with thrush and God knows what if I don't get 'em on dry land."

"Well, I don't want your Walloon friend to pop in on an innocent group of Canadian Engineers mining his premises. Corps would take a very dim view of such relations with the peasantry!"

"I'll have a couple of pickets to deal with that."

The captain called to a sergeant and I heard the words "charges . . . gelignite . . . crater" and presently a corporal and four sappers appeared, one carrying a pack, the other three with a post-hole digger, a couple of shovels and a crowbar. Two more joined them, one with a plunger and the other carrying two reels of light cable. The party marched off to "that battery horse lines" with a certain amount of admonition to the man with the pack to keep his distance from them. The captain's horse was brought round and together we rode off to see what I can only call "the shoot."

On the way over to our lines, the captain readily agreed to lend us picks, shovels, sledges, masons' hammers and as much cement as he could spare. We passed the little band of sappers, the lone one with the pack twenty-five yards behind. At the horse lines, I posted the pickets to keep an eye out for the farmer and sent all the horses out on an exercise ride. I didn't want them to know the strategy. The sappers arrived, the captain chose his three spots in the barn and the place for the crater, and they went to work. About twenty minutes later, the sappers blew the four charges and the captain and I went over to inspect the result. It was a perfect job! The barn and an adjoining wall presented the most precious rubble imaginable. The horses would have the driest standings in Belgium.

"That's what you wanted, I think. Just send a wagon over and I'll let you have the tools you need. Put six inches of fine rubble under the stones for drainage."

He mounted his horse just as Sergeant Fryer and the ride clattered up the road.

"Thanks a million," I said.

"Don't thank me . . . thank those Kraut gunners! Come over for a drink anytime you like."

130

He rode away.

For nearly fifty hours, we worked around the clock in two shifts and, at the end of it, we had two long standings of dry stone on rubble, enough for our one hundred and forty horses and all covered over with tarpaulins and canvas sheets. It had rained almost continuously while we were working and had stopped just as the work was done. The Major came over from the guns to see it. "Good work," he said, which was the equivalent of a mention in dispatches. I told him that the whole farm had been badly shelled. Major Van looked me straight in the eye.

"Yes, gunnery in the Canadian Engineers is at a very high level. Now I'll have a look at these horses. Oh, by the way, they're clearing out all the Belgian civilians from the forward area." He smiled. "Just in time!"

18

In early February, the Canadian 2nd Division was in front of Messines and our battery covered part of the line where the Douve River crossed No Man's Land, which was about one hundred and fifty yards wide. The two front lines were in a valley between Messines, a small town on a ridge of high ground, and Hill 63 on our side. It was a pretty hot area with almost continuous sniping and artillery action, with frequent night raids. We had two O. Pips, one on the forward slope of Hill 63 and another just behind the front line which could only be entered at night. This gave a wonderful view of No Man's Land and was perfect for cutting wire and shooting up snipers.

But the one near the crest of the hill was a beauty and, with the telescope which de Buttes had brought back from London, you could have a wonderful time. I spotted a trench set way back in Messines. The dugout with its viewing aperture was perfect. We had all worked at night when doing our turns to conceal the post and it was obvious that we had succeeded, for the Germans just shelled around us with light stuff, searching for what they were sure was there.

This was my second tour of duty on Hill 63. The night before, just as I left for the O. Pip, the Major had told me that I was to remain with the 13th indefinitely. I was still "on approval" but it was mighty good news.

The morning was sunny and clear and I felt on top of the world. It was on the chilly side and Bill Wilkinson was stoking the brazier with "iron ration" dog biscuits which were much better than coke. Art Vokes was on the phone. I took a look at what seemed to be a new sniper's post with a view to shooting it up when the gas blanket was pulled aside and a young British voice called:

"Is the officer there? The Corps Commander would like to speak to you."

I stepped out into the bright sunlight. There stood Lieutenant-General Sir Edwin Alderson, a full colonel and the Corps Commander's A.D.C. who had just spoken. I have never been so dazzled in my life. It was in the time before steel helmets were issued and the three of them were a gorgeous coruscation of red cap bands, gold staff badges, ribbons, buttons, red brassards. There was even an orderly with a guidon on a lance. What was most horrendous was that they all stood on the crest of the hill in full shining view of the Hun at his most alert. The General spoke.

"Well, my lad, how goes it? . . . Everything pretty quiet, eh?"

"Yes, sir."

"Beautiful day, what? Let's have a look at your little snuggery . . . . " He peered into the dugout. "By Jove, these chaps know how to make themselves comfortable!" This to the colonel. "Capital, capital. Well, my lad, good hunting!"

He walked along the crest with his G.S.O., as I afterward found out it was, the A.D.C. and the orderly. I lost no time.

"Get the phones and clear out the left down the hill. Quick as you can!"

I grabbed the telescope and followed Bill and Art down the reverse of the hill and to the left. It came quicker than I expected. A salvo of two 5.9 howitzers. You could hear them roaring in. They were plus a hundred yards or so and almost even with us on the flash. The next got one direct hit on that beautiful O. Pip. They gave it another for good measure but it wasn't needed. The dugout was a crater. Away down the hill on the reverse side, the General strode along with his little party. I don't think they even turned to watch the bursts. I could see the red that long way off and I saw red quite close, too. There was nothing for it but to use one of the craters for the rest of the day to observe and keep the phones back of the hill. That night we built a new dugout nearby which was named "Alderson Snuggery." It was never as good as the one the general visited.

The next time I was observing on that front, I used the O. Pip just behind the front trench, the one you could only enter and leave in the dark. I was ordered to use it (I certainly didn't choose it!) because we were going to cut some enemy wire with shrapnel and shoot up a couple of snipers' posts and the view from this forward O. Pip was perfect for that. The post was just a little burrow in the roots of a splintered tree trunk and there was only room for one signaller and the forward observation officer. Just a tiny hole in the trunk was the viewing range. You could hardly use binoculars but they weren't necessary as the targets were so close. The weather had turned really cold again and there had been some wet snow. We started out from the guns about 4:00 A.M. and got to the communication trench we needed with an hour to spare before dawn. We left the trench and felt our way across the ground toward the tree. It was a mass of shell craters, big and little, all filled with muddy water. The signaller led the way, trailing a second telephone line which we tried to conceal as we approached the tree. It was pitch black and the flares didn't help much. The rifle fire was continuous. I found the biggest crater there was and tripped into it, up to my neck in icy water. I was carrying our rations and blankets which, of course, were now soaked. I called out to the signaller who was paying out the wire to give me a hand. He came back, found me and I succeeded in pulling him in with me. It wasn't my finest hour.

After what seemed an eternity, but was really only five minutes, we got ourselves out of the "pond" which must have been an eight-inch shell crater, reached the O. Pip, both of us soaked to the skin. We faced the pleasant prospect of sitting in a damp burrow for at least twelve hours while the sleet fell, with no chance of moving so much as a foot to keep warm and no heat of any kind. My companion showed qualities of forgiveness, fortitude and guts.

I encouraged him by authorizing a rum ration, obviously my duty as the senior officer of a detached unit, and we each had a great big slug of S.R.D. from my flask.

Rum, at least the issue brand known as "Service Rum Demerara," is the only alcoholic liquor which is a genuine stimulant with a nutritive effect. It has no letdown as the grain distillates have, and in the Great War rum saved countless lives. It certainly gave us a good rise in our temperature. After our snort of that glorious, smoky rum, we could say, "We are warm-blooded animals and we will now each warm a can of bully beef on our chests!" The experiment failed in part and we put half the can inside us instead but everything seemed better and we both kept remembering about therapeutic animal heat!

The existing telephone wire was good, as was the second, and when the cold grey dawn came, I was ready for a little shooting. I got a good view of what seemed to be a steel rifle port in the Hun front line and in a few rounds of high explosive, we pretty well clobbered it. It must have been a sound target, for back came some 5.9 inch howitzer rounds on our front line, some of them very close to us. I was apprehensive as to whether they were after our tree. It had begun to snow, big wet flakes, and I saw that the part of our tree with the aperture of simulated wood made of steel would give us away because snow falling on that part would immediately melt. But as the morning wore along and I did some more shoots, including wire registrations with time shrapnel, and there was no more attention to the tree, it seemed as if we were not "in the nude in Piccadilly Circus."

The ghastly day came to an end at the O. Pip about six when it was dark and, still sodden wet but with another good slug of rum aboard, we negotiated the craters without a misstep and reached the battery and some glowing braziers an hour later. We had already inadvertently had our cold bath but we exercised that almost-forgotten rite of changing our clothes.

19

Soon the battery was moved to a position in the Wytschaete sector which the 2nd Canadian Division took over in early March. It was nearer the Ypres salient. As usual, the move was at night.

My job was to take the battery to the new site, the other officers being busy with various duties. A guide was to pick me up at a certain point and lead the battery in to the gun positions.

I knew the map well and could have found my way without a guide. A battery in column was about a quarter of a mile long. When the star shells and the small arms fire got closer, I began to lose confidence in the guide.

It was pitch dark, with no moon, and rain was beginning to fall. My horse stumbled into what must have been a shell hole and I landed in barbed wire coiled across the road. "Halt!" I shouted, and as I struggled to get my horse out of the crater, a shadowy figure appeared, flashing a light in my face.

"You're just a hundred and fifty yards from the front line, sir. This is the Vierstraat-Wytschaete Road. I think you've come too far, sir," said a good Canadian voice. "These are the M trenches and we're the 19th Battalion."

I turned to the guide. "What have you got to say, bombardier?"

"I'm sorry, sir. I missed the turning — about a mile back."

I was in for it, I knew. I was responsible. I had muffed my chances with the 13th.

We were stalled in a narrow, sunken roadway and would have to turn around. A six-horse limbered gun or ammunition wagon can't do a nice U-turn and there were twelve of them. There was nothing to do but unhitch the teams, unlimber the guns and wagons and manhandle them around. I gave the order. Like the perfect outfit the 13th was, every vehicle was faced about in the dark, ready to move back inside of ten minutes. When we reached the turn we had missed, I knew we would be at the new gun position no more than a few minutes later than scheduled.

As we arrived with number four gun in the lead, I thought it best to confess my mistake to the Major.

He said, "The wire you wandered into was put there for the express purpose of preventing you from leading my battery into Wytschaete which, as you probably know, is at present in German hands."

It was an adequate rebuke.

"By the way," the Major added, "orders have come through, appointing you to the 13th. I've just received them from Brigade."

I could scarcely believe what I'd heard. I was no longer just "attached," "supernumerary," "for training," as I had been ever since I was commissioned. Now I belonged and to the best battery in the whole corps. I hadn't time to gloat over my good fortune — which had come so suddenly after my darkest moment. The guns had to be in the pits, laid on the zero lines left by our predecessors, the ammunition stored and everything ready for action by dawn, an hour from now.

All through our time in that position facing Wytschaete Line, the Germans pounded the field next to us intermittently with 5.9 howitzers. I never saw so many shell holes close together back of the forward area. And yet, despite the enemy's observation balloons, the closest burst was twenty-five yards from our nearest gun pit.

Once, at a Vierstraat O. Pip, I was watching the road from

Wytschaete to the German front line when I saw a tall figure in a long greatcoat walking down the road. Although he was six hundred yards from me, I could see through my telescope that he wore a monocle and, as his coat was open, the ribbon of the Iron Cross in his jacket buttonhole. He stopped at a pile of rubble we had registered as a machine gun post. He stood there peering at our front line, an audacity that was scarcely believable. I couldn't understand why our snipers hadn't picked him off.

I ordered number one gun to stand to, gave the target number, and ordered one round of high explosive. The tall officer stood there motionless.

I heard the shell whining overhead. It was right on target. There was a burst of yellowish smoke and rubble — and no tall officer. I don't know if it got him but I felt rather sick. Some people said the field artillery was an impersonal service.

Toward the end of March, I had nearly completed a tour at Vierstraat. I was having a warm-up in the dugout of the 15th Battery. Its captain, a Toronto friend named Jim MacDonnell, had a red-hot brazier going, fuelled as usual with inedible iron ration biscuits. Jim was in a grim mood. We had just heard that Ottawa was going to do nothing about conscription that year (eventually a phony Conscription Act was passed in 1917) and Jim made some sizzling comments on people he thought were playing politics with the war. His principal target in this outburst was Mackenzie King, the future prime minister of Canada, who had been in the service of the Rockefeller Foundation in the United States ever since he had lost his cabinet post when the Liberals were beaten in 1911. From this self-imposed exile, King had made several pronouncements which, according to Jim, had not been exactly in full support of an all-out Canadian war effort.

Jim whittled on a biscuit as he warmed to his theme. He felt strongly about what he thought was apathy toward the war on the home front. Finally he held up the biscuit muttering, "I'm afraid it doesn't look much like King but any piece of cast-iron dough comes near enough."

Then he threw it into the brazier. As the biscuit glowed red-hot, there were two shattering crumps close by.

I rushed out to retrieve the telescope from the observation hole. A voice yelled, "Get in your dugout!" Running for cover, I tripped on a wire. My first instinct was to protect the telescope, which took both arms, and I landed on my nose, breaking it. Struggling to my feet, I made the dugout, pulling the gas blanket across the entrance. Instantly there was a shattering blow. I was on my face, right up against a signaller who had been sitting at the far end of the shelter. The other signaller had been thrown against the end, too. I couldn't get my breath and I fought for it.

The first signaller, Sigré, a Frenchman from Martinique, was badly wounded. He had caught a big splinter in the stomach. I could hear his screaming. The other signaller ran out to get a stretcher, while I went for a blanket. Only a few tattered shreds remained of the gas blanket. The shell crater reached into the dugout. The sandbag I had been sitting on was ripped open, yet I did not have a scratch on me nor did the other signaller. Poor Sigré had taken it all.

The telescope, which I was holding, was a total loss.

Two more shells had come over but they had burst in the ruins. Jim MacDonnell, who had got his wire through to battery, said he would look after the 13th. He would try to have an ambulance waiting at the first-aid station.

There was no time to go by the communication trench. We would have to make it straight across the open, about five hundred yards to a ridge of ground.

Sigré was a heavy man and there were plenty of shell holes to negotiate. It was the longest quarter-mile I ever covered. Sigré was quiet now; I did not hear him make a sound. Perhaps he was out. His innards seemed shot away. A German field battery fired at us, but we got him to the casualty station.

Long afterwards, I learned that Sigré had recovered.

A few days after the Vierstraat incident, we were entertained by the introduction of a Portuguese field battery to active service. The

Portuguese had been in the war on our side since the beginning but they had been fighting the Germans in West Africa and hadn't appeared on the Western Front. Unheralded and unattached to our division, in mid-morning of a clear "balloon" day a six-gun battery of field artillery trotted onto an open field on our left flank, executed a beautiful "action front" and the gun teams were unhitched and trotted off. Ammunition wagons then arrived and were precisely drawn up by the guns. The gun crews proceeded to dig in the spades of the trails, and ammunition doors of the wagons were dropped. It was like a peacetime display at a military tattoo. The uniforms were an unfamiliar blue-grey; the officers wore gold tassels on their boots and kepi caps. We couldn't believe our eyes; nor could the German observers in the balloons, for it was a full ten minutes before the first round came over about two hundred yards short. The Portuguese didn't seem to pay any mind to the Hun attentions and went on digging in. Only after a ranging bracket of two hundred yards had been found and the first salvo came over a bit short, did the horses appear again, wagons and guns were limbered up, and the battery was trotted off the field. Where it came from and where it went nobody knew. After two ineffective salvos, the Kraut counter battery ceased firing, seemingly bewildered by this parade-ground demonstration. A year later the Portuguese contingent served effectively in France, presumably reading up on trench warfare in the intervening period.

About the time of the mysterious visitation of the Portuguese battery, the apocryphal story of the General Routine Order was first heard. It read something like, "The practice of referring to the Portuguese forces as 'those bloody Dagoes' will cease forthwith and they will be henceforth known as 'our gallant allies the Portuguese'!"

20

We were now close to the Ypres salient, a mile and a half from St. Eloi, the hot corner at the southeast elbow of this blood-soaked appendix which was the heritage of Field Marshal French's obstinacy.

A pet scheme of General Plumer, commanding the British Second Army, was to straighten this elbow by advancing our line on a six-hundred-yard front to a depth of some three hundred yards. The general thought this limited operation would eliminate the enfilade fire that the enemy could bring on our existing line from two directions. The plan required the capture of two strong points between the German first and second lines. It was decided to mine this area.

Three galleries were tunnelled sixty feet under the water-logged ground by British and Canadian sappers. This mining operation was started in August, 1915, and completed by the beginning of March, 1916. Secrecy was successfully maintained until the British 3rd Division, chosen to make the assault, were given their orders. The Brigade concerned rehearsed the operation on specially prepared ground. Then rumours of the impending attack spread through the whole 2nd Army area. Dozens of German agents must have picked them up.

Plumer ordered the 2nd Canadian Division to relieve the British 3rd twenty-four hours after the initial assault, a decision that resulted in inevitable chaos. In spite of protests from General Alderson and our 2nd Division Commander Major-General Turner V.C., Plumer's plan was carried out.

We remained in the Wytschaete Line.

Our O. Pip had been moved from Vierstraat to a ruined barn two hundred yards forward. I was observing on the night of the attack. I had a good view of the St. Eloi area, about a mile and a half away, but my perch in the half-timbered ruin was about as secure as a kite balloon. A shell burst within twenty-five yards could have brought me down in a pile of rubble.

Zero hour was 4:15 A.M. and there was to be a short bombardment just before it, with medium and heavy howitzers. Though I was still partially deaf from the direct hit on the dugout, I heard this shoot begin. At zero hour, three huge orange blasts of flame erupted. Almost at once the barn swayed violently. Seconds later, the rumble came. I thought of all the men who had died that instant. The Germans had held the line very lightly, knowing the attack was coming, but even so, three companies of Jager riflemen went up in that blast. In March, 1916, it was the biggest man-made explosion ever set off.

Our Canadian infantry went in the following night to relieve the British. Instead of three craters, there were six. After confused and desperate fighting, the craters changing hands again and again, our actual front line remained where it had been before the action. Behind the huge craters, the Germans were in a stronger position than ever. All that had been accomplished was a widening of No Man's Land, which became a vast, treacherous swamp providing excellent defence for the enemy.

During the battle for the St. Eloi craters, which lasted twelve days, the Canadians lost nearly fifteen hundred men, mostly from the 6th Brigade, which had suffered appalling bombardments from German heavy artillery.

Some of the troops remained in isolated posts waist-deep in icy water for as long as three and four days. There was no continuous line.

Nobody knew beforehand what effect the three terrible explosions would have. The nature of the terrain had been changed and to this day no one knows who held the largest craters at critical times in the action.

In the end, those who gained undisputed possession of the craters were the citizens of the villages of St. Eloi and nearby Voormezeele. They now own two deep, circular ponds well stocked with fish. Fifty-two years later, when I visited St. Eloi, I saw a brightly painted boat floating at a little dock on Crater 4. There was scarcely a ripple on the water.

My mother

My father

Eliza Ann Massey,
my grandmother, aged 84.
The last of the pioneers

Hart Almerrin Massey,
my grandfather.
The machine-age pioneer

Plaster saint, 1901

May Crammond, my earliest
friend and implacable foe of
dust and dirt in the house and
on small boys

515 – Grandma's house

Our back yard at 519

The "gallery" at 519

Van on the box with Barney and Dolly about to leave for the horse show in Queen's Park, Dominion Day, 1902. You can't see the cockade because Van was going to snap it on his hat on Wellesley Street when father couldn't see him.

519–our house

The drawing room at 519. Except when May Crammond dusted it, nobody ever entered this room.

Aunt Fanny and partner at the Coaching Parade, Dentonia, 1904. Perhaps she liked acting, too. She had the temperament for it. May Crammond, who made her costume, was bitten during a fitting.

Opposite: "The Anarchist," Toronto, 1902

Line-up of Coaching Parade entries, Dentonia, 1904. The water tower which I climbed that summer is just visible in this old print. Seventy-three years later it still scares me.

Dolly just hadn't the stage presence which Vincent had in spite of her ribboned garter. She never was at her best without Barney.

My cousin Madeline driving the only non-equine entry in the parade at
Dentonia. This female champion from the Dentonia piggery proved quite
intractable even in the charge of the girl who had invented the game of
"Adventures."

Uncle Willard and my cousin Dorothy at the Coaching Parade. The old athlete
as a clean-shaven Uncle Sam seems a bit lonely in that nest of Union Jacks.

My brother Vincent and Cousin Nan Warnock at Dentonia in 1904. Frustrated actor, he had to settle for being Governor-General of Canada.

R.M. and the Armstrong cousins, Muskoka, 1905. I suppose I was like that once.

R.M. and Cousin Riley Armstrong, a great-grandson of old Hart, at the Elgin House, Muskoka, 1905. Riley is observing the old naval barefoot custom even on the rough Muskoka rocks.

Opposite: "Proud sportsman," also at Elgin House, 1905. On this triumphant occasion, Mr. Seldon just rowed the boat and the "muskie" weighed 22 pounds.

"Muskoka Still Life," Elgin House, Lake Joseph, 1905. Mr. Seldon has caught
father's stockbroker in a tense moment. He confided that they bite more
frequently on Bay Street.

Opposite: Norddeutscher Lloyd Kapitän Kneuth mit einem kleinem Kind

Walter Seldon, encyclopaedist, aboard the Norddeutscher
Lloyd S.S. *Kronprinzessen Cecilie*, 1909. You can see that
Mr. Seldon knew everything about everything.

Opposite: Upper Canada College Prep, 1907. Cleanliness is next
to Godliness but watch out for behind the ears.

Waiting for the Lindsay train, Sturgeon Lake, 1910. What Vincent had called the "village cut-up" is clearly identifiable.

Opposite: "The Wanderers," Upper Canada College Preparatory School, 1908. The sole activity of this exclusive club was the nocturnal and clandestine consumption of cold baked beans in the lavatory of "D" dormitory.

Appleby school prefects, 1913-14.
Standing: Donald Macdonald, A.
de V. A. Turquand, John Marshal
Harlan, Jack Gillespie. *Seated:*
Alec Gillespie, R. H. Massey,
Andrew MacLean

Left: Willie Caven and R.M.,
Kawartha Lakes, 1912

The cast of Galsworthy's *The Pigeon*, produced in Burwash Hall, Victoria College, in early 1915. The fire-irons and fender in the footlights indicated that the audience and the players faced each other through the "dancing flames" and caused much of the play to be in soliloquy. I have never seen this self-conscious device used since.

R.M. on Aunt Fanny, Toronto, 1907. This was our last ride before I went to boarding school and she departed to take charge of two young boys who lived near Oakville.

R.M. on Aunt Fanny II, Petawawa Camp, 1918, with the 85th Battery training for Siberia. I had heard from Mr. Seldon (who else?) that old Aunt Fanny, my pony, had died, aged 19 years, still gainfully employed and in her third job.

My father and stepmother on father's 70th birthday, Toronto, 1920

Yale, 1917–1918. I tried to teach gunnery and trench warfare to the R.O.T.C.

Major V. H. de B. Powell, M.C., "de Buttes," schoolmaster, brother-officer and dear friend.

Instructional staff of Yale University R.O.T.C., May, 1918. Captain Massey CFA, Major Reed, Captain Dupont of the French Army, Major Overton USA, Captain Bland CFA.

Balliol College VIII. Henley, 1920

The Oxford University Dramatic Society, Oxford, 1920. Nevertheless, two years later the author went on the professional stage.

Group of Canadian officers, Vladivostok, 1918. These occupants of the East Barracks jail demonstrate the delightfully simple hair style then in vogue in the C.E.F.(S). The author is identifiable by his pointed cranial feature.

A factory hand attempts Ibsen at the Hart House Theatre when he tried to act Rosmer in *Rosmersholm*, 1922. Rosmer was not Dracula and the Halloween mask make-up was a mistake.

21

After the crater battle, the horror deepened.

The trenches now resembled muddy ditches. The traverses, or cross barriers, had been beaten down by flank fire. Even the rats had retreated. Subject to incessant crossfire, the infantry could hardly be blamed for thinking their own artillery was at fault. The shells roaring into their trenches seemed to be coming from the rear.

I was in the battalion command dugout in the support line. My signallers were outside with the phone in a shelter. The colonel sat on an ammunition box, sullen and silent. A man of about fifty, he looked older, grey and haggard. Two of his officers were asleep on duck boards. The normal tumult of the front line was continuous. It was not long before dawn.

All at once shells were bursting in the trench outside, field-gun stuff coming in from the right flank. I could tell the direction. It was enfilade fire across what was still an ugly salient. But it did seem as if it was coming from the rear.

The battalion adjutant ducked into the dugout as we heard the yell of "Stretcher bearers!"

The colonel stared at me . . . and he sprang up screaming, "You bloody murderer!" His fingers were digging into my throat when the adjutant pulled him off me.

"Go on outside," he said.

I went out. My signallers managed to get through to the battery. When the adjutant came out of the dugout, I told him we hadn't fired a shot for at least half an hour.

"I know," he said. "So does the old man. He's as good as God makes 'em, but this show has been a bastard. He's . . . " He shrugged.

In plain view of certain stretches of our trenches in the St. Eloi area, there was a big white house that had survived apparently undamaged for nearly two years. All else around this white chateau was desolation, including the nearby village of Hollebeke. Not a tree was standing. Yet there, not six hundred yards behind the German line, stood this beautiful reminder of peacetime. A three-storey building in that Flemish plain, it obviously housed enemy observation points. Nobody could understand why we had spared it so long. Someone in authority decided that the chateau must go.

Two twelve-inch howitzers of the corps heavies were ordered to eliminate it. We at 13th Battery had been given notice of the shoot. That bright May morning, I had a grandstand seat for it — our new O. Pip in the second line. I don't know where the "heavy" observer was but he couldn't have had a better view than mine. With binoculars, ignoring the discomfort of my broken nose, I could see every detail of the building. Bright sunlight made its desolate setting more repulsive than ever.

Almost on the dot of the time set for the shelling, I heard overhead the fearful runaway roar of the first big projectile.

It took eight rounds to level the target. Looking at the smoking mound, I thought it was a little like murder.

I could not take my eyes off the ruins. There was movement in the debris, the occasional glint of a steel helmet. The concrete masses of several pillboxes could be seen in the rubble.

Everything was surprisingly quiet. Observation balloons were up but there seemed to be no retaliation.

I was about to call the battery when a large part of Belgium fell on me . . . You never hear the big one that is really close. This time it was just like Vierstraat, the shocking impact that hit before the noise. I couldn't breathe . . . or move . . .

The two signallers and an infantryman dug me out with their bare hands.

It seemed forever before I could gasp my lungs full of air, though it was only a few minutes before I was breathing normally again.

More shells came over, sweeping along the trench away from us. The first one — it must have been a 5.9 or bigger — had caved in the parapet on me. For a minute or so, I had been buried alive yet I hadn't a scratch on me. Only my tin hat was missing. I had worn my chin strap behind my head. If the strap had been under my chin, my head might have been missing with the helmet.

After I got to breathing again, we shelled the ruins with our eighteen-pounders. De Buttes relieved me. Back at the battery, I had a splitting headache, but my hearing was no worse. The Major summoned the medical officer, who gave me pills that made me sleep all that night and next day.

In the evening, I got up and had a bath in the "sock-it-to-me" manner. Anchor, my batman, hurled three buckets of lukewarm water at me in succession.

The following day, I was ordered to the wagon lines for a week by way of a rest.

After supper, Major Vansittart sent for me.

"I've just heard," he told me, "that I'm to be brigade major of the new 4th Division Artillery. Would you like to come with me as staff lieutenant?"

I was startled by the honour.

"I wouldn't like leaving the battery, sir. I'm proud to belong to the 13th. But I — I'd like to follow you wherever you go."

He listened gravely.

"The battery won't be the same, as far as that goes. De Buttes is certain to have his own battery soon. George Drew will take over another at once. I'm putting in half the signallers for commissions, including your particular friends. Several of the N.C.O.'s will go too. No, it won't be the same."

181

It was agreed that I would take the job. Then the Major ordered me to get some sleep.

I didn't sleep. My head kept on aching. I worried about the Major's offer. What if I wasn't up to the job?

I awoke early and walked about restlessly. In the officers' dugout, I found Norman Gianelli, a newly arrived subaltern, lying in his bunk. The Major was lacing up his field boots and there wasn't much room on the ground. Nick Rimmer, the orderly sergeant, was standing just inside the opening. I was immediately behind him, my left hand on his shoulder.

Once more that horrible impact . . . that frightful sense of noise I couldn't hear. Rimmer and I were down on our backs, Gianelli was sprawled behind the Major who had fallen over on his side. Sandbags, steel beams and debris covered us all. The dugout had taken a direct hit by a chance 4.1-inch shell.

The sergeant-major, Nick Rimmer's brother, and several gunners were in the dugout almost instantly, freeing us from the fallen beams and burst sandbags. In seconds, stretchers arrived. The Major, seriously wounded in the back, had turned a ghastly colour. Unable to speak, he was barely conscious. Gianelli, a gaping wound in his stomach, was in excruciating pain. Rimmer had been thrown on top of me, his thigh shattered. I escaped with only a clean wound on the back of my left hand.

Twenty minutes later, the ambulance arrived. The 2nd Divisional Commander, Major-General Turner, V.C., had stumbled to us from his car across a cratered field. The Major could not say a word to him. The general's eyes filled with tears as he grasped his friend's hand.

The three badly wounded men were placed on stretchers in the little Ford ambulance. The general and I climbed in with the driver and we bumped our way, agonizing for the wounded, to the Casualty Clearing station. Major Vansittart died soon after arrival.

Rimmer's leg was amputated high above the knee. Norman Gianelli was evacuated to a field hospital and began weary months of recovery. Though his active service was over for the First World War, his military ambition was not to be thwarted. Twenty-seven years later, when I met him again during the Second World War, he was commanding a brigade of tanks.

I persuaded the doctors to class me as "wounded remaining on duty." I was afraid if they sent me back to hospital, I might not be returned to the 13th Battery. Still, they kept me at the C.C.S. that night. My hand, with what the medics called "gas poisoning," was the size of a boxing glove.

I couldn't sleep. I couldn't talk without effort. My hearing was worse. The sleeping pills I was given didn't help.

I could not get Major Vansittart's death out of my mind. Now that he was gone, everything was different.

George Drew, who took over the 13th Battery, suggested I take a week's leave in England. When I stupidly refused, thinking he was trying to get rid of me, he told me to stay at the horse lines for the present.

I consoled myself by riding the Major's mare. Her nerves were in as bad shape as my own. She had been near a shell burst and horses didn't recover easily.

A week after the Major's death, de Buttes came to the horse lines and told me to go on leave at once. I was not to argue about it. I trusted de Buttes and complied.

I don't remember much about that leave. I think I spent most of my time taking baths and wandering about London. My hand was healing well.

On my last day, I took a train to Folkestone to call on Major Vansittart's mother and sister. Mrs. Vansittart, who had just received the Major's pack with his few possessions, insisted on giving me his binoculars. She told me he had mentioned me in his letters.

All week I had been dreading my return to the battery. I knew I was now useless as an officer.

At the station in Boulogne, news of a great naval battle had just arrived. There were conflicting rumours — one that we had sunk the German fleet, the other that the Royal Navy had taken a beating. The second version seemed more probable to the pessimistic British. The truth — that the battle of Jutland was a stand-off — was not heard.

At railhead, I had great difficulty in finding where my division was, let alone my battery. I received only the vaguest clue from another Canadian gunner-officer. He had heard that the 2nd Canadian Division was now moving into the Ypres salient in the Hooge area.

He and I made our way as best we could. I didn't know the area, nor did he. Soon, though, we felt we were on the right track. Ahead of us we could hear a terrific bombardment.

A little later we were startled by a battery overtaking us. Guns and wagons passed us at a gallop, the gunners clinging desperately to the bumping limbers.

As they passed a crossroads a short distance ahead, two German shells screamed in and blew a limbered wagon to pieces. It was horrible.

One shell had killed both the wheelers and badly wounded two of the horses. Two drivers were hit, too. The gunners on the limber I can't think about even now.

The rest of the battery galloped on. The guns were needed and there were stretcher-bearers near.

As I myself shot the wounded horses, the lead driver was crying. God knows, I wanted to.

That was my last memory of the war.

I must have found the battery, for I was with it the next two weeks. It was June 2 and the first day of the battle of Mount Sorrel and Sanctuary Wood. It lasted until June 16 — according to the history books. I myself have no recollection of that action, nor do I remember anything but isolated incidents during the next two months.

One is a clear picture of an officer with red staff patches standing beside me as I sit on a chair. His hand is on my shoulder and he is repeating in a gentle voice, "Don't try to speak . . . dont't try to speak . . . . "

22

Sometime about the beginning of August, 1916, I came home to Toronto.

The previous two months were hazy and most of June a complete blank. I had trouble speaking because of a stammer; my hearing was poor and I suffered intermittent periods of double vision followed by severe headaches.

I recalled a hospital in London and a medical board before which I appeared, in London, I think. I had no memory of rejoining the battery after that carnage near Ypres. Perhaps I hadn't gone back at all to the 13th. . . . It was frightening not to know.

Father pieced together for me what had happened, so far as he knew. He had not heard from me after reading in the casualty list on June 17 that I had been wounded. After that, he knew nothing until a friend who had traced me to a hospital in north London cabled him that I was listed as "shell shocked" and was to be evacuated to Canada. This news arrived just a week before I did.

"Shell shock" was a term used in the First World War for the condition that results from "close proximity to the burst of a large-calibre shell." Most often there was no actual wound. Because of this, shell shock usually carried the stigma of "lack of nerve" or even cowardice. Though the reproach was almost always self-imposed, it could be very real and shaming. The term shell shock was later abolished. Neurologists have since labelled the condition "battle fatigue."

Whether it's called shell shock, battle fatigue or whatever, the doctors know there is a physical condition resulting from a bruising of the nerves by violent concussion. They recognized early in the First World War that it was a serious problem. To this day, they have found no better treatment for shell shock than rest, sleep and, above all, quiet.

I don't remember the hospital in London very well. I was astonished to find myself in the Venereal Ward, thanks to overcrowding in the surgical wards. I remember reassuring myself that I couldn't have caught shell shock off a towel.

The ward seemed the noisiest place I had ever been in. Sleep and rest were almost impossible. Sleep meant dreams and it was better to lie awake than face my recurrent terrors. I was struggling to remember what had happened when I returned to the battery. How long had I been with the guns after I got back from leave? There wasn't a spark of light in the darkness of what could have been months or days or hours. Had I been a coward?

This was my worst anxiety, the fear that I might have failed my comrades.

There were other shell shocks in the ward, four or five, I think. In the bed next to mine was a young sapper officer whose hair was completely white. It looked odd with his young face. His eyes stared and didn't seem to focus. I remember this man clearly. He never spoke to anyone. Sometimes he tried to smile. Somebody told me he had been blown up in a mining operation by a "camouflet," a counter-mine dug to destroy a gallery without disturbing the surface. This man had been in a gallery sixty or seventy feet underground when the Germans had blown it in.

I don't remember how long I was in that hospital. The days were without end. Most of the time I sat on my bed fully dressed with nothing to do. The noise was incessant. At last the young sapper and I were taken in an ambulance to face a medical board in a hotel in the Strand. Three officers asked me questions. I don't remember what they were. I left the room and the sapper went in.

In a few minutes he came out smiling. The ambulance took us back to the ward.

That night I didn't take the sleeping draught. The sapper did. He moaned a lot but he was quiet most of the night. In the morning, the sapper was dead. Heart failure, they said. I did not think so. I think he was scared to death by his dreams.

Home at the beginning of August, I remembered nothing about the voyage from England. I had been given two months sick leave. After that I would face another medical board. I was back in civilian clothes. The cloud of that lost month still hung over me. Home was a sad place. Father was not well and Van, our coachman, had died just before I returned.

My stepmother took charge and, realizing that the city was not the best place for me, she arranged that I should stay with my old friends the Cavens at their summer cottage on the Kawartha Lakes, a place I had always loved.

Dr. Caven, a general consultant, had his own family problem, for his son Willie, my friend and contemporary, was suffering from a grave disorder from which he would die the following year.

Willie was a frustrated soldier. Dr. Caven knew the best thing for both of us was to forget the war — he did not allow us to mention it. Willie and I loafed, sailed and fished, but mostly did nothing, enjoying the silence as only friends can. Except for the cry of the loons, there was stillness around the lake, with sometimes the rustle of a breeze through the woods. The buzzing in my ears diminished and speech came more easily to me. Still, I was troubled by the gnawing thought of those lost weeks.

The night I returned from the Kawartha Lakes, I celebrated my twentieth birthday with my stepmother and father. A new issue of *The Illustrated London News* had just arrived. Idly leafing through it, I saw a picture of the officer whose face had been haunting me for weeks, his kindly voice my only memory of that blank month of June. I had begun to doubt his existence. Now I knew his name: Colonel Sir Bertrand Dawson, medical consultant to the B.E.F. and head of the standing medical board in Boulogne.

I don't know why identifying the colonel should have given me badly needed confidence in myself but it did. To this day, the colonel remains my only link with reality for that month in France in 1916. After the war, Sir Bertrand became Lord Dawson of Penn, physician to King George V. About ten years later, I was sent to Lord Dawson by my doctor about a stomach complaint. He never got around to discussing that; we talked only about the war.

After a further spell of rest in the lake region of Muskoka, I came home to be "boarded," confident I would be sent overseas again. It was late September.

I found a letter from de Buttes Powell. It had taken only three weeks to come from the front. It was written on pages of a field-service message pad during a lull in the battle of the Somme, where the Canadian Corps had been in the thick of it for a month. The letter began: "Directly you had left, old chap, I sat down and wrote you an eight-page letter telling you not to be such a silly chump as to think that you had failed in any respect." He sent loving greetings from the commanding officer and the battery.

I could not recall anything about the letter de Buttes mentioned. Probably I never received it.

I read the opening words of this second letter again and again. De Buttes hadn't told me anything about my two lost weeks with the battery, but the cloud had been blown away. After more than fifty-nine years, the pencilled writing in the letter before me is still clear though the paper is in shreds, taped and retaped many times. De Buttes described at length the agony and butchery of the first of the great frontal attacks that were to be repeated so often for the next two years. It is the letter of a very kind and tired man — an old friend from my school days.

De Buttes served for two more years as a battery commander, winning the Military Cross, being wounded three times, and dying from the effects of the third in 1918.

The medical board, to my delight, passed me "fit for active duty." In a few days I was ordered to report to Petawawa Camp in northern Ontario, where the field artillery was now training.

I felt better, my hearing, speech and headaches much improved. I remember leaving Toronto for Petawawa. And then — nothing.

That was the start of a second blackout. The next thing I remember is riding alone through unfamiliar woods, with a blinding, double-vision headache. I remember giving the horse his head and being carried back to horse lines where I found myself unable to speak coherently. Again there was a time in hospital. Again I was on sick leave with the prospect of another medical board at the end of it.

When, in the Second World War, I was back in the army in the adjutant-general's branch in Ottawa, I had access to my personal file in Petawawa. I found that for two of my blacked-out weeks I had been an artillery instructor. It seems the firing range had brought on my amnesia again with the other symptoms.

Among the officers I had worked with was a young subaltern named Walter Pidgeon. He and I have since worked together in pictures several times. Comparing memories, we both come out with empty reports on Petawawa. Pidge was pretty sick then himself.

The outlook was dim. After a few weeks of aimless loafing at home, I felt more or less fit. But it looked as if civilian life lay ahead. I loathed the prospect of university again; factory life seemed equally repellent. I found several friends around Toronto in a similar predicament, back from France and unemployable. Drawn together by our uselessness, we were of little help to each other.

To relieve the tedium, I bought for $65 a Chevrolet touring car of 1914 vintage, a potential death-trap on all counts. To my father, this vehicle was chiefly ominous as a means of my visiting a young female to whom he had taken what he called an instinctive antipathy, based, I believe, on the well-founded opinion of Mr. Seldon.

Shortly after acquiring the Chevrolet, I rose from the supper table at 519, muttered some mendacious plan for the evening and left.

It was icy December weather. Smooth tires and defective brakes combined to cause a head-on collision with an east-bound streetcar on Carlton Street near Jarvis.

I passed through the windshield with the steering wheel in my hands and some twenty pieces of glass in my face. The car was a wreck. Luckily, I had escaped serious damage.

About eleven o'clock that night, I was in the hospital bed where the doctor had insisted I spend the night. My father, who had been told of the accident, entered my room. He had dressed completely, with stiff collar, detachable cuffs and fur coat. He never asked how I felt or how the accident had happened. All he said was: "You were on the way to see that young woman, weren't you?"

"Yes, I was."

"We may all be thankful that you did not die with a lie on your lips."

In a few days, still bandaged but to some extent "rested," I appeared before the district medical board, fully expecting the discharge with which I had been previously threatened.

Just as I sat down in a chair facing three doctors, there was a crash outside the room, as of countless tin trays being dropped. As I picked myself off the floor, I thought it was all over with the army. Instead, one doctor murmured, "Quick reactions."

After answering a few questions about hearing, speech and such, I was dismissed. Three days later, I was appointed adjutant of a new machine gun school that had been established in Toronto.

23

Relief from the boredom of army paperwork came in June, 1917. I received an informal offer to be an instructor in the gunnery of trench warfare with the artillery unit of the reserve officers training corps at Yale Unversity. It was a personal letter from the chief of the general staff in Ottawa.

The U.S. had just entered the war. The training of American junior officers was in full swing. While I was at Yale, I would be seconded from the Canadian Army and paid by the university, about four times my army pay. The job also meant promotion to captain. The appointment was to begin in September. Meanwhile, I would be instructor at an eight-week officers' training course at Princeton University.

It was a wonderful break. It turned out to be a fascinating year. During my time at the machine gun school, I had qualified as an instructor, an advantage at Princeton, for this was infantry training. There were about eight hundred officer candidates in the Princeton course, commanded by a West Pointer named Major Stanley Rumbaugh.

Another Canadian officer, Captain Leys Brown, who had served in France with the 42nd (Highland) Battalion, took over the supervision of trench warfare training. I did the machine gun instruction.

The Yale appointment was quite different and, being a gunner, I found it a good deal more interesting. The U.S. War Department reasoned that the war would probably be a long one and that a great many officers would be needed in the following years. So the R.O.T.C. program of training was planned with a view to enabling seniors and juniors to finish the current academic year while qualifying for commissions.

The Yale R.O.T.C. was solely for training officers for the field artillery. More than half the curriculum was devoted to military work, on the assumption that one academic year would give enough time for the training of an officer.

The Yale appointment was a strange mixture of academic and military practice. The corps was ostensibly under the command of Captain Overton, a West Pointer who had been pried out of retirement for the job. Crippled by a knee injury, he could walk only with crutches. He was out of touch with contemporary artillery weapons and methods. Luckily, a faculty member managed, with tact, to do the captain's job for him. He was Professor E. B. Reed (class of '94) and he held the rank of major. A demon for work, the major always delivered what we needed, for he knew who held the academic purse strings.

The instructors were, besides myself, another Canadian, Captain Bland, and Captain Dupont of the French Army. Other instructors were faculty members holding military rank. Dupont was to give instruction in the French 75s of which we had four guns. Bland and I would handle the instruction on the British eighteen-pounders. The American expeditionary force field artillery was to be equipped with these guns.

Bland and I divided the gunnery instruction, the gunnery of trench warfare, map-reading, communications and weapons. I took on the riding and driving and battery drill. Captain Dupont was to conduct a course in the artillery usage and methods of the French Army. A course in the care of horses, of one hour a week, was included at my suggestion. I had seen enough of the needless neglect of horses to press for its inclusion. It fell on me to teach it.

I was to do about twelve hours of lecturing a week plus the equitation which took up every afternoon. I enjoyed my chances to

192

repeat Ringwood's excellent command: "Sit back on your asses, gentlemen." There were also a number of sessions at the sub-calibre dummy village range which all the instructors divided up. It seemed ludicrous to me that at twenty-one with no academic experience, I should stand before two or three hundred men, most of them older than I and some within a few months of graduation, and hold forth on the advantages of fixed as compared with unfixed ammunition or the prevention and cure of epizootic laminitis. Looking up at me with poised pencils were Henry R. Luce, Brit Hadden, Jed Harris, Stephen Vincent Benet, and others within a few months of graduation listening to one whose sole examination success had been passing out of the Royal School of Artillery at Kingston in Canada.

I am always in awe of the physical resources of America's great universities. One year before the U.S. had entered the First World War, a big riding school, gun park and stables for a hundred and fifty horses had been completed. This complex, called the Yale Armory, was ready for us at the end of August, 1917. A building known as Artillery Hall, adjoining the Baseball Cage, was completed before term began. It housed the four French 75s and the sub-calibre practice range. No facilities such as these were ever available to batteries in training in any other country. I had only to ask for a practice ride and Professor Reed would go to work — and there it was, complete with jumps and Russian downhill run.

There arrived as if from on high one Master-Sergeant Hildebrand. A regular U.S. Army N.C.O., he was one of the smartest I ever knew. He had fifteen years in the regular cavalry behind him, followed by three years in the reserve, which he spent as tiller-man on a hook and ladder with the New York Fire Department. For the past year, he had been with General Pershing on the Mexican border. I grabbed him for the mounted work. I told him that he had a new rank — sergeant-major.

It seemed to please him, for he said, "The captain is making a Marine out of me. Maybe it's a promotion for all I know, sir."

In October, the officers of the 305th Regiment of Field Artillery of the A.E.F. came to Yale in two sections for a week's instruction in trench warfare gunnery. There were about twenty officers in each group. The first included Lt.-Col. Henry L. Stimson, second-in-command of the regiment; and the second, its commanding officer, Colonel Doyle. These two courses were fascinating to the instructors, for it seemed as if the searching inquisitiveness of these officers, a number of whom were lawyers, could not be satisfied.

Colonel Stimson in particular showed a knowledge of field artillery usage which was astonishing for anyone without previous experience of active service. At this time he was fifty. At seventy-three, in the Second World War, he was given his greatest task by President Roosevelt, as Secretary of War. How brilliantly he justified the appointment is history, but it was no surprise to those of us who met Colonel Stimson at that short course at Yale in 1917. In France, he was to command the 31st F.A. Regiment.

I confess to shamelessly bragging that I once was instructor to the late great Henry Stimson.

Of all the remarkable people I met at Yale, and there were many, the man who made the deepest impression on me was Stephen Vincent Benet. I was lucky enough to work with him in the early years of the Second World War and to play in a stage version of his epic poem, *John Brown's Body.* But I speak of Steve Benet when he was an undergraduate, the most eager member of the R.O.T.C. and the leading figure in the Elizabethan Club, the delightful haunt of those interested in English and American plays and poetry. There, as a guest, I constantly attended readings of poetry and intimate performances of plays, all of which seemed to be sponsored and stimulated by Steve.

Son of a regular army colonel, Steve's childhood and youth had been spent on army posts all over the country. This service peregrination had given him insight into America. He loved his country passionately and he loved his father's profession. He longed to win his commission and go overseas. But active service eluded him. His health and eyesight were none too good; even in 1918 there were signs of the arthritis that eventually crippled him. A good soldier, he won his commission two days before the armistice.

During my year at Yale, I was able to gorge myself on theatre. New York was only two hours away.

194

My tastes were as broad as could be. Lamentably uncritical, I liked everything I saw. I remember few of the plays — only the players. The character Lionel Barrymore created in *The Copperhead*, for example, remains a vivid memory but I can't recall the play at all. It's the same with the plays in which I saw George Arliss, Grant Mitchell, Tyrone Power (the elder), John Drew, Ina Claire, Francine Larrimore, Marjory Rambeau, Patricia Collinge and many others. Maybe it wasn't a good season for plays, but the acting was great.

I saw the Washington Square Players. They were doing a season of one-act plays. A brilliant company, it included such talent as Walter Huston, Helen Westley, Louis Calvert, Ian Keith, Arthur Hohl and Edna St. Vincent Millay. But I recall only one performance in one of the plays — a piece based on a Mayan legend. A girl with no lines to speak who only beat a drum made the little play her own by her compelling personality and beauty. She was Katharine Cornell, the girl from Buffalo.

I went backstage after the show. We had supper at the late-night Child's Restaurant near Columbus Square. Kit Cornell had already made a start as a professional actress on Broadway. Now she was going back to Buffalo for a year of stock with Jessie Bonstelle. She wanted as much acting experience as she could get. That night I was again severely bitten by the theatre bug.

As always in wartime, it was a year of musicals — less musical comedies than big so-called extravaganzas or revues. There was the annual *Ziegfeld Follies* with a cast of fifty. In the 1917 show, there were W.C. Fields, Fanny Brice, Will Rogers, Peggy Hopkins, Bert Williams, Dorothy Dickson and Carl Hyson, Walter Catlett and the reigning show-girl beauty, Dolores. These were just the headliners. It was a fabulous collection of talent. W.C. Fields did two of his sketches — *Billiards* and *Motoring*. I had seen Harry Tate do both in England. I never found out which of the two created those hilarious acts; there were at least half a dozen that both Fields and Tate did. Will Rogers, then a newcomer, was limited to a ten-minute, rope-spinning monologue — but he was superb. Fanny Brice did a burlesque of Ethel Barrymore who had just played in *The Lady of the Camellias* at the Empire. I can still hear her: "I've been a wicked woman, Armand, but awfully good company!"

The man who interested me most in the 1917 Follies was Bert Williams, one of the greatest Negro comedians who ever lived. There is nobody today who can compare with him, or who has his range. He was supreme at pantomime, at song or comic monologue. He also appeared at the New Amsterdam Roof every night in cabaret. I saw him so many times that I knew his routines to the last breath and gesture.

There was a show, a musical of course, with the significant title of *Hitchy-Koo*, which had in addition to its star, Raymond Hitchcock, a wonderful comedian named Leon Errol and also Johnny and Ray Dooley, two hilarious graduates from burlesque.

I have no idea why I was particularly intrigued with the comedians in the musical shows. But my aimless, diligent study of the techniques and routines of low comedy stars would stand me in good stead within a few months time in Siberia.

Before winding up my job at Yale, I had a day to spare for a final visit to New York. I had a date at the Plaza for tea and to dance to the music of Whispering Jack Smith with Marilyn Miller. This young divinity had just opened in the 1918 Ziegfeld Follies. I was going to see the show that night. Mr. Ziegfeld never knew of the jeopardy in which his lovely dancing star was placed by my field boots and spurs, but she survived. What's more, she made it seem as if I could dance, too, as the envious eyes of the Ivy League looked on.

I had gone to Toronto over a weekend in May to seek medical approval for going overseas again. I felt sure I was fit to serve once more with the guns. But the M.O. who examined me was dubious. He recommended that I transfer to another branch of the service. This was an official entry in my record and I gathered that if I "stuck to my guns," I would remain at home.

A reserve squadron of the Royal Canadian Dragoons, a regular cavalry regiment, had been training in Toronto and was due to go overseas in July. They were one officer short.

I called up Percy Arnoldi, the squadron commander, with whom I had been at school some years before, and told him my story. He suggested I apply for transfer to the cavalry, and he would ask for my appointment. Meanwhile, I should finish at Yale. My service with the guns practically qualified me for cavalry service.

I wrote my application and returned to New Haven.

I was bound to remain at Yale until the end of June, 1918, but I gave notice to President Hadley that I was applying for active service again and would not be with the R.O.T.C. the following academic year.

I left Yale with regret and gratitude for the friendship of the great men, faculty and students.

24

The morning I arrived in Toronto, newspaper headlines were announcing that Canada was about to send an expeditionary force to Siberia to help the White Russians against the Bolsheviks. The expedition was to consist of an infantry brigade and, what interested me, a battery of field artillery. All the units of this force were to be organized and trained in Canada. The officers and as many other ranks as possible were to have had experience in France.

There it was in public print — field artillery — and here I was about to report for duty with the cavalry. The more I thought about it, the more frustrated I became. I didn't want to leave the artillery. I knew I was fit for active service with the guns, particularly in the kind of action to be expected in Siberia. But my transfer to the cavalry had gone through orders and was therefore sacrosanct. Any application "through channels" for a return to the guns would be blocked by the first deputy assistant adjutant-general who read it.

The more I thought about the Siberian expedition, the less I liked the idea of going overseas with a reserve squadron of dragoons. Father interrupted my brooding.

"Are you considering this Siberian expedition they've announced?"

I knew he was thinking that even his three, overlapping great-coats plus his fur-lined one would be inadequate for such a climate. I had an idea.

"What's Vincent's job in Ottawa, Father?"

"Secretary of the War Cabinet. I hope you're not going to importune Vincent for an appointment in the Siberian expedition!"

"I'm going to do exactly that, Father. I don't think it will embarrass him in the least. If it does, he knows how to say no."

I telephoned my brother and was on the train to Ottawa that night.

Vincent had been in command of a school of musketry for the first two years of the war in Military District 2. Not only had it been a training job, which he greatly disliked, but he had been training troops with the Ross rifle, which had been discarded by the Canadian Corps in favour of the British Lee-Enfield. The Ross rifle, an excellent target weapon, was completely unsuited to the rigours of trench warfare and battle conditions. Its adoption by the Canadian Army in Canada was the sole responsibility of Sam Hughes, the Defence Minister; and its use in training a scandalous waste of effort and money. My brother knew this, yet despite his obvious frustration, he had done a fine job through two years of training men for overseas.

His abilities in administration had been recognized in Ottawa and now, in 1918, he was military secretary to the War Committee of the Cabinet, with the rank of lieutenant-colonel.

From the station, I went straight to Vincent's office and was waiting for him when he arrived at 8:30 "ack.emma."

I told him what I wanted — field artillery. I had come to the right place, though I had ignored proper "channels." Vincent's committee had, according to him, dreamed up the Siberian expedition, perhaps with some encouragement from the British.

Vincent told me that the C.E.F. (Siberia) would consist of field artillery with ammunition column, a machine gun company, a field company of engineers, a field ambulance section, a field hospital and the necessary supply units. In short, it would be an independent force, then known as a mixed brigade.

The officers and N.C.O.'s of the combat units would all have experienced active service in France; as many discharged veterans as possible would be in the ranks. The commander was to be Major-General James Elmsley, who had just completed three years in France as a brigade commander. I knew of his brilliant record. The expedition was to help complete what Winston Churchill had termed the "Cordon Sanitaire," which was to contain the Bolshevik revolution. Specifically, the Canadians and any allies would operate in support of the White Russians who, Vincent said, were more or less in control of Siberia as far west as Omsk.

My brother told me all this rapidly and without further discussion picked up a telephone.

"Get me the C.G.S., please."

As he waited, he covered the mouthpiece of the upright telephone and said to me, "I think you're right to try for this Siberian force. It will be the first independent military expedition Canada has undertaken. There's no time to waste. We'll go straight to the top. I'm going to get you in to see the C.G.S., the Chief of the General Staff."

Major-General Gwatkin, Chief of the General Staff, was a weary, gentle British officer. He showed the effects of several years of service with, or rather under, Sam Hughes, Canada's former Minister of Defence. He motioned me to sit down and went on reading my file. After some moments he looked up. "I suppose you know this is a matter for the Adjutant-General's branch? It's highly irregular to come to me. I don't blame *you* but your highly persuasive brother . . . . Well, it's the first time I've ever heard of anybody pulling wires and breaking regulations to go to Siberia . . . . I'll see what can be done."

Three weeks later, I was at Petawawa again, with the 85th Battery, C.F.A., training for the C.E.F. (Siberia). It was nearly two years since my last unfortunate visit to Petawawa but this time I knew I was fit for active service. It was a wonderful feeling to be in a battery again. We were a six-gun unit and I had the centre section.

The battery commander was Major Douglas Storms, M.C., "Granny" Storms, who had gone overseas with the 1st Division and had commanded a battery for nearly three years.

I last saw Granny at a regimental dinner a few years ago. There were about twenty-five of us there. The youngest was seventy-two. Granny made a speech in which he said he had been turned down for the gunners in the Second World War because he was too old. "Fifty!" he snorted. So he became a sapper, since that was what he did as a civilian. One morning in England, he woke up and found he was a brigadier-general in command of fourteen thousand Canadian sappers. "But I'd rather have had a battery," he finished.

It was a dandy battery, the 85th. There was a fine spirit about it. We knew it wouldn't be trench warfare in Siberia but lots of movement; and if we had the same experience as the two Canadian batteries then based on Archangel in North Russia, we would sometimes realize the gunner's dream of "open sights," that is, see our targets. Training went on perfectly. Everything looked too good to be true, when I got orders to go to Vancouver with fifty gunners from the ammunition column to sail with General Elmsley and his staff and an advance party of men for Vladivostok. Bill Mulock, a lieutenant from the ammunition column and an old friend of school days, was to go with us.

I disliked leaving the battery, even for what was to be a few weeks. Granny Storms didn't want me to go either, but nothing could be done about it.

We went west from Petawawa on a C.P.R. troop train that carried about half of the advance party, troops of all descriptions.

I remember that trip for one reason only. All troop trains have a caboose at the back like freight trains, and I rode in ours for the breathtaking ride through the Rockies and Kicking Horse Pass with its spiral tunnel, the most amazing engineering feat I have ever seen.

After a week under canvas in the rain at Esquimault, British Columbia, we boarded the C.P.R. liner *Empress of Japan*. She was, I would say, about the size of J. P. Morgan's yacht, *Corsair*, but that was the only similarity. We took two and a half weeks to get to Vladivostok through the Straits of Hakodate. As German submarines had never operated in the Pacific, no evasive course was necessary. Our time was the best the old ship could do.

Before we had left Canada in mid-September, the black influenza epidemic of 1918 was at its peak, having spread over the whole North American continent. This particular flu was unlike the epidemics of more recent times. Almost invariably the victims developed pneumonia. Since there were no sulpha drugs or antibiotics, mortality was shockingly high. Strangely, the young seemed most vulnerable.

It was inevitable that we bring the virus with us on the voyage. Scarcely a day passed without one or more burials over the stern of the ship. My gunners had to supply the firing parties.

The weather was atrocious, even for the Pacific. Once in a pitching sea, the whole lot of us were nearly washed overboard as the fantail stern dipped below water and the corpse prematurely disappeared. At one point in the voyage, there were thirty cases of flu among the six hundred troops.

The advance party was top-heavy with officiers, over sixty of us crowding the little saloon where we messed. The only complete unit aboard was General Elmsley's force headquarters which accounted for some twenty officers and about thirty other ranks. His actual staff numbered six. The general was a tall, handsome regular officer, with a splendid combat record as a brigadier in France. His nickname, "Gentleman Jim," suited him. He won the respect and loyalty of all ranks. His G.S.O. 1 was of the same breed, a fine staff officer, Lt.-Col. "Sid" Morrisey, D.S.O., M.C. He and Gentleman Jim made a perfect team.

In Siberia, the Canadian expedition was to be under command of the Japanese General Otani. But General Elmsley had the right of appeal to Ottawa in the event that any order of Otani should jeopardize the Canadian brigade. This, of course, upset the War Office in London, represented by General Knox in Vladivostok. It also annoyed the Japanese. Since we were going to have one or two British battalions brigaded with us, life was not going to be easy for General Elmsley.

The Japanese were supposed to have only five thousand troops in Siberia, but when we got to Vladivostok, we found no less than seventy thousand of them spread around the port and all the way up the railway to Lake Baikal.

Shortly after we arrived, Sid Morrisey and another Canadian staff officer were invited to dinner at the Japanese headquarters mess.

At the bridge table after dinner, General Otani and his chief of staff were pitted against the Canadians. Otani had bid a little slam for a rubber and, the way Sid told it to me afterwards, it was obvious when the dummy was laid down that the general had to finesse a queen to make his bid. As Sid held the solitary king, he was extremely happy. With quiet glee, he played it on the general's queen. The general had another plan. Gently pushing Sid's hand back, he replaced his queen with the ace from dummy, hissing, "Solly, pliss." Sid swallowed his tongue and said nothing. A week later he received the Order of the Rising Sun, 3rd Class. He had many decorations, but this one, he always said, was really hardly won.

There were two private soldiers aboard for whom no military records could be found. Both appeared on a list known as Base Details, assigning batmen, orderlies and so forth for certain administrative officers, but all others on the list of about fifty men had records of previous training and service. Not so with Privates Rockcliffe Fellowes and Daniel Groesbeck. Militarily speaking, they were stowaways.

In civilian life, however, they were by no means waifs or strays. Cliff Fellowes had quite a standing as a leading man in what was then a budding Hollywood. He was also married to a well-known actress, Lucille Watson, whose brother, Major-General Sir David Watson, was commanding the 4th Canadian Division. Groesbeck, for his part, had been a successful illustrator for the *Saturday Evening Post*. In their forties, both men had enlisted in the East very recently, were untrained and determined to remain so. Fellowes became batman to the Judge Advocate General, Lt.-Col. Gregory Berkeley. Groesbeck was finally thrown into my detachment of gunners.

How I became involved with these two oddballs I cannot remember. I daresay I was a kindred soul.

About midway on our voyage to Vladivostok, Private Fellowes

mentioned that he had written a little farce that he thought might amuse the officers' mess. He let me read it.

The script made me laugh, and I showed it to a couple of friends. Hertzberg of the sappers and McKellar of the machine gun company agreed we should put it on.

With the general's permission, I became a producer. The show was for officers only and, though cleaned up considerably, was pretty raw for those days. It dealt with the adventures of a beautiful woman spy aboard the *Empress of Japan*. The cast included the officers commanding the machine gun detachment, the engineers, myself, the author and, to play the master counterspy, Captain Duffus of the Royal North West Mounted Police, who in the dramatic finale got his man — or, rather, woman.

It was a smash hit on its only performance in the little saloon. The general laughed uproariously. So did the rest of the captive audience. I think they would have laughed at a reading of the Vancouver telephone book. I have the script in front of me now and it's just terrible. How we dared perform it I cannot imagine. The one dissenting member of the audience was a colonel I had taken off in the skit. For the ensuing nine months, my fifty gunners and I were to pay for this performance. We were assigned the most repellent jobs in that colonel's bestowal — guarding docks, sanitary fatigues and the like.

At last we seemed to drift into Vladivostok harbour.

It was early October, the weather was much like a bad day in Cleveland, Ohio. I tried to detect something of the mysterious East I had looked forward to finding. All I could sense was a repellent and non-mysterious smell. It remained dominant during my stay in Siberia.

Next morning we marched through Vladivostok to our quarters in what was known as East Barracks. The barracks were not too bad after they had been cleaned up. We officers were luxuriously housed in the military jail, each of us having a cell to himself with a board bed.

A brief inspection of Vladivostok late next day confirmed our first impression that here was one of the strongest inhabited smells on earth. The sanitation of this Far Eastern spa was served — or should I say, stirred — by Manchurian coolies. In great numbers, they passed to and fro with huge wooden barrels on wheels, drawn by tough little horses, each of these "honey carts" an olfactory catastrophe. The coolies themselves added a malodorous piquancy to the general stench.

This drab and treeless town was the eastern terminus of the five-thousand-mile Trans-Siberia Railway. Its harbour, with the aid of ice-breakers, could be used the year around. The railway station was the only sizeable building in town. It looked like a huge, sprawling church. Since the station was to a certain extent heated, it provided shelter for nearly seven thousand refugees every night, a heartbreaking sight. Vladivostok's normal population was about forty thousand; but during the winter of 1918-19, an additional one hundred and fifty thousand derelicts crowded into the town and its vicinity. Their living conditions were appalling. Their only hope was to go south to China and that hope was faint. Money was the major necessity and most of the refugees were penniless. Inflation had wiped out their savings. These victims of the Bolshevik terror were from all classes.

The Red Cross did magnificent work in Vladivostok, as did other relief organizations. The trickle of refugees south to China was speeded up and some made their escape direct to America by sea. But a large number met death in Siberia.

One of my first jobs after we landed was to inspect barrack accommodations for the main units of the expedition which were due to arrive shortly. To this end I was assigned one of the few H.Q. cars and took with me a Sergeant-Major Ryan and a White Russian officer, who came along as a guide and interpreter. I knew Ryan well from O.T.C. days in 1914 when he had been a musketry instructor. He had been in the Irish Guards and was a permanent force fixture of notable proportion in Military District 2.

In theory there were sufficient barracks to house a hundred thousand troops in the Vladivostok area. In fact, ninety percent of these buildings were only partially completed and quite useless. There must have been forty or fifty of them, planned to house a company and placed in groups of four scattered about in the vicinity of the city. They were without windows and only partly roofed over. Each unit had an overhanging plumbing facility on the second floor, obviously incomplete. From this upper floor, protruding earthwards about three feet, were six pipes of about ten inches in diameter, and that was that. After visiting four or five of these half-done shells, I asked the Russian officer why the buildings were all left in the same unfinished state. His cryptic reply was, "Many rich people in Russia!" I knew what he meant.

Sergeant-Major Ryan, standing below the projected latrine facility, looked up at the six pipes musingly:

"Smooth bore, sir . . . the Russians appear to disregard the elements of ballistics . . . no compensation for windage or drift . . . they contemplate only a light propellant, apparently relying on gravitational pull."

I signalled to him the presence of the Russian officer but he blissfully rambled on:

"I would surmise, sir, that the area on which we are standing is properly reserved for punishment drill."

We got in the car and the Russian doubled up with laughter.

One of the few important buildings in Vladivostok was the morgue. It looked as if it might have been a church before being put to its present use. When I saw it in mid-winter, it was too full to be sure of its original purpose. The winters in the Amur Province were very cold and graves impossible to dig, so the naked bodies (clothes were too valuable to be discarded) were piled in haphazard confusion, to freeze until spring thaw would allow mass burial.

The red-light district, which I visited officially with a combined allied patrol on several occasions, was another unforgettable horror. It was known as Kopek Hill and, of course, was out of bounds to all troops. The allied patrol was solely to apprehend violators of this quarantine. I have seen the cribs of Marseilles and some of the more repellent erotic marts of Europe and America, but there can be nothing comparable to the degradation of Vladivostok's Kopek Hill in 1918. Every night, there was at least one murder on the Hill.

In Siberia, the Bolsheviks were less than effective. During our stay, all they achieved were minor though brutal attacks on White Russian troops. We continually found the bodies of these men, bearing obscene evidence of torture before death. Many times through the winter, we were alerted to take action stations according to prearranged anti-riot plans, but nothing ever happened "above ground." The fact was that the mass of Siberian Russians had little or no sympathy with the revolution. Corporal Filip Konowal, V.C., an intelligent man who had soldiered with the Russians, told me he doubted there were a thousand genuine Bolsheviks in the whole of Amur Province.

Early in November, I was ordered to take my gunners north of Vladivostok in the hills to a large barrack compound called Gornastai Bay and prepare it for the two infantry battalions due to arrive shortly. I had about fifty Austrian prisoners as added labour. We needed them. The barracks were fine and well-built, quite different from the uncompleted shells I had seen in the town. But they had been briefly occupied by Bolsheviks in 1917 and were in a state of filth.

We managed to get them into habitable state in about two weeks.

Gornastai was a beautiful place. According to Corporal Konowal, the barracks had been constructed for a guards regiment and we found in the former officers' mess the liveries for twenty mess servants, all neatly packed away in chests. There were also stables for two squadrons of cavalry and we readied them for the Mounties. Captain Duffus was at Gornastai with me; an inspector in what was still in 1918 the Royal North West Mounted Police, he had been in the force when Charles Dickens' son was an inspector.

We had a pleasant little cottage and one of the Austrian prisoners was a good cook. He even produced a schnitzel that wasn't veal.

Czarist vodka was an unknown quantity to most of us, Duffus included. We both discovered its effects one evening at Gornastai when we divided an Imperial quart. We consumed it in the approved Russian manner with no heel taps. As the contents of the large bottle diminished, our intellectual powers and clarity of vision increased. The problems of the ages were solved with incredible facility. It all seemed so simple. I remember that perpetual motion was the final subject of discussion. As the inspector solved this riddle, he rose from his chair with dignity and deliberation and collapsed on the floor. I inquired, "What's the matter, Bill?" Next

207

moment I found myself prone beside him. I heard Bill Duffus, "I may not be able to move but, damn it, I've never been able to think better." I had to agree.

We had been in Vladivostok a month when the Armistice in Europe was declared. The news was two days old when we heard it. On November 15, elements of all allied troops in the area marched along Pushkinskaya in what was proclaimed to be a peace parade. It wasn't too happy a description. Many of the thousands who watched us pass were refugees for whom peace was a meaningless word.

But the parade confirmed what we had been told many times by people who knew the facts of the revolution: that the presence of allied troops, however small in number, made possible the growth and spirit of resistance to the Bolsheviks. Without us, the newly organized White Russian troops would "melt away," as Sir Robert Borden, Prime Minister of Canada, wrote just about this time.

As our little collection of odds and sods of the advance party marched by the crowds, we heard wild cheers. The American regiment of infantry, a British infantry battalion of the Middlesex Regiment, and the French instructors all got the same reception. But a battalion of Japanese passed to resentful silence. The crowd was cool even to the Czech battalion.

It was understandable that the Japanese would get the cold shoulder. After all, it was just fifteen years since they had given the Russians one of the most humiliating lickings in history. But the Czechs had literally saved Siberia from the Red revolution.

Two Czech divisions had been formed from the prisoners of war in the Ukraine. Under their own officers, they had made their way across the Urals and, almost unaided, gained control of the Trans-Siberian Railway and so of Siberia itself. These two superb divisions, deployed across a continent, had made possible Admiral Kolchak's White Russian government in Omsk. The new White Russian divisions could not have been organized without the Czechs. Yet the Czechs were only trying to get home the long way round. The Russians couldn't help regarding them as invaders.

Xenophon, the ancient Greek historian and writer, told the

story of a band of Greek mercenaries who, when their officers were murdered by the Persians, fought and connived their way home, a tortuous two thousand miles, capturing a king on the way and living on his ransom. The Czechs' story is a bigger one. They covered twenty-five thousand miles in the end and, instead of a king, they captured half a continent. They never produced a Xenophon to tell about them.

The night of the peace parade, there was a big party at the town hall. It was a strange affair, impossible to describe kindly except as a colossal bore. It wasn't a "ball," for very few women were there. It was not a concert, for the only music was provided by a Russian band which butchered every national anthem, including their own, and omitted the Czech hymn. It was no banquet, for there were only the inevitable Russian hors d'oeuvres which defied analysis. There was, however, plenty of good Imperial vodka. I don't know who gave the party, but I imagine it was the White Russians. Vodka was practically "on tap" to them. After the anthems and a couple of speeches by the Jap general and a Russian, which did nothing but create a good thirst, the gathering proceeded to get drunk as quickly as possible.

Three of us Canadians — Hertzberg of the sappers, Scully, a medical officer, and I — bagged a table and went off to forage for food and drink, leaving McKellar of the machine gun company to watch our claim. We had decided that with the international cast assembled, it would be advisable to keep sober so we came back to the table with Russian beer, or *Pivo*, and some indescribable food. In stony silence, McKellar was facing five Czech officers squatting at the table. In civilian life, Mac was a commercial traveller and one of the most agreeable fellows I ever knew, but the Czechs weren't having any truck with him. There he sat with an empty chair on each flank. "I don't think I'm going to make a sale," he sighed.

The Czechs had in a long time travelled a rough, lonely road. They had taken a beating on all sides and they suspected everybody. It was said that rank was designated in the Czech officer corps by the number of chips on the shoulder.

Of the five officers who had joined our table, one was a shaven-headed general with a black patch over his eye. He sat to the left of the other Czechs. Spying an empty chair at a nearby table, I tried putting it between our three and the invaders. It was not an easy manoeuvre, particularly while carrying a tray full of drinks. "Do you mind if I join you, sir?" I said before tripping over the chair and depositing four glasses of Russian beer on the head of "black patch."

The Czechs sprang to their feet and formed a "football huddle." I tried to apologize but it was useless. Scully, the medical officer, urged me to get out of the way — which I did, with Hertzberg and McKellar.

"This one-eyed character," Scully said, when he finally rejoined us, "commands one of the Czech divisions. He's a major-general, named Jan Sirovy. If you'd poured Pilsener on him, it wouldn't have been so bad . . . but Russian suds was too much. He wants to settle this . . . *insult* by a duel at the race track . . . tomorrow morning at six o'clock."

"But I haven't a sword on me," I faltered. "It's back at Gornastai."

"Don't be a bloody ass . . . you're not going to fight any duel. You'll get back to Gornastai in a droshky as quick as hell and stay there until these Czech jokers cool off. I've given them my card and I'll take on the trouble."

"What do you think, Hertzy?" I asked the sapper.

"The sawbones is right. Elmsley would blow a fuse if you played around with this Czech."

Tucked into a droshky by McKellar, I went back to Gornastai, with the comforting advice that it was a good time for a trip to the country. Gornastai was eight miles north of Vladivostok in the hills.

As was the custom in civilian life, we carried personal cards, exchanging these on occasions of inter-allied hospitality. Scully was a gregarious fellow who had dined at various messes, collecting cards which he carried in his wallet. Apparently these were mixed in with his own and from this little pack he had picked a card and exchanged it with the Czech officer.

210

At 8:00 A.M. the following day, two Czechs called on the executive officer of the U.S.S. *Brooklyn* at the Vladivostok docks, inquiring about the whereabouts of a Canadian officer who had failed to appear at the race track to settle an affair of honour.

That same day, the *Brooklyn* sailed for home with a much confused "exec."

Twenty-four years later, in 1942, my wife and I were dining in the cabin of Captain Ellis Stone, who commanded a newer *Brooklyn*. I noticed a photograph of the previous ship on the cabin bulkhead. I told Captain Stone about Major-General Jan Sirovy and the beer deposited on his head, and I made my belated apologies.

In 1938, when Czechoslovakia was betrayed at Munich, the man who formed the government which followed that of President Benes and who handed over his country to Hitler was the then inspector-general of the Czech Army, that one-eyed general named Jan Sirovy.

Shortly after the Armistice party, two transports arrived from Vancouver. One carried the police squadron with its horses; the other brought the balance of the sappers, the machine gun company and some other detachments, making our total strength in Siberia twelve hundred men. The ships had sailed before the Armistice. There was still no sign of the two infantry battalions or the 85th Battery.

Just about this time, an advance party left for Omsk: Lt.-Col. Morrisey, the G.S.O. 1, with eight officers and about fifty other ranks. My friend Bill Mulock went with the party.

In spite of my efforts to join him, I was told to wait for the battery in Vladivostok. Sid Morrisey would be in acting command of the British battalions at Omsk, part of General Elmsley's brigade. The point of the Canadian expedition was to establish a presence in Omsk as focal point of the White Russian effort against the Bolsheviks. There was nothing for the rest of us to do in Eastern Siberia.

The incredible vacillation of the Canadian government regarding the Siberian expedition now began. We, the troops in Vladivostok, knew little of the proceedings at Ottawa. We knew only that for the next eight months we were useless and ridiculous. Only General Elmsley knew what was going on, and never was a commander put in such a frustrating and humiliating position. In the original operation plan for the Canadian Expeditionary Force (S), the disposition and employment of troops was to be left to Elmsley's judgement. But the Canadian Cabinet hog-tied the general by refusing to allow his troops "to engage in military operations or move up-country without its express consent." This was in mid-December, after the two battalions had sailed for Vladivostok.

Knowing of this shackling of Elmsley's initiative, the British War Office recommended the withdrawal from Omsk of the two British battalions and the recall of the Canadian battalions then at sea. Ottawa disregarded this recommendation. The 259th and 260th Battalions duly landed at Vladivostok and, headed by a brigade band, marched to Gornastai barracks, long since cleaned up for them by our now forlorn detachment of gunners.

The new arrivals were rifle battalions. They wore silver buttons. Their officers carried swords. They were very smart and they sat on their behinds for five months.

Because there were conscripts in their ranks who had to be considered above volunteers, they would be the first units to leave Siberia for Canada, in April, 1919.

I was now back in East Barracks in my old cell in the jail. At least I was fairly close to other messes, and the two restaurants, Ah San's and the Zolotoi Rog or Golden Horn. The base depot mess was of the boil-everything order. Bill Duffus and I had been spoiled by our Austrian-prisoner cook.

I dined out as often as I could. Once I was at the sappers' mess in the town, where I had a first-rate dinner. Hertzberg had worked up a new hick monologue which was riotously funny. We broke up about two o'clock.

There was not a droshky in sight. It was bitterly cold, below zero, and I didn't like the idea of walking two miles to East Barracks. I hadn't gone more than a quarter of a mile when a coolie porter hove in sight.

The coolies in Vladivostok were Manchurians, big fellows who, without effort, could carry bales and crates in excess of their own weight for miles. They had a sort of cradle on their backs and the burden was distributed in the same way as a tumpline.

When I saw the coolie with the empty cradle, I beckoned to him. We came to terms for four rubles. He leaned over and I climbed aboard and dozed off. My weight was nothing to him.

I was awakened by, "Halt, who goes there?"

The guard had been mounted by my own gunners.

"Grand rounds!" I answered, dismounting from my coolie.

"Advance and be recognized!" from the sentry. I stepped forward. The sentry must have thought I had suddenly been promoted. He called, "Grand rounds, guard turn out!"

Sergeant Fraser, with a broad smile, gave the order, "Present arms!" There they were, all eight of them. They had turned out in just half a minute.

Dismissing them, I remounted my cradle and proceeded to the jail.

25

A few days before Christmas, a ship arrived with a cargo of combat supplies, including the six eighteen-pounder guns and twelve ammunition wagons of the 85th Battery. I went to the docks to have a look at them. Despite rumours of a Canadian withdrawal, it looked as though we were here to stay. The guns remained with the ordnance section to wait for Major Storms and the battery.

Within days, I was ordered to report to General Elmsley. I reached Force H.Q. on the run and was shown straight in to the general.

"Sit down," he said. "You remember that little show you did on the ship coming over?"

"Yes, sir."

"Have you done much of that sort of thing?"

"No, sir."

"Well, you'd better get some experience at once. I want you to put on some entertainment . . . a full-length sort of thing . . . music and all that . . . make it funny, you know . . . and I want it ready in two weeks. D'you think you can do it?"

It was as though Fanny Brice, Leon Errol, Johnny Dooley and Bert Williams were standing there with me, saying, *Go on, kid, what's stopping you?* I'd never met any of them, but there they were.

"Yes, sir."

"Good. You can call for any men you want from any unit, officers or other ranks. I'll relieve you of all other duty . . . and all personnel connected with the show, too. You can have all the transportation, trucks and cars you need."

"Sir, when will the 85th — the battery, I mean — be arriving?"

"I'm afraid you can forget about the battery, Massey. It was demobilized in Vancouver last week."

"But the guns and wagons just came, sir! I've seen them."

Gentleman Jim got up from his chair and walked to the window that looked out on Pushkinskaya.

"We're up against a situation that's tougher to handle than a fighting war. That's five thousand men with nothing to do . . . in this cesspool of a place."

He turned to me.

"Report progress to me at the end of this week. That's all."

I walked back towards East Barracks in a daze. I felt heartsick at the news that the 85th was finished, and was filled with terror at the job assigned to me. The show had to be ready in two weeks!

The cold air cleared my mind. I was no longer a gunner subaltern; I was a theatrical producer — with plenty of backing and no need to bargain with talent. They would be under orders to perform — at military pay.

By the time I reached the jail, I'd pretty well decided on a minstrel show, following the style of Primrose and Dockstader and the Christie Minstrels. Half the show would be in the conventional style, with Interlocutor and End Men and three or four others a side. All but the Interlocutor would be black face. The second half would be a succession of vaudeville acts. I could see daylight.

Fortunately, the two I needed most to help me — Hertzberg of the sappers and McKellar of the machine gun company — were at East Barracks. I told them of my orders and both agreed to do anything to help. They too felt that a minstrel show was the most practical formula. They knew the old Primrose and Dockstader Minstrels who had played the Grand Theatre in Toronto before the war. As for gags, between the three of us we remembered thirty-five and typed them up at once.

The general had said the show was to be played for all allied troops in the area, so some of the audiences wouldn't understand English. A lucky break, Hertzberg observed, considering the material we had exhumed from our memories of Joe Miller's joke book:

INTERLOCUTOR: "Rastus, why didn't you bring that water back from the creek last night?"

RASTUS: "I done got scared, Mr. Interlocutor."

INTERLOCUTOR: "Why were you scared?"

RASTUS: "There was a great big alligator in the creek."

INTERLOCUTOR: "An alligator? Why, that's nonsense."

RASTUS: "Yes, sirree . . . there was a powerful big alligator in the creek. I sure got scared . . . . Yes, sir!"

INTERLOCUTOR: "You go right down to the creek and get that water . . . the chances are that alligator is more scared than you are."

RASTUS: "If that am de chances dat de alligator is more scared than I am, that water ain't fit to drink!"

Years later in the entrance hall of King Vidor's house in Hollywood, I saw a large oil painting which was one of King's proudest possessions. A huge Negro stands in the foreground with an obviously empty bucket in his hands. He is gazing apprehensively at a wicked, grinning alligator which peers at him from a river in the background. It is a brilliant and witty work and, as King told me, it was Thomas Hart Benton's appreciation of the alligator story.

Every question was asked two or three times and the gag was milked to the limit except the pay-off line. This one was sure fire:

ONYX: "'Tambo Johnson' has sure got a real hard head."

RASTUS: "Yes, sirree, dey was working on the barracks at Gornastai and a fellow right on the top of de barracks . . . he dropped a brick and it smashed onto Tambo's head."

ONYX: "Right on his head. Did it kill him?"

RASTUS: "Kill him? No, it don't kill him . . . . Tambo jus' look up and he say, 'Quit throwing dat sand!'"

RUFUS: "I was away the other day and while I was away, my mother-in-law died."

216

INTERLOCUTOR: "Why, that's too bad. I'm sorry to hear that.
. . . . What did she die of?"

RUFUS: "My mule kicked her. When I got back, a lot of my friends — Eph Cole, Sam Johnson, Gus Smith — was all there in my yard."

INTERLOCUTOR: "Oh, yes . . . . I suppose they were there to sympathize with you?"

RUFUS: "No, sir, they was there to buy the mule."

In preparation for my new role as theatrical producer, I conducted a combined audition and rehearsal. "Suspected" talent was summoned from units all around. At the end of eight hours, we had a cast of twenty-five chosen from double that number who had been paraded at East Barracks.

Within twenty-four hours of the initiation of the project, the show was cast, written and in rehearsal. But we had a long way to go. Out of the audition, I got a passable barbershop quartet — two of my gunners and two of Hertzberg's sappers. Among my own men, I found three professional vaudevillians from the Pantages circuit in the States who were good for a hoofing and singing act. Of course, Hertzberg himself would do his monologue, a sort of forerunner combination of Will Rogers and Tennessee Ernie Ford.

Beyond that, there was a good deal to fill. For myself, I had picked Bert Williams' "Solo Poker Game" and his great song, "No----body." I knew the poker game by heart, and I was going to steal it, every single second of it. It was a hand of poker in which Williams pantomimed the sad fate of the holder of a full house facing a "pat" hand. In the vaudeville half of the show, I planned more thievery with a burlesque of a sort of Ruth St. Denis dance. I had watched the comic genius of Fanny Brice, Johnny Dooley and Leon Errol. As I worked out the "choreography" in rehearsals, my debt to Fanny Brice seemed the greatest. I was able to acknowledge it in Hollywood when I met Miss Brice in 1937. She was kind enough to say that she was pleased to have had her Siberian reputation in my hands.

Captain McGill of the Signals showed me the script of a dramatic sketch called *In Flanders Fields*. It was well written with, in

217

retrospect, a touch of *Journey's End.* I wanted to play in it instead of doing my dance. Hertzberg and McKellar dissuaded me, as they thought my "talents" lay in the comic vein.

Gunner Groesbeck at last came into his own, painting our scenery with great wit and skill. He remained the most unsoldierly and sloppiest member of the C.E.F. (Siberia) but he made a large contribution to *The Roadhouse Minstrels.* The next time I saw Dan Groesbeck after Siberia was in Hollywood in 1941, when he designed the settings for C. B. de Mille's *Reap the Wild Wind,* in which I was playing the villain.

For the minstrels, I used the liveries of Russian mess waiters I had found at Gornastai Barracks. They were perfect: plum-coloured, claw-hammer coats with yellow facings and black trousers. We looked just like the Primrose and Dockstader Line. There were plenty of corks in Vladivostok to burn for the makeup. Women's black stockings with wool sewed in little clumps made excellent wigs.

Many of the soldiers had musical instruments and, with a piano discovered in the barracks, we had no difficulty getting together a five-piece orchestra.

We opened in the big hall in our barracks one day under the two weeks the general had given me to have the show ready. There were over seven hundred troops in the audience and we went over far better than we had hoped to.

Gentleman Jim was in front with his staff. Afterwards he came backstage and thanked everybody. He really had enjoyed himself and seemed genuinely proud of his show. I know how he felt. It was his idea.

We played about twenty performances, usually twice a week, sometimes to as many as two thousand men, sometimes as few as three hundred. With no amplification in 1919, we just had to speak up. But we were heard and, with the help of the sappers' lighting, we were seen. Here is a program:

THE ROADHOUSE MINSTRELS

1.   WAY DOWN SOUTH

CAST

Interlocutor	Gnr. Moffat, C.F.A.
Gus	Spr. Longdon
Rastus	Lieut. R. H. Massey, C.F.A.
Sambo	Capt. K. B. McKellar, Base Depot
Onyx	Lieut. K. N. B. McKenzie, Base Depot
Abe	Pte. Kane, No. 10 Sn. Section
George	Sergt. Wheeler, Remounts
Great Scott	Spr. Scott, 6th Signal Co.
Eph	L/Cpl. Cross, Base Depot
The Spiritous Quartette	Gnr. Berrill, Gnr. Curtis, C.F.A. Spr. Brown & Spr. Cassidy, O.E.
The Tired Trio	Gnrs. Beere, Girardin & Kenny, C.F.A.

2.   A RURAL INTERLUDE   Capt. C.S.L. Hertzberg, MC

3.   WAY DOWN SOUTH (2nd Spasm)

INTERMISSION

4.   BY HECK

Si Perkins	Sergt. Lewis, Base Depot
Josh Fry	Bdr. Sylvane, C.F.A.

5.   IN FLANDERS FIELDS

Pte. Foster (a Batman)	Sergt. Scott, Base Depot
Capt. Frampton	Capt. T. C. McGill, 6th Signal Co.
Sergt. Totten	Capt. J. G. Gauld, MC Base Depot

Capt. Thompson   S/Sgt. Denniss, Base Depot

The scene is a dugout in the front line in Flanders.

6. IN THE SHADOW OF THE PYRAMIDS
                              Lieut. R. H. Massey, C.F.A.

7. A GEOGRAPHICAL MONOLOGUE
                              Spr. Longdon, C.E.
8. IN A SIBERIAN CABARET

   Tania   Gnr. Curtis, C.F.A.
   Fred   Gnr. Berrill, C.F.A.
   Waiter   By himself

9. A LITTLE BIT OF SCOTCH   Spr. Scott, 6th Signal Co.

Critical reaction was good. *The Siberian Sapper,* published by the 16th Field Company Canadian Engineers, was enthusiastic, although biased in our favour by the presence of Captain Hertzberg in the cast.

Our performance for the U. S. 31st Infantry won a rave in their regimental paper:

THE ROADHOUSE MINSTRELS
On Saturday evening, Feb. 15, the "Roadhouse Minstrels"— the all-star All-Canadian troupe — played to a crowded house at East Barracks. The American officers and men as guests of their Canadian friends were given an opportunity to see the best Allied show yet produced in Siberia.

Special mention must be made of Mr. Massey, as end man and as a dancer. His interpretation of Salome's Dance would have made Ruth St. Denis turn green with envy. And his solo poker game was one of the hits of the evening. In fact, the exhibition so impressed the American officers that they promptly extended him an invitation to their quarters in hope that he would again demonstrate his ability to lose gracefully to a "pat" hand.

The playlet, *In Flanders Fields*, was cleverly written and well

220

acted. Capt. McGill, the author and "leading man" was heartily congratulated for his work in this drama.

The success of the show was due in large part to the skill of Gunner Groesbeck, who painted the scenery, the actors and the drop curtain. This last was especially good, representing a mountain scene said to have been taken from a sketch made of Hakodate Pass while en route to Vladivostok. The black eye worn by the dancer in *In the Shadow of the Pyramids* was also worthy of remark as a work of art.

The whole show was noticeable for its energy and vitality. There was not a dull moment in the entire evening. The Canadians have set a pace with this show which the other Allies will have trouble in keeping.

This was my first press notice and I still know it by heart.

Performing to audiences such as the White Russians and Czechs who did not understand English went remarkably well, if there was a small section who understood what was being said and who could act as a sort of laugh track. But even to a totally non-understanding crowd, we apparently looked funny enough to evoke laughter, oddly in the right places.

At one performance in Vladivostok town hall, there were about a dozen women in unfamiliar uniforms sitting in the front row. There was, of course, the usual amount of "blue" material to be found in any army show that we could cut. In particular, I had a bawdy monologue in the minstrel show that began, "De-jected, hell ... "

I asked Captain Barker, who managed the show, who the women were. "Don't cut anything," he said. "They're Czech nurses and won't understand a word." The show went beautifully. After the final curtain, Barker brought one of the women back and introduced her to me with an ape-like grin. In a voice which could only have come from an English vicarage, she said, "Oh, Mr. Massey, what a delightful evening! You know, I thought your speech about 'dejection' was quite charming."

At the end of February, the futility of our expedition was admitted by the Canadian government. Although the whole force, with the exception of the 85th Battery, was in Vladivostok, Ottawa decided that no Canadian troops would be sent up-country.

General Elmsley was in a humiliating position. There were angry exchanges between him and the British General Knox, who wrote our general on December 27: "If the Canadians only think of playing the American-Japanese sitting game in the Far East, I honestly don't see much use in their coming at all." The advance party at Omsk was in an appalling situation, from which they were not extricated until April, when the first Canadian transport left Vladivostok for Vancouver.

At that time, the White Russian cause was in the ascendant. It reached its peak in May, 1919, when Lenin wrote to his Revolutionary Army Council: "If we don't conquer the Urals before winter, I think the destruction of the revolution is inevitable." At the end of May, less than one-sixth of the whole of Russia was in Bolshevik hands.

That was when the last of the Canadians, including myself, left Vladivostok. The expedition had been a complete fiasco, and we had left when victory over the Bolsheviks was in sight. One of the last things I saw when we boarded the transport was our six eighteen-pounder guns and our limbered wagons still in the dock shed and soon to be the property of the Revolution.

Churchill fumed at our betrayal of the White Russian cause. Three weeks later, Admiral Kolchak was murdered in Omsk; and the White Russian armies, when deserted by us, melted away.

One year later, the two Czech divisions returned to their home across Canada. Since they had gone to war against Russia in 1914, they had girdled the globe.

Though I didn't know when or where, I was certain of one thing: for me the theatre lay ahead.

I remembered Kit Cornell stating to me and the cows back in Cobourg that she was going to be an actress on Broadway. "Me, too, Kit," I said to myself.

26

In the Michaelmas term of 1919, I went up to Balliol College, Oxford. At this time, Balliol was the undisputed intellectual focus of the university. I believe it remains so to this day. I never could understand why I was in such an environment, and the college and I did not really come to terms. I believe the fault was almost all mine, except that my brother was an enthusiastic Balliol man with persuasive powers.

Balliol is the second oldest college in Oxford University, founded in 1263 by a flourishing Norman noble named John de Balliol and Dervorguilla, his wife. During the following centuries, Balliol College was joined by some thirty-three later foundations. In 1870, the Fellows of Balliol College elected Benjamin Jowett, Doctor of Divinity, as Master. He had been jockeying for the mastership for twenty years. It was a significant appointment. Hitherto, the colleges of Oxford had proceeded on a more-or-less even tenor of academic quality. But the new Master had definite ideas about the future of Balliol. An owlish, shrill-voiced little man, Jowett was a rare combination of scholar and activist, not only a don renowned in his classical field and the definitive translator of Plato, but also a determined and practical Master whose obsession was to make Balliol the intellectual leader of the university.

This he succeeded in accomplishing by unashamedly recruiting the best brains from leading public schools. He had an uncanny ability in spotting not only intellect but character in the young and he had representatives or scouts everywhere. Everybody knew Jowett and he knew everybody. He was the outstanding academic figure of the Victorian age.

Within a generation of Jowett's death, Balliol had produced men pre-eminent in nearly every phase of English life: prime ministers, churchmen, cabinet members, judges, pro-consuls, ambassadors, leaders in letters and the arts and every manner of public life. The University Honours List each year sparkled with "firsts" attained by the college. There was a fierce loyalty and pride deepset in Balliol men, usually concealed in British reticence, but expressed with emotional extravagance by Hilaire Belloc, who went up in 1892 and so had had two years of "The Jowler":

> Balliol made me, Balliol fed me,
> Whatever I had she gave me again;
> And the best of Balliol loved and led me,
> God be with you, Balliol men.

My brother, who had been up in 1912 and 1913, had filled me with Balliol lore. I must admit that I went up to the college with a feeling that perhaps I was misplaced. I never overcame this apprehension.

Oxford had been hard hit by the war. The university had always been small in the number of its undergraduates, usually about three thousand. In the war years, two thousand and seven hundred Oxford men had been killed, an academic generation virtually wiped out. The university was generous in the extreme in the accommodation of ex-servicemen. We were excused all examinations but the final Honours Schools and even these, if we wished, we could take on a so-called shortened course. I could in six terms write for my degree. Jowett must have turned over in his grave. There is no such thing at Oxford as a class based on a graduation year. One enters or goes "up" to a college in any of the three terms and becomes a member of that college.

During the year 1919, some hundred and seventy-five of us came up to Balliol, just out of the army or navy. Most of us were a few years older than the usual undergraduates; yet we faced with equanimity, even with pleasure, the restrictions that a wise and ancient institution saw fit to impose on us "junior members of the university." After all, it was rather cosy to be regarded as still youthful.

On my staircase was Frank Sandford, a commander in the Royal Navy, who had taken the first submarine through the Dardanelles minefields in 1915. In the Zeebrugge Raid in 1918, he had rescued the crew of the blockship commanded by his brother, who won the V.C. My next-door neighbour was Andrew Rothstein, lance corporal in the Royal Engineers, and later London correspondent of T.A.S.S. and director of the Information Department of the Russian Trade Delegation in 1921-24. He informed me that in the coming revolution, I would be the first to be put up against a wall and shot.

Rothstein was the first Communist I had ever met. He was indignant that I had visited Siberia with a military force intended to interfere with the revolution, and I lost no opportunity of goading him into a rage.

There were six of us occupying rooms in this staircase which looked out on St. Giles. It was one of two seventeenth-century buildings in the inner quadrangle. With the exception of a small, fourteenth-century Gothic library, these two buildings were the only ones to escape a devastating renovation in the nineteenth century. The new dining hall and chapel of Balliol, built sometime about 1860, are examples of the Victorian style of which John Ruskin had been the supreme advocate. The chapel, with its horizontal stripes of dark and light brown stone, is particularly offensive.

Oxford conjures up pictures in most minds of oak-panelled rooms, glowing fireplaces, upholstered wicker chairs, pipe smoke and endless, enlightened talk. Such pictures are true but not totally. There was in my time no inside plumbing at Balliol.

In the late eighteenth century, the college had received the gift of some twenty-four water closets from a thoughtful and generous noblewoman, the Lady Elizabeth Perriam. These facilities were housed in a flat-roofed building known as The Perriam against the wall bordering Trinity College and at a minimum distance of one hundred yards from all the staircases. It is proper that all the inevitable graffiti inscribed on the walls of this Balliol structure have been in impeccable Greek or Latin verse.

It was gracious living but with chamber pots. Since my Oxford days, I have acquired a collection of chamber pots, ranging from cloisonné and Spode to the simplest china with ribald inscriptions. I possess some twenty-five of these treasures to remind me of Balliol.

The hardest-worked men I have ever encountered, with the exception of coal miners, were the college scouts, or room servants, who had to carry huge ewers of hot and cold water up as many as four storeys for "sitz" baths and then carry the waste down again. They had to serve the breakfasts and clear away the debris, clean the rooms, make the fires and quite often serve luncheons in the rooms of their young men.

The scout on my staircase, Number IV, was an old fellow named Bliss. He had been a scout at Balliol for over forty years. In the long summer vacations, he used to work as a waiter in a hotel at Lynton on the north Devon coast. I had met him when I was there with my family in the summer of 1912. He told me much about Balliol, where my brother had been the previous year. Bliss said that his work at Mr. Hole's Cottage Hotel at Lynton was a perfect rest after serving six young gentlemen on staircase IV. I saw his point seven years later.

The high point of Bliss' career was serving the future Marquess of Curzon in 1878, when he was living in the rooms I later occupied in the college.

In my time, none of the occupants of Number IV staircase matched the elegance of Lord Curzon; but with the departure of Rothstein in my second year, the tone was considerably improved. He was replaced by my old school friend from Appleby, John Harlan, who came up to Balliol in 1920 as a Rhodes Scholar. This made the number of future lawyers four out of the six of us: Mr. Justice Harlan of the U. S. Supreme Court; Lord Evershed, Lord

Chief Justice of England; Mr. Justice Barry and Bertram Bevan-Petman of the Inner Temple. The last, named "B-P," had been in the Indian Cavalry six or seven years. When I knew him at Balliol, I was able to understand the gold standard perfectly: B-P's finances were entirely based on an 18-karat gold cigarette case. All I remember now about his involved but sound theory is that "it has to be a very good cigarette case." I also recall that he sometimes pawned the case. Such emergencies he referred to as "recessions."

Normally one spent the first two years living in college and the rest in lodgings or "digs." But as most of us were up for a shortened course of six terms, we remained in college all our time.

No resident of the college could leave it after nine in the evening or re-enter after midnight. Huge wooden gates were locked with enormous padlocks at 9:00 P.M., the only entrance being by a tiny postern gate. I was relieved of this restriction by the generosity of a friend, Harcourt Johnstone, who bequeathed me a large key to the rear postern gate in St. Giles when he was sent down in the Hilary term of 1920. I also had a room looking out on St. Giles and the Martyr's Memorial. It allowed ingress through a window from the top of a hansom cab driven up on the pavement. Several hansoms were still plying in Oxford largely for this purpose, I think. I myself never used this means of entry, preferring the key. One night, about 1:00 A.M., a tap on my window from a cabby's whip summoned me to open it. Four merry friends were passed into my room, where for several hours they continued a party they had just left at Magdalen.

Lunch and tea could be served in one's rooms when requested and it was a popular form of hospitality. Late in my first term, I invited two friends from Worcester College to lunch. As I had been entertained well at Worcester, I was anxious to prove that you could have good food at "that dreary hydro on the Broad," as Balliol was often referred to by other colleges. Bliss had set the table and brought the wine up, a bottle of sherry and some claret. I thought I would give my guests mulled claret, a popular drink in those days. I set a bottle on the trivet in front of a good hot fire.

No young bride ever fussed about her first meal for her in-laws more than I did for these guests of mine. I straightened the knives and forks, dusted the glasses over and over and finally came to rest standing with my back to the fire.

I was looking at my watch when the explosion took place. I had forgotten about the bottle coming to a boil on the trivet. Luckily, I was wearing a pair of heavy corduroy trousers and the glass didn't penetrate them. My guests and I picked up the fragments scattered all over the room.

Bliss brought up another bottle. "Try it at room temperature, sir," he said. "Mr. Curzon always did."

Oxford learning was based on the tutorial system. Each scholar or commoner in the college was assigned to a tutor, perhaps to two or even more, in the "school" for which he was reading. My school was Modern History, my tutor Kenneth Bell. He was not only a brilliant scholar but a remarkable human being, kindly, witty, humorous and understanding. He was in many ways like de Buttes Powell and we became close friends. Kenneth had been up at Balliol about the same time de Buttes had been at Keble. Kenneth had earned a "First" in Modern History and a Fellowship of All Souls (here there was no similarity to de Buttes). He had lectured in Toronto University for three years and, during four years service in the Royal Field Artillery, had won an M.C., been wounded and commanded a battery. Now he was back at Balliol as one of three History tutors. As Junior Dean of the college, he was in charge of the discipline.

Six or eight of us would go to Kenneth for tutorials twice a week and sometimes I would have a little extra time. These sessions were informal, no two of them alike. The aim of Kenneth Bell, though never expressed, was not to impart knowledge but to make us think. History was to be approached in a legalistic, analytical manner. We had to speak up in those tutorials of his. If we were silent, it was evidence of not thinking and that was failure. I realized almost at once that my fellows in the tutorial were just plain better than I was, better prepared and more articulate. In my second term, I asked Kenneth point blank, "I'm in fast company. Can I make the grade in Schools? Or shall I just try for a diploma?"

228

"You're mentally lazy," he answered directly. "Possibly it's timidity. But Schools are not competitive and, as far as the college is concerned, we can do with a leavening of intellectual vagrancy."

For the first two terms, I went to the Dean, Francis Fortescue Urquhart, once a week for another tutorial. He was known as Sligger and his sessions were just as easy-going as Kenneth's. Sligger was a devout Roman Catholic who spent many of his vacations on a round of visits to the houses of recusant nobility. A good tutor, he dealt with the political philosophy of Modern History, which entailed the reading of such enchanting works as Hobbes' *Leviathan,* John Locke and John Stuart Mill. Even Sligger, who had a pretty wit, could not alleviate my boredom with Mill.

The Master kept tabs on us by requiring an occasional essay. I have one that I submitted in the Hilary term of my first year. It is entitled, "The Separation of the Functions of Government Is the Greatest Discovery of Political Science." I have read it again after fifty years and I find it has not improved with age. I have this satisfaction: my essay must have bored the Master as much as a lecture of his on "The Poor Laws in England in the Nineteenth Century" bored me. This was the only lecture I went to at Oxford. Attendance at lectures was voluntary and I found I could borrow the notes of friends and avoid the crush of eager women undergraduates who thronged these gatherings. There were three or four women's colleges at Oxford in my time, but lectures were the only university activities in which the sexes met. I convinced myself that the written word was more compelling than the spoken, at least it was less liable to be mislaid.

The Master was a cobwebby little man with a high-pitched voice. His name was A. L. Smith. A formidable scholar, he was steeped in the tradition of maintaining Balliol's intellectual supremacy. Beyond a couple of ritualistic tea parties at the Master's lodgings and the submission of my essay, I saw little of him until my last term.

A curious phenomenon of Balliol was the singing or moaning of a strange ditty called "Gordooley" on every conceivable occasion, by any number of Balliol men, drunk or sober. It had a simple libretto of two lines and the tune was reminiscent of a mournful bugle call such as "The Last Post." The words were: "Oh, Gordooley — got a face like a ha-a-am. . . . Bobby Johnson says so and he ought to know!" That's all there was to it. Who or what Gordooley was, nobody ever knew, except that apparently he was no rose to look at. As for Bobby Johnson, his identity is shrouded in mystery. For the previous hundred years, no member of the college had been so named. The chant was used nocturnally, as a rallying cry like an American college yell; or, in spite of its lugubrious, wailing tone, as an outburst of elation or just to annoy our next-door neighbours in Trinity College.

Since most of us undergraduates of the post-war years were older than the usual run of students, less "youthful exuberance" might have been expected of us. In fact, we were as boisterous as previous generations. I remember two enthusiastic outbursts with pleasure.

The British government, in December, 1919, had distributed a vast number of captured German weapons as war trophies to cities, institutions and villages. Often these obnoxious relics were resented and consigned to the nearest pond. or dump. Balliol was included in this governmental generosity. After the Christmas "vac" that year, we found a large German minnenwerfer squatting in the centre of the Fellows' garden. It was an ugly contraption mounted on two wheels like a gun, weight eight or nine hundred pounds; an unpleasant memento which, it was unanimously agreed, would have to go.

No plans were made. But a few nights after term began, there was, for no accountable reason, an unusual call for the doughty college ale in hall. Shortly afterwards, the sad strains of "Gordooley" drifted from the Fellows' garden like a tocsin. Gowned scholars and commoners swarmed to the ramparts. No orders were given. It was the will of us all that this metallic insult should be passed over the fifteen-foot wall into the gardens of Trinity. Where there's a will there's no weight; in a few minutes, the damned thing was on the roof of The Perriam, all eight hundred pounds of it.

There was now only about six feet of wall to carry. Trinity was offering some resistance, flowerpots coming over in a kind of barrage. But we were close to success now and twelve of us managed to

230

get a hold. With a shout of "Look out below, Trinity!" over it went. There was a crash of breaking glass as a cucumber frame in the Trinity president's vegetable garden perished.

The operation closed with three triumphant "Gordooleys" and the happy discovery that Kenneth Bell, the Junior Dean, had joined the group on the Perriam roof, which had given the final heave. There had been no police brutality and academic freedom had been preserved.

In the next term, the university was visited by Princess Mary, the Princess Royal, who honoured Balliol by planting a tree in the Fellows' garden where the Hun mortar had been. The whole college witnessed the little ceremony and H.R.H. was heartily applauded.

That night after hall, the Communists and radicals of the college, about fifteen of them, tried to dig the tree up. They were driven off with light casualties by a small band of royalists and conservatives. A picket was left to protect the tree.

About an hour later, the attack was renewed, both sides having been reinforced, and in this engagement, the tree suffered some injury. The attackers were again driven off and the tree was placed in protective custody in my rooms. It was replanted with splints applied to its fractured trunk by a small party of conservationists early the following morning.

This highly successful exercise in political science had an unfortunate culmination. The Junior Dean, who had performed so commendably in the affair of the German minethrower, appeared in his academicals and gated us for a week for interfering with college property. This decision resulted in the confinement to college at night of five loyal monarchists, including two future High Court judges. But, even if somewhat scathed, the Princess' tree survived.

27

The day I came up to Balliol, I became a rowing man, and in my six terms I never missed a day on the river.

Those early autumn days were lovely and relaxing, and I thought how wise I had been to have chosen to row instead of wallowing about a rugger field in the muddy grass.

Flowing out of Oxford under Folly Bridge, the Thames bends almost due south and, with Christ Church Meadows on the left bank, runs almost straight for a mile and a half to Sandford Lock. This provides the racing course with a fearful jog in the middle called The Gut, where a good cox can gain a half-length and a bad one lose as much. For the River is too narrow for boats to race abreast; and the Lent races and the summer Eights are run in single file, a complicated system of competition in which a number of boats start at equal intervals and try to bump the next ahead.

In my time, there were three divisions of about twelve boats each and racing took place on six consecutive days. The lead boat in each of the second and third divisions rows in the higher division for the second time in the day. It is possible to get a triple bump if the crew in front has bumped, leaving two vacancies ahead, but this is a remote chance.

The moment a bump has been made, the bumper and bumped must get out of the way; and this is sometimes difficult with two exhausted crews. Once, long ago, a cox was gored by the sharp prow of a shell in such a mix-up, so that all boats now have a rubber ball fixed on the bow like the button on a fencing foil.

The winning Head of the River crew earns the supreme reward of college rowing, second only to the varsity boat that races on the tideway against Cambridge in March. The little Master of Balliol, A. L. Smith, had rowed bow in the Head of the River Eight in 1872, and he still kept a grandfatherly eye on Balliol rowing.

Along the east bank near the finishing pole, the college barges were moored. Some of these ancient and ornate craft had been built in the early eighteenth century for the liveried companies of London. They served as changing rooms for the crews. In 1919, they were all very decrepit, although they looked gay enough. They have since been replaced by boathouses.

Rowing was more than a sport at Oxford, it was a cult. It was ingrained in the university, a great deal of the coaching being in the hands of dons. My first days of "tubbing" in a heavy clapboard, four-oared contraption with fixed seats were directed by an antique don who apparently had come out of the woodwork. He wore a frayed, faded Leander cap, which meant he must have been an old Blue, a trials man or have rowed in a Head of the River boat. The Leander Club is exclusively restricted to such heroes of Oxford and Cambridge. His instruction was, I gathered, faithful to the orthodoxy of Oxford and Cambridge rowing, as developed at Eton, which always has supplied the universities with good oarsmen. Rowing, he explained, was an art in which the oar was moved through the water by the legs and the swing of the back: the arms were merely the connection of the back with the oar. This made the "English" method of rowing a rhythmic movement of beauty.

He warned us that there was in being, in actual practice, a deplorable heresy preached by a man named Steve Fairbairn, an Australian, in which the back was disregarded in its proper emphasis and the arms were used to finish the stroke. This Australian had taught his baleful ideas to the crews of Jesus College, Cambridge, with the sad result that Jesus had gone Head of the River on the Cam before the war. Fairbairn had also taught the Jesus style to the Light Blue or Cambridge Eight with disgustingly successful results. He had even imparted his revolutionary ideas to a tideway rowing club which had done depressingly well at Henley in 1914. Fairbairn was quoted by the old don as having said, "It's better to go fast than look good!" The blasphemy was whispered to us.

With due reverence for tradition and style, a very sore behind from the fixed thwart or seat on which we slid in those horrible heavy fours, and a savage determination to excel as a galley slave, I was weaned from the tubbing.

I was lucky enough to be in the winning four in some time tests and in the last week of term was picked as number three in the second Torpid for the bumping races in the Hilary term.

The winter had set in; it was late November and a time to try our souls. The Torpid boat was a heavy barge-like vessel with the same agonizing fixed seats as the four. We never missed a day at the Balliol Boat Club. Sometimes with chapped hands, ice in our hair and blood-stained shorts, we would return from an hour's workout and try to thaw ourselves around the tiny stove in the barge.

After the Christmas vac, Kenneth Bell took over the coaching of the second Torpid, or "togger." In the dictionary, torpid is said to mean lacking in energy, vim or vigour. Some Victorian don with a sick sense of humour must have given the winter term races the name. It was not appropriate for us. Though we may have lacked style, we certainly possessed vim and vigour.

Despite Kenneth's voluble efforts to make us conform to the traditional long-leg stroke, we kept using our arms. It wasn't rebellion, it was the torture of those fixed thwarts on which we rubbed our hinder parts to the bone. Our arms seemed to give us some relief. We tried to do as we were told — but in spite of ourselves, we were rowing in the Fairbairn manner and we were very fast — for about five hundred yards!

The full course was about a mile and a quarter. Just before the Torpid week, we rowed our last full course. Kenneth gave up. "Your time was not too bad, but you're not teetering on your backsides. You're trying to slide on fixed seats which accounts for the barge looking like a butcher shop. You're not using your legs. You should get a bump a night if you do it before the Gut. After that, I won't answer for you."

The word "night" was always used instead of day in reference to both Torpids and "Eights" week — I suppose for the same reason matinee tickets are marked "morning" in England.

We bumped Jesus, Wadham, Exeter, St. John's II and Pembroke, missing our sixth because the boat ahead, Worcester, got a bump and we rowed over in a stately but ineffectual effort to abandon the Cambridge heresy.

Kenneth was wrong in one prophecy: that we couldn't last through the Gut, for we caught Pembroke along the willows, near the barges.

The Balliol First Togger had held its place; I think it was fourth. We had a rousing bump supper and all of us got suitably tight, including Kenneth. With the whole college we sang innumerable "Gordooleys" and hurled flowerpots into Trinity. The Master, who had watched the racing from the Balliol barge on the fourth night, never saw us, for most times we had bumped at the Haystack, and on the last night he thought our row through was "quite passable."

The Oxford system is to do most of one's reading in the vacations which take up more than half the year. I spent the Christmas vac of 1919-20 at Lyme Regis in digs with Hume Wrong, an old Toronto friend. In spite of having only one good eye, Hume had bluffed his way into the British Infantry, serving two years in the trenches as a subaltern. He was later the first Canadian ambassador to Washington, my brother having been the first minister. It was a tough winter and, as we struggled to keep golf balls within the ill-defined limits of the Lyme Regis golf links, I thought of those icy hours on the river that lay ahead, when we would practise for the Torpids. Hume played golf at Oxford and was very smug about my rowboat activities.

In the Easter vac, Hume, his brother Murray, and I did a walking tour of the battlefields for about ten days. Nothing much had been done to clean things up; dud shells were lying about, the towns were still in ruins.

235

When Trinity term started, I found to my astonishment that I had been picked as three in the college first Eight, which I held down for the Eights Week races. We rowed in a new *Lady Dervorguilla* shell with sliding seats, and my days of pain were over. With two Blues and several old Etonians in the boat, we weren't too bad. The college started the week in third place with Christ Church and Magdalen ahead of us. That's the way we finished.

Magdalen, with four Blues in her eight, went Head of the River by bumping "The House" opposite the Christ Church barge on Monday and Balliol rowed through every night. We did gain on The House (so-called because of its Latin name "Aedes Christi") by half a length almost every one of the five nights but couldn't pull off a bump.

Eights Week was a lovely sight that year. The weather was perfect and every night the barges filled with pretty women in bright summer frocks. The towpath opposite was a contrast with howling mobs following each boat, and signal pistol shots and shouts of "You're going up, Merton," "It's a canvas, Trinity!" And of course, "Well rowed, Balliol, well rowed!"

After Eights Week in 1920, the University Boat Club persuaded six colleges to send their First Eights to Henley Regatta. Oxford was making a determined effort to swamp the expected Cambridge invasion. Magdalen, Christ Church, Trinity, Exeter, Merton and Balliol were set to go, and Oxford had entries in every event in the Regatta. We were to row in the Ladies Plate, a race for colleges and public schools. The captain of the Balliol Boat Club was an Australian Rhodes Scholar named Hugh Cairns. A Blue, he had rowed in the Oxford boat the previous March and had rowed at seven in the college eight. He took himself out of the boat in order to coach us. We still had one Blue, Stanley O'Neil, at number six.

Hugh Cairns served four years in the Australian Army Medical Corps, held two degrees (B.M. and B.Sc. from Adelaide University), and became a Fellow of the Royal College of Surgeons. He rowed twice for Oxford against Cambridge, and married a daughter of the Master of Balliol — all of this before he was twenty-five. By the time he was thirty, he was Hunterian Professor of the Royal College of Surgeons and a neuro-surgeon with an international reputation. When General George Patton suffered an automobile accident in Germany in 1946, Hugh was sent for and made a desperate but fruitless attempt to save his life.

Hugh was a gentle, gregarious man, with many friends, among whom was Rudyard Kipling. Hugh brought him to our training table in hall one night before we left for Henley. Mr. Kipling appeared much interested in rowing and our chances at Henley. After dinner, some of us adjourned to Kenneth Bell's rooms, Hugh and Mr. Kipling along with us. It was a cheerful evening with much good talk, and Mr. Kipling fitted in smoothly with the group.

A hero to us all, Kipling might have been just another don as he curled up in a big chair with his mug of Balliol ale. He listened, talked a bit, laughed a lot and seemed to have a good time, whether he heard about the merits of swivel rowlocks, the virtues of the newest *Lady Dervorguilla,* the shell we were taking to Henley, or the usual small talk of training table. By the time we broke up, it had been arranged that Mr. Kipling would accompany us to Henley. We had adopted him in a peremptory manner. He complied cheerily. Hugh Cairns said the house the college had rented for our two weeks at the Regatta would accommodate Mr. Kipling in addition to the fourteen of us (Hugh was taking five substitutes as well as the eight).

Two days later, we made our first appearance on the river at Henley. There were thirty-five eights and twelve fours, to say nothing of pairs and sculls entered, and the course had to be reserved for time tests. All day long, one or another of the eights, fours, pairs and single scullers would be rowing a "course," with a coach and followers with stop watches, all on bicycles, making the towpath as perilous to a casual pedestrian as Fifth Avenue or Piccadilly. The course was on a beautiful straight reach of the Thames from a little island with one of those eighteenth-century temples on it to a finishing post with the Leander Club lawn on the Buckinghamshire side and Phyllis Court Club on the Berkshire bank, one mile, five hundred and fifty yards long with booms on each side the entire

237

distance. The towpath ran along the Bucks bank. No other course in the world compares with Henley for beauty or for racing.

Mr. Kipling was all attention, a stop watch concealed in his pocket, timing the crews who were rowing "courses." Since he could see starts from the Leander Club enclosure opposite the finishing post, he was able to time all our likely competition in the first two or three days. Nobody knew what he was doing. He was as furtive as a Newmarket clocker at early-morning gallops. He said the only other spy he detected was a bishop whose pink Leander cap clashed so violently with his purple bib that nobody in the enclosure could take their eyes off him. This chromatic disturbance fascinated Kipling. Greatly impressed with the influx of rowing clergy, he was convinced that a superb and stately crew composed entirely of bishops and deans, who were members of Leander, could be put on the river for a five-hundred-yard display.

After ten days at Henley, the Regatta opened with Balliol in fairly good shape. Hugh had made a couple of experiments at six and five but we went to the first heat against the Royal Military College with the same order we had started with - that is, with Hookey Walker at seven instead of Hugh Cairns. We made a good start and at the end of ten strokes had a third of a length lead. We were never pressed and rowed through in eight minutes at about thirty-six strokes a minute. R.M.C. had an electric bell which their cox sounded for a spurt instead of the usual "Give her ten!" This was unexpected and extremely helpful to us. It was a good race and we won by nearly a length.

In the draw for heats, we had been told the bad news. We were to row against Eton on Thursday. Although Eton was a public school, its crew was almost always better than the average college. This year was no exception. We faced an eight that had been superbly trained and was a good five pounds per man heavier than we were. Mr. Kipling had timed them over a trial course at 7'47", exactly their time in the heat against us. They won by a length. It was a galling defeat. We were rowed out. I couldn't breathe and held my head down between my knees. As we drifted under Henley Bridge, I remember a kindly Cockney voice calling, "Good old three — don't worry, you'll live!"

We paddled back to the boathouse and carried *Lady Dervorguilla* to her rack. Hugh Cairns and Mr. Kipling appeared. They had watched the race from the umpire's launch and looked far from dejected.

"You rowed well, the best form you've showed," Hugh told us. "Now take it easy and about half-past seven tonight I'm going to put you over the course again, against the clock."

We relaxed until about seven o'clock that night, then we took the shining shell out and paddled up to Temple Island. There we did some starts and short bursts of rowing. One of the substitutes got in the starting punt and steadied us for a start. Hugh called from the bank: "I'll start you with a gun . . . COME FORWARD . . . ARE YOU READY? . . . THE SHOT!" We were off. Arengo Jones, our stroke, set us about forty the first minute and then he settled down to what seemed about thirty-five. Something astonishing had happened. The boat was moving forward without our effort. As we came forward, she seemed to slide ahead of us. It was an extraordinary sensation of smooth movement. I felt I was slacking but I dared not press for we were, for the first time, completely together in a rhythmic cycle. Arengo was giving us great length and maintaining the rate of stroke. From the bank, Hugh Cairns on his bike shouted, "Oh, well rowed, Balliol!"

We were passing the 1500-yard post. I could hardly believe we had come that far. Kimber, the cox, cried, "Give her ten, Balliol!" and counted us through, Jones bringing us up to forty. We were nearly at Phyllis Court now. We could hear an orchestra playing. It was so easy. Good Lord, there's the enclosure on the Bucks side. Again Kimber shouted, "Now row her in, Balliol, give her ten!" Ten good long ones we gave her, and it was over. "Easy all, Balliol!"

From the bank by the Leander enclosure, now empty in the dusk, came Hugh's delighted words, "Well rowed, Balliol, oh, well rowed!" Mr. Kipling was shouting the time, but we couldn't hear him. We paddled back to the boathouse and, as we lifted the *Lady Dervorguilla* over our heads and placed her on the rack, Hugh, Mr. Kipling and the substitutes came into the boathouse. We heard the good news that our time had been 7'10" — three seconds better than Eton's in the morning. It was the best row I ever had, practically in the dark, racing against the clock, with no one to see us except Hugh Cairns and Rudyard Kipling.

28

I spent the long vac of 1920 in Cornwall with an old school friend, Crawford Grier. His uncle was a doctor in the little village of Mevagissey, and we were his paying guests. The doctor, among his many activities, ran a fishing boat which he took out twice a week for mackerel. Crawford and I, determined to study, had brought the best of intentions and a ton of books with us. But the good doctor saw in us two healthy recruits for his understrength fishing crew.

We joined the first expedition with enthusiasm. The edge went off our keenness when we experienced the back-breaking work involved. Required at the dock at 3:00 A.M., we were returned to the moorings as late as five in the afternoon. When we had any luck, which was extremely variable, each of us made as much as five or six pounds.

I don't know how Dr. Grier managed his practice, because he came along as skipper on every occasion. His method of fishing was purse-seining. The seine net was over three hundred yards long and twenty deep, with floats on the top edge and heavy brass rings on the bottom through which the purse lines passed. When a school of mackerel was sighted, the big powerboat with the net made off and circled the fish, the net being secured to a small boat called the "vollyer," or follower. Our duty in the vollyer was to row like hell in a direction opposite to the big powerboat so that the net was pulled off. Once the circle had been made around the suspected fish, we'd board the powerboat in a state of utter exhaustion and immediately help with hauling in the purse lines and then the net itself. Then, with no skin left on the palms of our hands, we'd scoop the slithering, stinking mackerel into the hold. The mackerel, I think, is the only fish which smells just as bad alive as dead.

This was a good day, but sometimes we'd make a blank cast. If it was too late to prepare the seine for another cast — and that took hours — we just went home with empty pockets. It may be asked why I repeated this dismal operation. Why will a man spend thousands of pounds for the privilege of standing up to his hips in cold water from dawn until sundown, trying to lure a fish who steadily refuses to be conned by futile antics? At least Dr. Grier offered us the chance of some financial gain.

Back at Oxford, I was in the thick of activity. The number of clubs, societies and organized groups within the university was prodigious. The colleges themselves are virtually clubs, their senior and junior common rooms being operated in the manner of social clubs. The most exclusive club in the world, excepting the Order of the Garter, is the graduate College of All Souls. It is the wealthiest and possesses a cellar of fabulous quality. The port served on gaudy nights and special occasions is famous. It is sipped and revered in a special room to which the fellows and guests retire after dinner in the hall. On one occasion, my brother told me, a cobwebbed bottle of the precious vintage was placed before an aged Warden of the college who reverently and gently filled his glass and passed the bottle to his neighbour. As he gazed at his glass, he admonished his guests in tones of dismay, "Gentlemen, pray desist . . . I think, I am not sure, but I think I saw a bubble!"

I belonged to the Raleigh Club, a collection of imperialists whose interests may be indicated by the toasts at the annual dinner in 1920 — "The Empire of the Bretanes," "The Dominions," "India," "The Crown Colonies"; and by the speakers, who included Lord Milner, Lord Meston and my brother Vincent, who had been president in 1913. I remember there was some laughter at the "Bill of Fare." It had a distinct British ring to it; among other courses, "cutlets of yonge lamb with little peas," "a capon roasted with a choice of legumes and grene sallads" and "frozen fruits of rosy hue." Nobody could understand why, after Wolfe had defeated Montcalm on the Plains of Abraham, we should not have the choice of "2 veg." instead of "legumes." After all, we did eat "little peas" with the lamb and not "petit pois"! All this was only sixty years ago, but there was not a sign of Tanzania, Volta, Ghana, Zambia or any of the newborn states that have replaced the Crown Colonies. The Empire was still a reality. South Africa was a staunch and loyal Dominion, of which Lord Milner had been the architect. Only over India was there a cloud in the sky and it was a little bigger than a loincloth. The war seemed to have made the Empire more solid than ever, at least so it seemed to me after every meeting of the Raleigh Club.

The Brakenbury Society was an old and informal institution. It met periodically for discussion of some timely subject, often with a distinguished visitor. The club had about thirty members, most of whom attended meetings in the old Senior Common Room. At one meeting, T. E. Lawrence came to us. It was a disturbing occasion. I am always ill at ease in the presence of cold intellect. Sheer brain frightens me. Lawrence was bitter and brilliant. He had been allowed to make commitments and promises to the Arabs which were not kept by the British. But the sad fact is that in 1920, he foresaw exactly what is now happening in the Middle East. I have never forgotten that evening with an extraordinary man. We had the privilege of meeting other great men at "Braker" meetings: Lord Asquith, a Balliol prime minister, was one of them, but there was never another like Lawrence.

As I joined every club, society, group or faction that would have me, except the Communist Party, I soon found myself a member of the Union. This was the university debating society. Its sessions were modelled closely on those of the House of Commons; and for more than a century, future statesmen, prime ministers and members had learned the ways of the House by debating motions, grave and frivolous, in the Union. The four principal speakers wore white tie and tails, as did the Speaker. A sergeant-at-arms was in attendance and sometimes he was not only ceremonial but necessary.

Following the tradition of Westminster, all speeches were extemporaneous, even notes being unfavourably regarded.

Those were still the days of rhetoric and eloquence in public life: before the prepared statement and the speech-writer appeared, before the idiot cards and the teleprompter. I was used to hearing fluent speech. My uncle John, the Methodist bishop, had spoken with great coherence and vigour whenever the occasion demanded. His son, my cousin George Vincent, was the most articulate and rapid public speaker I have ever heard. His command of words and his diction were incomparable. When I hear the inevitable, "Well . . . " preface every utterance of an ad-lib interview these days, when "I mean . . . " and "In other words . . . " are refuges of the incoherent, I think of my uncle and his son.

The young men who spoke at the Union were worthy followers of Gladstone and Asquith. I remember Anthony Eden, who made quite a reputation for himself as a speaker in 1920 and 1921. It was my misfortune to speak against a motion that had just received Eden's eloquent support. My friend from Balliol, the future writer Beverly Nichols, was in the chair as Speaker. As he "recognized" me, there was a look of kindly pity on his face. With something approaching horror, I remember those minutes I stood in a crowded Union and tried to take Eden apart. The funny thing is, I haven't the foggiest recollection of what we were talking about. I spoke again several times but only after careful preparation; my attendance at the Union was primarily to hear my fellow members perform.

It is probably unfair to judge the Oxford University Dramatic Society by its activities in 1919-1920. The OUDS, in abeyance since 1914, had started up again after the war with an entirely new membership. I joined as soon as I could, and this was not so easy as it might have been. The society, which occupied some rather austere rooms in George Street, was run in the manner of a social club. Naturally I knew none of the members to propose and second me. The president, Maurice Colbourne, decided to waive such formalities in view of my obvious enthusiasm for the theatre. He exercised his presidential authority to make me a member forthwith. Other than myself, I think, he was the only member of the OUDS of that year of its revival who became a professional actor. He certainly was one of the few who gave performances of professional competence in the Society's first production.

The OUDS had given a number of noted actors their initial experience; but at the time of which I write, only two were active in the theatre — Arthur Bourchier and Sir Frank Benson. Benson had for many years been actor-manager of a first-rate Shakespearean repertory company and I believe he owed much to his Oxford days, though not particularly to the OUDS. His performance had an athletic, "undergraduate" vigour and for many years his touring company could field a respectable rugger or cricket team. He once wired a London agent to send him a good halfback who could play Laertes and Hotspur. He had learned the Oxford lesson of exercise — and who is better qualified to play Laertes than a good running half?

The program of the OUDS had never been ambitious: a few casual visits to the society's rooms by critics, managers, writers or actors, evenings of questions and mulled claret; the annual production in the Hilary term. I remember only Harley Granville-Barker coming for an evening's session, a great experience for me. It was my first encounter with a great professional theatre man. He was a Renaissance character — the actor, producer and playwright combined. As a playwright, he could write any kind of play from a farcical comedy like *Rococo* to *The Madras House*. As an actor, he couldn't help writing good dialogue.

It always puzzled me that Granville-Barker undertook the job of adapting or rather editing Thomas Hardy's *The Dynasts*. This epic poem about the Napoleonic Wars was written in dialogue and published in three sections in successive years beginning in 1906. Of incredible length, when it finally reached the public, the literary critics delivered paeans of adulation. Barker undertook to edit it down to stage dimensions. I never read the full-length version. I never will — but Barker's abbreviation remained, as I am sure the original omnibus was, as lifeless as Madame Tussaud's waxworks.

We played it at the New Theatre. John Drinkwater directed the

245

production and about forty young gentlemen of the OUDS had speaking parts. I doubt if the best professional cast in the world could have handled Hardy's leaden verse. And we were amateurs. I played Caulaincourt in a brief scene of Napoleon's abdication before exile to Elba. I still remember my one speech. You don't forget a decisive defeat. I don't remember who played Napoleon. I had my own problem. It was deeply personal and I faced it in the best amateur tradition, without regard for my fellow performers. Eight times I spoke those deathless lines in front of an audience:

"We should have had success. But fate said no.
And abdication, making no reserves,
Is, sire, we are convinced, with all respect,
The only road."

This sample of Hardy's verse was about the level of much of the rest of the play. I also played a dragoon, a very fortunate one, who had no lines, at the headquarters of Sir John Moore at Coruña. The heroic general was performed by Charles Morgan, later the dramatic critic of the *Times* in London. As a discerning critic, he forbade "Morgan the actor" ever to perform again.

Alone of the company, Maurice Colbourne brought his character to life. As Nelson, he was extraordinarily good. He was also the moving force behind the revival of the OUDS.

The choice of play was unfortunate. The war of a hundred years ago was not the most intriguing theatre fare for people who had lived through 1914-1918. The next year, the OUDS returned to the traditional Shakespearean production with a professional star in the leading feminine role. *The Dynasts* had been cast from the vast number of dons' daughters available for women's parts. In 1921, the committee selected *Anthony and Cleopatra*, with the beautiful Cathleen Nesbitt as Cleopatra. Cathleen afterwards married Cecil Ramage, who played Anthony; and at the age of eighty-six, she is one of the loveliest, most talented and active ladies on the stage.

I dropped out of the OUDS during my second year and, with a college friend, Guy Vaughan-Morgan, organized a small play-reading club of fifteen members, mostly from Balliol. We met about every fortnight to read a play. We had about ten readings — plays by Ibsen, Galsworthy, Granville-Barker, Shakespeare, the usual selection of the eager and stage-struck. The "performances" were sometimes quite effective in what was soon to become a radio technique. One thing is certain: we got more out of our nameless little group than the OUDS ever offered.

London was only an hour and a half away by train and matinees were possible without applying for leave. A night away from college was a different matter. All colleges were stern about such leaves. James Morris' excellent book, *Oxford,* tells of an undergraduate applying for an absence to attend the funeral of his uncle. The reply of the dean of the college was, "Oh, very well . . . but I wish it could have been a nearer relative."

Sometimes I am inclined to ridicule the caricatures of Victorian male attire which many of the young and would-be young of today have adopted, particularly for evening wear. Such travesties of former styles are termed Edwardian, although they are really derived from the mauve decade. But I curb my taunts when I think of my own garb when I went down to London for a day or an evening in '20 and '21. I had two suits, both pin-striped, a dark grey and a brown. White spats or a pair of grey-topped, black-buttoned boots always called for an agonizing decision. Light-coloured waistcoats and broad, striped club ties were in order, and good loud shirts. The ensemble was not in the least conspicuous at that time, nor did it lead my fellow passengers in the third-class carriage to expect that I would shortly produce a deck of cards. But it did raise the eyebrows of my friend Katharine Cornell when I called on her in her dressing room after a matinee of *Little Women,* at the New Theatre. She had just scored a great success in London playing the part of Meg. She was utterly delightful in the play. Kit went to tea with me even after she had noticed my bowler hat and a borrowed Malacca cane with a gold knob. Years later, when I played Ridgeon with Kit as Jennifer in *The Doctor's Dilemma,* she suggested I wear the grey-topped buttoned boots. Alas, they were no more, but it seems they had made an impression.

Like a great many undergraduates, I was soon caught in the web of credit. Booksellers, shirtmakers, bootmakers, tailors, even the college stores, flaunted credit at you. In my first term, a Mr. Stratton called at my rooms with a bag of cloth samples, a measuring tape and an agreeable personality. I ordered a suit of clothes from his firm, Messrs. Lesley and Roberts of 16 George Street, Hanover Square. I was to have a fitting when I could come to London. The suit was to cost £8-8-0 as a trial and the subsequent charge would be £10-10-0. I thought this fairly steep but the suit worked out very nicely. The cutter, Mr. Robinson, was excellent. I thought so then and I've thought so ever since. In 1970, he cut a suit for me as Tom Garrison in *I Never Sang For My Father,* which I played at the Duke of York's. Old Tom was eighty years old in the play and Robbie was persuaded by me to cut the suit loose. It nearly broke his heart. At eighty-five, Robbie was still working hard and was fit as a fiddle. He hadn't changed a bit since 1920 but the price of the suit had.

As the Michaelmas term of 1920 progressed, I continued to live Oxford life to the full. It was a life crowded with meetings of clubs, societies and groups, of luncheons and dinners, and through it all endless talk. I had ears as well as a tongue. This life was worthwhile and I enjoyed it.

I could not escape the spectre of the "Schools" that lay ahead, now only a few months away. My work was far behind schedule. The vacations had not produced the required solid reading that I had planned. Not that I wasn't up to the job. My misgivings that I was not up to Balliol standards were just self-pitying hypocrisy. I had done well at school in Canada. I had a fair mind and anyway the examinations were held by the university and not the college. The truth was I lacked the self-discipline that the Oxford system demands. At preparatory school, work had been constantly scrutinized, tested and disciplined. I thrived on that method. But without the whip crack, I lay back on the traces. It's a sad admission.

About mid-November, I submitted to Kenneth Bell a "collection," which was an informal examination on the basis of Schools paper. By informal, I mean that it was written in my own room without the stress and strain of regular examinations. These were held in an awesome hall called the Examination Schools and candidates were required to wear a dark suit and a white dress-tie. The

Schools also included an oral examination, or *viva voce* questioning. It took the courage of F. E. Smith, later the Earl of Birkenhead, to put the *viva* in its proper place. When gently admonished for his obvious lack of preparation on a certain subject, F. E. answered, "I am here to be examined, not to receive unsolicited advice." Alas, there are few F. E. Smiths, and I was not one of them.

My "collection" was handed back to me by Kenneth, with the following notation in red ink: "One good and interesting answer on the Elizabethan drama; an unfinished answer on Elizabethan archbishops, and that is all! It is most important that you revise a term's work and force yourself by an act of will to write in an examination. I'm sure in your case it is the will which defeats you."

I spent an evening of contrition, resolution and Scotch with Kenneth, ending in our singing a few "Gordooleys," my tossing flowerpots into Trinity, and Kenneth donning his gown and gating me for a week. His parting admonition had been: "It's our purpose here to make you think rather than know, but please remember that in order to think, it is necessary to know!"

My pursuit of knowledge in the long vac had been somewhat impeded by the pursuit of a young lady in Cornwall, to say nothing of the fishing, and this quest seemed at the time to have ended in failure. My mention of it in a letter to my father brought a typical reply: "I sincerely hope that as the days go by you are steadily wearing off the trouble which you have experienced. If taken rightly, it will work to your good. I was just thinking of your cousin, George Vincent, who was engaged to Mina Miller and she dropped him for Thomas A. Edison — that was a sorrow far worse than yours . . . "

His letter brought bad news of my stepmother, whose health had been poor for some time. Though he was vague about her condition, he said they were leaving for Pasadena which was then considered a health resort, "on the advice of physicians."

I made arrangements to leave for California at the end of the term. In 1920, the trip involved eleven days by ship and trains. My plans for concentrated reading during the vac went out the porthole of a second-class cabin of the *R.M.S. Aquitania*.

I found my stepmother very ill and my father desperately worried. Her condition was breast cancer, which in those days was terminal. After five days, I felt callous leaving them, and I never saw my stepmother again.

In the Hilary term of '21, much of that Oxford life I had been so strongly urged to follow by my brother was dropped. I "sported my oak" most evenings; that is, bolted the heavy oak door of my room and did my damnedest to catch up with the reading I had neglected. I did row in the Balliol four but that was exercise and had to be done. We got through two heats but lost to Merton. There were two or three London trips that neither helped my work nor my bank account. Having a chaperon was still the custom for a theatre or dinner dance. That meant the cost of a foursome, no small burden for an undergraduate with a bank book frequently incarnadined. But after some hard work in the Easter vac, admittedly in London, I made progress in my studies.

At the beginning of the Trinity term, five weeks before my Schools in June, I felt fairly confident. Kenneth Bell wasn't quite so sanguine. He still thought I should have a dry run at Schools and wait another term for a real try. I assured him I no longer had the jitters. It was my unfortunate sense of immediacy, I suppose. Everything looked fair for a degree in June, a low degree perhaps but an Oxford degree. True, I was rowing in the college eight again, but that was a wise precaution against Oxford torpor, and anyway, my tutor was coaching us.

There came a day about a month before the Schools when I found myself walking up and down the quad with A. L. Smith, the Master. He was patient and kind. There were questions about my work, how it was progressing and what I felt to be my chances in the Schools.

After about half an hour of traversing the quad under the scrutiny of the whole college, the little man paused and said quietly, "Perhaps it would be best for you and best for the college if you were to go down without facing the examiners."

"Master," I asked, "am I being sent down?"

"No . . . no . . . that decision I leave to you."

Then and there, I made the decision.

"What about rowing in the eight, Master?"

The man who had rowed at bow in the Head of the River Eight in 1872 answered, "You may continue to row in the eight."

As I look back to my Oxford days, my regret that I decided to leave Balliol increases. I had a good but lazy mind. I had frittered away my two years, mistaking information for knowledge and failing to exercise the self-discipline without which Oxford is a waste of time. The Master was a wise old man, and knew that only I could make the decision.

29

By inclination, I am a pessimist. I have never been given to long-range planning nor have I indulged in setting goals or ambitions. I think I have steered clear of conscious aspirations to avoid disappointment or defeat. The negative approach is to me preferable to a positive one. When you say, "You wouldn't have a match, would you?" you are prepared for a negative answer. A direct appeal for a light invites a rebuff. By the same token, I have always thought it best not to mess about with the future and, if possible, leave it to look after itself. I don't say that this is wise, in truth it is just folly, but it took me many years to learn otherwise.

I had decided to return to Toronto but had given no serious thought as to what I was going to do. There had been a vague understanding with my father, that I would go into the family business, but for how long and in what capacity I had no idea. I still wanted to be an actor but it was a remote dream which I hadn't spoken of to a soul, and now it seemed light years ahead. The sober truth was that I had married a London girl, Margery Fremantle, whom I had met in Cornwall the previous summer. She was an art student at the Slade School and a member of an old naval family, and she had never given a thought to living anywhere but London.

My homecoming in 1921 was not a happy one. My stepmother, whom I had last seen at Christmas in Pasadena, had died in the spring and I found my father a bewildered and lonely man. He had aged very much and was in poor health, with a doctor in constant attendance. Father's new secretary, Mr. Burns, was running 519. He was an agreeable fellow but without the ability to manage the household. Fortunately, Mr. Seldon was still there to supervise.

Father expressed his relief that I was home and his desire that I start work at the Massey-Harris Company as soon as possible. It was not from father but from Mr. Seldon that I learned the more ominous facts about the immediate future.

"Your father's got a prostate condition. He'll have to have an operation but he doesn't like surgeons — he lost your mother and your stepmother under surgery. It's going to be up to you to persuade him. It's a new operation they do at Johns Hopkins and I think quite risky."

When I suggested that my brother help in the matter, Mr. Seldon said, "No, you'll have to do it yourself. Vincent's done all he can. He's away in the country for the summer. You must start in at the factory right away. Your father's got his heart set on that. To have you working with the company will do him more good than the surgeons."

Mr. Seldon told me the company was having a difficult time. It had just finished its worst year yet and was laying off many workers. Father's small salary as honorary president had been cut off.

"I've found a small house for you and your wife in Rosedale, just across the ravine from mine," Mr. Seldon told me. "519 is no place for you. Your house is furnished with Aunt Lillie's things . . . although Mrs. Vincent got the best stuff."

My wife hated Toronto with a passion. She rarely left the little house furnished with the second-best from Euclid Hall. The company received me with what might be described as arms akimbo.

The days when grandfather and my uncles knew most of the men by name had long since gone and Old Hart, stalking through the factory in his shirt-sleeves, wasn't even a memory to most of the hundreds who worked in the Toronto plant. My father had retired in 1917 and my brother had left the office of secretary a few weeks before.

I walked into the head office to find a male receptionist sitting at a desk behind a bronze bust of grandfather bathed in the sunlight filtered through a stained-glass memorial window to my Uncle Charles. These were the only vestiges of the Masseys.

A hasty interview with the general manager, Thomas Bradshaw, established my salary at $25.00 a week. I was then turned over to the superintendent of the Toronto works. He promptly informed me that due to the difficulties the company was now facing, my $25.00 would be cut by $2.50, so that my weekly haul would be $22.50. This gentleman then said that I had better spend some time learning the business.

"I'm going to put you at setting piece rates," he grinned. "That will show you everything!"

I had had a little experience with piecework when I was working on the shells in 1916. I remembered how I had hated the rate setter. Piecework involved pay by the job or amount of work done rather than time employed, and it was loathed by most of the men.

There must have been nearly forty different farm machines produced at the Toronto works and each of them entailed at least a hundred distinct piece jobs. That meant more than four thousand piece rates to keep up to date. The jobs always seemed to be rated downwards; the carrot moved a little farther away from the donkey. The setters were mostly white-collar men resented by the factory hands.

A young man I had known for a long time was in charge of the department. His name was Alfred Walker. He was a son of Sir Edmund Walker, my father's friend, a prominent banker and director of the company. Alfred was a scrupulous man. He had stopped the practice of sneaking times for piece jobs — that is, timing the job when the man didn't know it was being done. We had to let a man know when his piece rate for any operation was being set.

Some of the jobs, particularly in the foundry, were difficult to judge on a time basis. I was setting a rate on making moulds for a seed-drill part which had a difficult die problem. On the average it took about a minute and a half a mould; but during the hour I watched, this expert broke three moulds. "This shouldn't be piece jobs," he said. "How can you average out the duds which are nobody's fault?'' I didn't even put a timing in. Alfred took the whole moulding shop off piecework. Also, I got myself booted out of the piece-rate setting. I had proved too generous.

The factory hours were a little easier than in my munition-making days in 1916. We now had Saturday afternoons off. Even so, it was a 52-hour week. The whistle blew at 7:30 A.M. and the shafts and pulleys started to turn. They came to a halt when another whistle blew at 5:30 P.M. After September, it was dark when both whistles blew. There were no unions in 1921 and the paternalistic benefits of Old Hart's day had vanished. Working conditions at the Massey-Harris Company were probably no worse than other companies, but a 52-hour week was a miserable grind however one looked at it. The days seemed interminable. It was the crushing monotony which made it so unbearable.

Relief came for me when least expected. Father and Vincent, both executors of the residual portion of my grandfather's estate, had some years earlier embarked on a project of building a students' centre for the University of Toronto. This was to be named Hart House after my grandfather. When it was presented to the university in 1919, it was to house all manner of student activities outside the academic curriculum — from a great dining hall, gymnasium, swimming pool, common rooms, library, music rooms, to a theatre. The theatre was an afterthought as the architects puzzled over an unused area beneath a large quadrangle. Vincent had seized on the idea, and father readily agreed. The old stage-struck Puritan was finally convinced. How mother would have laughed! Instead of becoming a theatre-goer, he presided over the building or, rather, the digging of a theatre. The Hart House theatre was underground, the only one I know with a lawn on its roof.

When I returned to Toronto, I was eager to know how the project had worked out. Hart House had then been open for a year. I had expected that some student organization, similar to the OUDS, would have come into being to take advantage of a real theatre building. My brother told me that Hart House had been enjoyed to the fullest by the undergraduates of the university; but he was noncommital about the theatre.

255

I gathered that the theatre had been like an infant on the university doorstep, put up for adoption. The foster parents' roles had been assumed by Vincent and his wife, who headed a committee made up of faculty members and citizens, but no undergraduates. This body enjoyed the archaic title of "The Syndics," without realizing that the up-to-date connotation of the word was censor. They were trying to run a theatre by committee.

Though I did not realize it then, theatre can only work under autocratic control. There must be one individual in complete power.

The Hart House Theatre Committee had appointed a professional director the previous year, a Toronto-born New Yorker, Roy Mitchell. It had not been an ambitious season. One of the productions had been *The Chester Mysteries*, which father had seen and thought highly of. He considered Mitchell's production the work of a genuinely religious man. But Roy was also a theosophist, not quite what father had in mind.

After his first year of theatre in Toronto, Roy Mitchell gave up. Before he returned to New York, he confided to me that his troubles had been less severe than Job's, but not much. He had anticipated running a university theatre with undergraduate talent and the support of the academic community; instead, he found the students apathetic and the theatre regarded as a "town" project in which the "gown" would have little part.

It is a perplexing fact that while Toronto — and the rest of Canada for that matter — supported whatever professional theatre came its way, up to the 1920s Canadians had little interest in developing local theatre, amateur or professional. Canadian stage talent had to seek work in the States or England. It is astonishing how many Canadians managed to gain professional fame in those days before there was a Canadian stage. Margaret Anglin, the daughter of a speaker of the House of Commons in Ottawa, was the first of the great Canadian-born stars. Many others followed. Mary Pickford, Walter Huston, Marie Dressler, Beatrice Lillie come to mind. But they didn't even get a start in Canada. In 1921 the grass was only trying to grow up through the concrete.

256

In the 1930s, amateur theatre began to flourish under the encouragement of the competitions initiated by Lord Bessborough, as Governor-General. But it wasn't until after the Second World War that an indigenous professional theatre came alive.

Roy Mitchell's successor as director of Hart House Theatre was an Englishman named Bertram Forsyth, a handsome actor with a diffident disposition, who arrived in August with a charming French wife and a small daughter. He had worked with Nigel Playfair since the war, having acted in Drinkwater's *Abraham Lincoln* and St. John Ervine's *John Ferguson* at the Lyric Theatre, Hammersmith. He had also worked on the production of Playfair's revival of *The Beggar's Opera*, then in the midst of its triumphant run of nearly four years. In addition to being a fine actor, Bertram was an accomplished scholar in the Elizabethan, Restoration and Regency drama. He also knew Ibsen and Shaw thoroughly. He seemed ideal for the job. His modesty and tact suited the committee, who might have feared a more intense and dynamic personality.

It was decided to open the season with Bernard Shaw's *Candida*, which in 1921 was just a shade on the daring side, chiefly because it was by Shaw. Bertram persuaded the committee to cast me as Marchbanks, which is every juvenile's dream part but not an easy one to act. In Shaw's lengthy description of Marchbanks, he is, among a host of characteristics, "effeminate with a delicate childish voice." It was not a temptation to me to "camp" Marchbanks and, with Bertram's excellent direction, I got by. It was a fairly good production. Bertram played Lexy Mill, the curate, and the cast of six were very good; and, most important in amateurs, they were eager.

In my job at the factory, I was now working in the experimental department on a new reaper-thresher, eventually called a combine. I liked working with tools and was pretty good at it. Two mechanical engineers, fellows with college degrees, were working on this huge contraption. It looked about as unwieldy as the thresher great-grandfather Daniel had brought to Canada from Watertown in 1830.

We were sometimes joined by an old gentleman named Charlie

McLeod, a legendary figure in the company. He was known as the "Prince of Salesmen," not only because he was good at his job but because he closely resembled the Emperor Napoleon III. Charlie McLeod had joined the old Massey Manufacturing Company while it was still in Newcastle in the late 1870s and had worked with Old Hart and my uncle and father. He was, as he called himself, "a Massey man." Not only a salesman, Charlie was a field man and a phenomenal mechanic. He had worked all over the world — in Europe, Russia, Australia — and contributed considerably to the development of the combine assembly at Massey-Harris.

Charlie McLeod awakened my pride and interest "in the business," which was then nearly eighty years old. He convinced me that the spirit of the old firm was still alive.

After my day at the factory, I would go straight to the theatre, grabbing some food on the way; and I would rehearse until midnight. Saturday afternoons and Sundays were reserved for really hard work. I hoped father wouldn't hear about this infraction of the Fourth Commandment.

For five weeks, it was a rugged timetable — 6:30 A.M. to 1:30 A.M., leaving me about five hours sleep a night, with luck.

Candida opened for a week's run, with the drama critics present. They dealt with us graciously, in the patronizing manner extended to amateurs. In truth, we weren't too bad. Bertram Forsyth gave a comic performance of the curate, Lexy Mill. I myself learned a very important lesson in playing Marchbanks, which I have never forgotten in my professional life of over fifty years — that is, never to rely on my own emotions in front of an audience. It was Bertram who taught me this.

Marchbanks, as Bernard Shaw conceived him, is a highly sensitive, emotional character; and playing the role gave me my first real acting opportunity. It was easy to go overboard in the poetic extravagances of the part. At a rehearsal a few days before we opened, in the final scene with Candida I could not hold back my tears, and I was utterly worn out when we finished. "That's very good," Bertram said. "Remember how you played it and look at it

258

next time from the outside. You cry at rehearsals, but let the audience do the crying at performances."

That sense of control took years as a professional to achieve.

Many actors and directors, notably of the continental theatre, disagree profoundly with this objective theory of acting. Stanislavsky, the Russian director, declared: "It is proved now that an actor cannot move the audience, or be in any way creative on the stage, if he watches himself acting." It must be remembered that in most non-English-speaking theatre, the actor is working under a repertory system, not concerned with keeping a performance of the same role fresh and spontaneous for protracted runs as we do on the English and American stage. Yet even in our own theatre, there are actors who insist that the only way to move an audience is for the player to be "inside" the character he is depicting, to involve himself emotionally in his performance. My own opinion is that such actors are either deceiving themselves or are frankly hypocritical if they claim they can sustain an effective performance for hundreds and thousands of times with this emotional identification.

I remember going to see a play in Hollywood some years ago with Humphrey Bogart. The play was a fine one which had run for a season on Broadway and was now on tour with its male star whom I shall call Bill. After the final curtain, Bogie and I hurried round to the stage door to see Bill, who had given a superb performance. Bogie knocked on the door of the dressing room. There was no answer. He knocked again. Silence. Bogie opened the door and there was Bill at his dressing table, his head bowed and his fists clenched.

"Bill," said Bogie. Silence. "Bill . . . Bill . . . "

Not a word. We retreated.

About a block away from the theatre, I broke the silence. "That was a great performance."

"Yes," Bogie murmured. "I think his finest moment was in the dressing room."

Marchbanks is an acting plum any young actor would love to pick; and as *Candida* is a perpetually popular play, most young

259

actors have played him — from Harley Granville-Barker, the original Marchbanks, to Marlon Brando. The part can be cast in many different ways. Yet all the time I was working on Marchbanks, I was hankering to act Morell, Candida's clergyman husband. I wanted to be able to tell Marchbanks what Morell and I thought of him and his poetry and his sensitivity. That's how unprofessional I can be. I had to wait twenty-one years for my dream, and the Marchbanks I took on was played by Burgess Meredith, who made the fragile poet very convincing. In fact, Buzz gave the best performance of the part I ever saw. This revival was made memorable also by the Candida of Katharine Cornell, who was born to act Shaw heroines.

At Hart House, the third production of Bertram Forsyth's season (I wasn't in the second) opened in early January. It was what might be described as a Masque of the Regency Theatre, written by Bertram himself. It had wit and charm — a play within a play, telling of a visit of the Prince Regent to a gala performance at Drury Lane Theatre. *The Masque* was reminiscent of *The Critic* and Sheridan, as manager of Drury Lane, was a principal character, played by Forsyth.

The cast was very large, even with a lot of doubling, and the number of both sexes who were able and willing to act was limited. Forsyth had to settle for quite a few who were just willing. I was in some short scenes only and played a part based on a real-life eccentric of Regency times known as "Romeo" Coates. This character was a wealthy, stage-struck young man with an overweening ambition to play Romeo on the professional stage. Completely devoid of talent, he engaged a company, booked a theatre and appeared in the part. He was so inept that his efforts were riotously successful. He became a short-lived vogue, attacking several of Shakespeare's tragedies to guffawing, capacity audiences before he sank back into oblivion. In Bertram's play, there were two scenes from Coates' *Romeo and Juliet*, which for me were a return to the slapstick of Siberia.

When Coates was brought to the Royal Box after his exhibition, and the Prince Regent mockingly commended his performance, inviting him to supper at Carlton House, Coates replied,

260

"Your Royal Highness will please forgive me when I decline your gracious invitation. I am much fatigued by my performing."

Whether it was my fault or not, Coates as I played him became pitiable rather than comic. I got plenty of laughs but I knew the audience was sorry for the buffoon I was acting.

Bertram's production of *The Masque* was well received and pleasing to the eye. Still, it was thin theatrical fare; and even if it had been acted by a professional cast and given style and period flavour, I doubt that it would have succeeded.

30

When father's state of health deteriorated to a point where surgery was imperative, I accompanied him to the Johns Hopkins Hospital in Baltimore where the famous Dr. Hugh Young was performing his new method of prostatectomy. I quickly learned about the financial methods of big medicine. Before the great man operated, I was questioned about my father's financial status, his annual income and assets. When I said I did not know about these matters, I was told that the fee for Dr. Young's operation was twenty-five percent of the patient's current annual income. That, I observed, would be an inadequate reward for Dr. Young's skill since my father had practically no income for the current year. The Massey-Harris Company, due to the slump in the farm-implement business, had passed up three dividends, and practically all father's assets were with the company.

An ugly scene followed, which resulted in a handsome flat fee being grudgingly accepted by the hospital. Vincent arrived the next day, much relieved that he would not be faced with so sordid a matter as money.

He and I had a few words with Dr. Young before the operation. I asked for his prognosis on father. "My record is one hundred percent successful — it is very important to me!" was the surgeon's reply.

The operation was successful. Father came back to Toronto better than I had seen him for a long time.

I was transferred to the sales department of the company. I also played Rosmer in Ibsen's *Rosmersholm* at the Hart House Theatre. I can class this adventure as disaster.

In Ibsen's original text, there is said to be considerable humour and wit. William Archer, in his translation, carefully omitted such relief and in *Rosmersholm* I found myself lost in the long gloom of Norse introspection. I did not understand Rosmer. I tried to get outside the character, as I had planned always to do, and found nothing I could comprehend. I don't remember much about Rosmer except my makeup. I affected a white skunk-like streak in my hair.

Back at the works, in the sales department, I was put under the tutelage of old Charlie McLeod. As a salesman, he was a super pitchman and he found me a good shill. I was "a Massey," a great-grandson of Daniel, the founder of the firm, and as such he used me as an angle for his pitch.

Charlie was well in his eighties but his vigour was staggering. It was late spring and we were pushing cream separators at the time. I had thought the factory hours pretty rugged, but old Charlie began the day at 5:30 in the morning. We would be in an awful hotel in some small Ontario town and the first sales roundup would be at a farm, usually at least thirty miles out in the country. About twenty farmers would be gathered at 7 o'clock, having had their breakfast. Charlie would introduce me as "Old Hart's grandson, his middle name is Hart!" Then he would go into his pitch: "Now he's going to give you a Babcock test on the best cream separator in the field that's going to knock the Laval out of business!"

The Babcock test was a simple estimate of the butterfat content of the cream drawn off by the centrifugal force of the separator. In the tradition of the medicine show in the old carnivals, Charlie made this test into an elaborate test-tube, abracadabra routine that would leave the farmers bug eyed, even though they knew how to do it themselves every milking day.

Charlie coached me for a day and taught me his dialogue. It had some tongue-twisting double talk in it that I firmly believe

Charlie had made up himself. We would perform this ritual at least four times a day at different farms, sometimes to as many as thirty or forty farmers. We travelled around in a model-T Ford truck or a buckboard, depending on what we could hire. We ate most of our meals at the farms; the food would have gagged a buzzard. Apple pie and salt pork was a breakfast regular — and pork kept reappearing at dinner, along with apple pie.

I did my first Babcock test at seven o'clock on a cold, drizzly morning. Charlie had given me a buildup as virtual inventor of the test as well as of the separator; which I was busily assembling as he talked. He continued to extol my virtues as I processed a five-gallon can of milk, trying to remember my spiel for the test. The machine was hand cranked. I got through the routine all right, remembered my lines, and came to the clincher, the pay-off statement of the amount of butterfat in the cream. I couldn't remember whether the tube in my hand held the cream or the skim. In a false note of triumph, I croaked, "Now gentlemen, there's the butterfat result!"

Charlie saw my predicament and rescued me: "Did you ever see such a skim! That's a zero percent residual!"

I did not remain on the road very long. Before my digestion was seriously damaged by Canadian rural cuisine, I was taken away from field work and transferred to sales accounting. Here I was a lost soul, despising the paperwork. At night I was in the throes of rehearsing Rosmersholm. These were dark days, brightened only by my father's improved health. I realized that my attempt at following in my father's and my uncle's footsteps was a failure, but escape from the bondage of factory life seemed impossible.

At this low point, the theatre beckoned me again, a good, strong "come hither." There was a club in Toronto called the Arts and Letters, which drew writers, painters, journalists and various eccentrics. It was housed in a former livery stable just off Yonge Street. A clever architect had converted the carriage-house part into a huge room which could be changed quickly from the club quarters into a little theatre. All kinds of shows were put on but what I remember now was a production of two of Eugene O'Neill's sea plays. In the script *In the Zone*, I was asked to do the leading part of Smitty. It was my first taste of the new realistic theatre and, since Siberia, the first time I had worked with a cast who had vitality and enthusiasm. I was learning that theatre is not bricks and mortar and lights and scenery; but people who write, act and respond.

Not long after this, when I became a professional actor — that is, when I was paid for acting — my first job was in O'Neill's play *In the Zone*, but I didn't play Smitty.

The touring season of plays from Broadway was nearing its end. That year I had not seen many of the plays that had come to the Royal Alexandra, then the only remaining legitimate theatre in Toronto. I had been too busy with Hart House.

I bought seats for *The Circle*, Somerset Maugham's play that was booked at the Royal Alex with the Broadway cast. The great John Drew, Mrs. Leslie Carter, Ernest Lawford, Estelle Winwood and a fine cast were coming. I had seen the London production, which was superb, and the play was one of Maugham's best. I had never seen John Drew act. He was the great exponent of high comedy in America and, as the uncle of the three Barrymores, the head of the "royal family" of Broadway. Having been enthralled by Lionel and John Barrymore in *The Jest* and Ethel Barrymore in *Declassé*, I could hardly believe that the family had another member with equal talent.

John Drew's Lord Porteous was the equal of Allen Aynesworth's in London. I cannot give higher praise. The whole cast measured up to Mr. Drew. It is sad to think that high comedy has disappeared from English-speaking theatre. Except for revivals, the play of manners is no more; it has no place on the current stage, where it is at the moment crowded off by ash cans, garbage, grunts and growls. I believe, however, that the public increasingly misses the style, precision and grace which the players of that almost lost art of high comedy brought to the stage.

That night at the Royal Alex in Toronto, the genre was to be seen at its best. During the second act, I made a sudden but irrevocable decision. After the final curtain, I wandered around to the back of the theatre, where I asked the stage doorman to take my card in to Mr. Drew. I never for a moment thought he would see me. I was also amazed that I was alone at the stage door. In a few moments, the doorman returned with Mr. Drew's dresser, who guided me across the stage. Nothing can be more dismal than a stage a few minutes after the final curtain falls and the dim work light makes any scene a murky cavern. I thought of Prospero's lines: "Our revels now are ended. These our actors . . . were all spirits and are melted into air. . . . "

Suddenly I was in Mr. Drew's dressing room — a dingy closet of a room, badly in need of paint, which it still needed when I used it eleven years later on a pre-Broadway try-out of *The Shining Hour*. There was a shabby sofa (still there in my occupancy) and an open wardrobe trunk that filled the little room. Mr. Drew, in a tatty dressing gown, sat at his dazzlingly lit makeup table. He bade me sit down on the sofa and turned in his chair to face me. I stammered my appreciation of the play and dried up.

"I'm sure you didn't come just to tell me you liked the play," said Mr. Drew.

"No, sir," I plunged in. "I'm going to be a professional actor . . . and I'm bold enough to ask if you'd give me advice as to how I might accomplish that."

"Are you any good as an actor?"

"I think I could be, but I haven't done enough to know."

"If you don't know for a certainty, don't try it. You have to know you're good. What have you done?"

I must say, I didn't seem to add up to much. What impressed Mr. Drew most were the Bert Williams, Leon Errol and Fanny Brice routines I had done in the minstrel show.

"You know what acting means — or do you? . . . It's a bare stage lit by a work light a lot of the time. It's this kind of dressing room, for months and months. Hotels . . . trains. It's much worse here than in England. But if you really want to act, and you know you're good, there's nothing in the world that's better."

He turned to the makeup table, searching for something. I realized that his sight was bad. His dresser handed him a pot of grease.

"Don't try to start in New York. It's a cruel place for a young man who is unknown. It's not so bad for women but the competition is heartbreaking for men. Go to London. There is so much

266

theatre there, and with your Canadian accent, you can play American parts. You may have good fortune in England."

Two nights afterwards, I went to a party for Mr. Drew and Mrs. Carter and the company, and I had a chance to thank him again for his advice. He had no recollection of me.

I wasted no time in clearing my way for action. First of all, I wanted to be sure I had no future such as father hoped for with the Massey-Harris Company. I went to see the general sales manager, my boss at the time. Charles Wisner, a dapper little man with a grey moustache and pince-nez glasses, was most conveniently deaf. He had a habit of demanding that one repeat what one had said, in order to gain time or to cause embarrassment.

Wisner was sitting at his desk, in vest and shirt sleeves with elastic arm bands. Without looking up from his mass of papers, he grunted, "What can I do for you?"

I sat down on one of the straight-backed mahogany chairs that might have been designed by Torquemada.

"Mr. Wisner, I have now been with the company nearly a year and I'm earning exactly $22.50 a week. I'd like to know what I may look forward to earning in, say, five years' time."

"Repeat that."

I did.

"You can expect the cut in your pay to be restored next year. That will make it $25.00. As to five years ahead, that is guesswork and will depend on the nature of your work. I would hazard a guess that you might be getting $30.00 a week in five years."

"Mr. Wisner, that's less than I earned as a lieutenant in the army. I'm twenty-five, I've had a decent education and I've served nearly five years in the army. At times I've been in charge of hundreds of thousands of dollars worth of government property and the lives of a hundred and fifty men. I think I know enough about this company to be entrusted with responsibility and the salary that goes with it."

"Huh?" said Mr. Wisner, who was now looking at me.

"I think you heard me, Mr. Wisner."

"Now listen to me, young fellow. I don't care if you're Hart Massey's grandson or who you are. The fact remains that while you were in the army and fiddling away at Oxford, other men have been learning this business and they are going to have the responsible jobs and the pay raises. Before you!''

"I'm quitting, Mr. Wisner. Please say goodbye to all my friends for me. Except Charlie McLeod. I'll speak to him myself.''

Now I had to tell father. I went straight to 519. I was sure he would understand about my giving up on the company. He knew how things were and he knew that I had done my best. I was not so sure he would understand about my trying the theatre.

It was only eleven o'clock in the morning. I found father lying down on that torturous sofa in the library. I told him about my talk with Charles Wisner. As I had expected, he was in sympathy with my quitting the company. He just said, "By George, it's insufferable.''

Then I told father I was going to England to go on the professional stage. He lay on the couch in silence.

After about ten minutes, he got up and took my arm. He led me into a room called the gallery, where most of his pictures were. He closed the door; we sat down by the fireplace. It was quite a warm day but father asked me to light the fire.

There was another long silence. At last father said, "I think you are quite right to go to England and to go on the stage. I think you will be a very good actor. I think you will be able to serve God as well in the theatre as in the implement business which your great-grandfather founded.

"There is one promise I want you to make. That is that you will not act or practise on Sunday."

This was a tough situation. I knew, of course, that I could not and would not keep such a promise. All year I had rehearsed on Sundays. But I had to give that wonderful old man peace of mind. I crossed my fingers and promised.

Then he knelt on one knee, the way he did for family prayers, and made a prayer to God for my success and honesty as an actor. I shall not repeat it here, although it has remained clear in my memory. It was a sort of actors' Hippocratic oath. My father expressed an astonishing awareness of the actor's obligations and duties. He asked God to help His servant Raymond to avoid self-conceit, to appear in good plays and to abhor indecency in the theatre. To the best of my powers, I have tried to do just that.

Vincent came in shortly afterwards. Father told him of my severance from the company and my intention to adopt the stage as a profession. The old man seemed quite proud.

Vincent turned to me.

"What name are you going to use?"

I did use my own name, and had the sense to follow John Drew's advice. Taking five letters of introduction, my Canadian accent, and a determination which amazes me now, I presented myself to thirty-four stage doors in London's West End.

I met briefly thirty-four doormen and one stage-manager. My letters netted me one lunch at the Garrick Club, where I got a glimpse of the great Gerald du Maurier, who was later to have such an influence on my professional career. But not that day. My host did not know him and the longed-for introduction did not take place.

About then I discovered the grapevine of casting news, and my first experience of the generous, kindly folk of the theatre. Wandering around those stage doors and pubs in St. Martin's Lane, Charing Cross Road and Shaftesbury Avenue, I would hear leads to a job, and who was casting what — sometimes shamelessly overheard, sometimes proffered by actors who were complete strangers to me. One such offered tip paid off. After three weeks and one day I had my first job — they actually paid me to act — which meant I was finally a "pro."

It was at a little theater — the Everyman in Hampstead. There was no stage door so I tried to open one of the exit doors. Engaged in this seemingly nefarious operation, the door was violently pushed open from the inside. I was thrown on my back. Stunned and prostrate but everlastingly determined I started my routine — "I am a Canadian actor . . ." I got no further. The somebody who had opened the door disappeared. But five minutes later I was rehearsing the part of Jack, the Yankee seaman in O'Neill's In the Zone. *It seems that my predecessor in the part was suddenly ill and they were fresh out of Yankees. My accent did the job for me. A few years later my partners, Allan Wade and George Carr, and I took over the management of the Everyman. I have a great fondness for that theatre.*

The volume to follow this one is a particular joy to write. The widespread comment that "writing is a lonely job" has no validity for me. For me, it is a reliving of a long professional life, spent with kindly, generous and merry people, whose single aim was to "do it well together." This includes the behind-the-scenes workers to whose skill and good nature we visible folk owe much.

It is not strictly true that one cannot live one's life over again. Memory of struggles, defeats, personalities and off-stage happenings returns to supplement the cold print of the factual press books. I cringe again as I hear the gallery, displeased with us or me, "count me out" vociferously during the last act of Topaze *— having loudly applauded the first act. But also, again I trot breathlessly beside the striding George Bernard Shaw on his way to his prompt lunch, while he tries without sucess to duplicate my Canadian pronunciation of "ou" as in "about" and "house." Again, I can't take my eyes off Katharine Cornell's Boldini hat, as I sit across the desk as Sir Colenso Ridgeon in* The Doctor's Dilemma, *while she rescues me from an on-stage attack of sulfa amnesia when I can't even remember my name. Gertrude Lawrence's yellow ball gown enchants me again as did her pronouncement that "gin was mother's milk to h-h-er."*

Charles Laughton's giggle before the first performance of his edited version of Stephen Vincent Benét's John Brown's Body *still delights when he said to all of us, "Now I've ruined your careers — all of you — Judith Anderson, Tyrone Power and you old bastard Ray — yes and you and your music, too, Walter Schumann." Tyrone's solo battle of Gettysburg prickles my skin to this day. My struggle as director to persuade Charles Laughton to waltz in a wheel chair in* The Silver Tassie *exhausts me all over again. I won, and when Charles finally accomplished this difficult feat, it turned out to be his most spectacular scene.*

And that Christmas Day when Robert Sherwood sent over to my house the script of Abe Lincoln in Illinois! *The cover was pasted all over with Christmas seals, and the card read "From Guess Who."*

The great playwright had kept his promise to write it for me. It was, I had thought, a sort of casual idea, made to me seven years before when he came to my dressing-room after my final performance of Hamlet *in New York. As we became close friends over the years I learned that ideas were not "casual" with Bob. And his compulsive vocal rendition of "When the Red Red Robin goes bob, bob, bobbing along" on all occasions of congenial jollity is still a subject of speculation, which I leave to the psychologists.*

In the early twenties, the theatrical trade papers in London, The Stage *and* The Era, *ran personal columns on their front pages. These announced the activities of various stage folk, such as "so-and-so has concluded South African tour," or "is at liberty." One that constantly appeared seemed to me most endearing. I will use the traditional stage pseudonym. "Mr. and Mrs. Water Plinge thank the Williamson Co. for long comf. engage."*

The abbreviation for "long comfortable engagement" allowed the insertion to go in for the minimum of ten shillings. The Plinges were perhaps not entirely intent on expressing gratitude to the Williamson Company. The insertion was also a delicate way of informing other managers that the Plinges would not be averse to another "engage."

The title of my recounting of my professional years with the Theatre and its mechanical offspring, motion pictures, radio, television, should perhaps be "Long Comf. Engage."

They have been long years of enchantment, of disappointment, of hopes lost and hopes fulfilled. The memories of the people I have been privileged to work with are in the bright foreground. The panorama of successes and failures hangs behind them, more dimly lit. But the people of the theatre are forever. I thank those dear people for those years of camaraderie and help. I thank the public for my "long comf. engage." It's only thanks. I am not looking for another job.